*baknowledgeacademy*
Advancing the art and science of business analysis

# ECBA™
## CERTIFICATION
### STUDY GUIDE

Your Guide to
Learning the
Business Analysis Profession

A Business Analysis Knowledge Academy Publication

© 2019 Business Analysis Knowledge Academy | All rights reserved.

Version 1.0

ISBN: 978-1-7342626-4-3

This document is provided to the business analysis community for educational purposes. Business Analysis Knowledge Academy does not warrant that it is suitable for any other purpose and makes no expressed or implied warranty of any kind and assumes no responsibility for errors or omissions. No liability is assumed for incidental or consequential damages in connection with or arising out of the use of the information contained herein.

Contents of this document may not be disclosed to any unauthorized person for any reason. This document may not, in whole or part, be reproduced, stored in a database or retrieval system, translated, or transmitted in any form or by any means, electronic or mechanical. Purchasers and owners of this material may not share or transfer ownership of their copy of this material to any other person for any purpose.

Business Analysis Knowledge Academy is an entity separate and apart from International Institute of Business Analysis (IIBA®). Business Analysis Knowledge Academy is an education, service and products provider for the business analysis community. Neither IIBA nor Business Analysis Knowledge Academy warrants that use of this publication and related material will ensure passing any exam.

BA Knowledge Academy, and the BA Knowledge Academy logo are trademarks owned by Business Analysis Knowledge Academy.

IIBA®, the IIBA® logo, *BABOK® Guide* and *Business Analysis Body of Knowledge®* are registered trademarks owned by International Institute of Business Analysis. CBAP® and CCBA® are registered certification mark owned by International Institute of Business Analysis. Certified Business Analysis Professional, Certification of Capability in Business Analysis and Entry Certificate in Business Analysis are trademarks owned by International Institute of Business Analysis. The ECBA™ logo is a certification mark owned by International Institute of Business Analysis.

Business Analysis Core Concept Model™, and BACCM™ are trademarks owned by International Institute of Business Analysis.

Cover picture designed by rawpixel.com / Freepik

Published by Business Analysis Knowledge Academy Publishing
P.O. Box 922
Independence, KY 41051-0922

*Preface*

# The Right Book!

You have the right book to help you become IIBA® ECBA™ certified. This Study Guide will be used by classroom students, IIBA chapter study group participants and individuals studying on their own to obtain the IIBA® Entry Certificate in Business Analysis (ECBA™) designation. This study guide is a comprehensive guide to help you understand the structure and content of *A Guide to the Business Analysis Body of Knowledge v3 (BABOK®* or *BABOK® Guide)*. The ECBA™ certification exam is based on the *BABOK® Guide*, so a deep understanding its content is crucial to passing the exam. The purpose of this study guide is to assist you in your goal to obtaining your IIBA® ECBA™ designation.

# Other Tools to Assist in Obtaining Your ECBA™ Certificate

The following tools are also available from Business Analysis Knowledge Academy:

### BABOK® Study Sheets
These robust study sheets are designed for students doing independent study or participating in an IIBA chapter study group. They provide a high-level overview of each chapter of the *BABOK® Guide*; which makes it an excellent companion to the ECBA™ Study Guide.

### ECBA™ Online Practice Exam Questions
With an online question bank of over 80 questions, you can take a 10 to 20 question quiz that covers one of the domains of the ECBA Certification Exam or take a 50-question simulated practice exam designed to give the student a real-life experience similar to the actual ECBA exam.

### Use All Three Tools Together
Use of the ECBA Certification Study Guide, BABOK Study Sheets and ECBA Online Practice Tests gives the student all the tools you should need to prepare to pass the IIBA® ECBA™ certification exam.

Please visit our website at https://baknowledgeacademy.com for more information on these products and training services available from Business Analysis Knowledge Academy.

# Contents at a Glance

1. Introduction and Overview — 1
2. Business Analysis Key Concepts — 19
3. Business Analysis Planning and Monitoring — 35
4. Elicitation and Collaboration — 65
5. Requirements Life Cycle Management — 93
6. Strategy Analysis — 129
7. Requirements Analysis and Design Definition — 161
8. Solution Evaluation — 199
9. Underlying Competencies — 225
10. Techniques — 247

# Table of Contents

## 1. INTRODUCTION AND OVERVIEW — 1

**OVERVIEW** — 1
**WHAT YOU WILL LEARN** — 1
1.1 Introduction to this ECBA™ Certification Study Guide — 1
1.2 Overview of IIBA® and the BABOK® Guide — 2
1.3 Introduction to the *BABOK® Guide* — 3
1.4 What is Business Analysis? — 8
1.5 Who is a Business Analyst? — 8
1.6 About the ECBA™ Exam — 9
1.7 ECBA™ Application Process — 10
1.8 General Exam Taking Tips — 12
1.9 Student Exercises — 13
1.10 Business Analysis and the BA Profession Pop-up Quiz — 15

## 2. BUSINESS ANALYSIS KEY CONCEPTS — 19

**OVERVIEW** — 19
**WHAT YOU WILL LEARN** — 19
2.1 The Business Analysis Core Concept Model™ — 19
2.2 Key Terms — 21
2.3 Requirements Classification Schema — 23
2.4 Stakeholders — 24
2.5 Requirements and Designs — 25
2.6 Student Exercises — 27
2.7 Business Analysis Key Concepts Pop-up Quiz — 31

## 3. BUSINESS ANALYSIS PLANNING AND MONITORING — 35

**OVERVIEW** — 35
**WHAT YOU WILL LEARN** — 35
**THE BACCM™ IN BUSINESS ANALYSIS PLANNING AND MONITORING** — 37
**TASKS IN BUSINESS ANALYSIS PLANNING AND MONITORING** — 38
**BUSINESS ANALYSIS PLANNING AND MONITORING STUDENT EXERCISES** — 41
3.1 Plan Business Analysis Approach — 43
3.2 Plan Stakeholder Engagement — 48
3.3 Plan Business Analysis Governance — 52
3.4 Plan Business Analysis Information Management — 55
3.5 Identify Business Analysis Performance Improvements — 59
3.6 Business Analysis Planning and Monitoring Pop-up Quiz — 63

## 4. ELICITATION AND COLLABORATION 65

| | |
|---|---|
| OVERVIEW | 65 |
| WHAT YOU WILL LEARN | 65 |
| THE BACCM™ IN ELICITATION AND COLLABORATION | 67 |
| TASKS IN ELICITATION AND COLLABORATION | 68 |
| ELICITATION AND COLLABORATION STUDENT EXERCISES | 71 |
| 4.1 PREPARE FOR ELICITATION | 73 |
| 4.2 CONDUCT ELICITATION | 76 |
| 4.3 CONFIRM ELICITATION RESULTS | 79 |
| 4.4 COMMUNICATE BUSINESS ANALYSIS INFORMATION | 82 |
| 4.5 MANAGE STAKEHOLDER COLLABORATION | 85 |
| 4.6 ELICITATION AND COLLABORATION POP-UP QUIZ | 89 |

## 5. REQUIREMENTS LIFE CYCLE MANAGEMENT 93

| | |
|---|---|
| OVERVIEW | 93 |
| WHAT YOU WILL LEARN | 93 |
| THE BACCM™ IN REQUIREMENTS LIFE CYCLE MANAGEMENT | 95 |
| TASKS IN REQUIREMENTS LIFE CYCLE MANAGEMENT | 95 |
| REQUIREMENTS LIFE CYCLE MANAGEMENT STUDENT EXERCISES | 99 |
| 5.1 TRACE REQUIREMENTS | 101 |
| 5.2 MAINTAIN REQUIREMENTS | 107 |
| 5.3 PRIORITIZE REQUIREMENTS | 111 |
| 5.4 ASSESS REQUIREMENTS CHANGES | 117 |
| 5.5 APPROVE REQUIREMENTS | 121 |
| 5.6 REQUIREMENTS LIFE CYCLE MANAGEMENT POP-UP QUIZ | 125 |

## 6. STRATEGY ANALYSIS 129

| | |
|---|---|
| OVERVIEW | 129 |
| WHAT YOU WILL LEARN | 130 |
| THE BACCM™ IN STRATEGY ANALYSIS | 131 |
| TASKS IN STRATEGY ANALYSIS | 131 |
| STRATEGY ANALYSIS STUDENT EXERCISES | 135 |
| 6.1 ANALYZE CURRENT STATE | 137 |
| 6.2 DEFINE FUTURE STATE | 144 |
| 6.3 ASSESS RISKS | 150 |
| 6.4 DEFINE CHANGE STRATEGY | 154 |
| 6.5 STRATEGY ANALYSIS POP-UP QUIZ | 159 |

# 7. REQUIREMENTS ANALYSIS AND DESIGN DEFINITION — 161

Overview — 161
What You Will Learn — 162
The BACCM™ in Requirements Analysis and Design Definition — 163
Tasks in Requirements Analysis and Design Definition — 163
Requirements Analysis and Design Definition Student Exercises — 167
7.1 Specify and Model Requirements — 169
7.2 Verify Requirements — 175
7.3 Validate Requirements — 181
7.4 Define Requirements Architecture — 183
7.5 Define Solution Options — 187
7.6 Analyze Potential Value and Recommend Solution — 190
7.7 Requirements Analysis and Design Definition Pop-up Quiz — 195

# 8. SOLUTION EVALUATION — 199

Overview — 199
What You Will Learn — 199
The BACCM™ in Solution Evaluation — 201
Tasks in Solution Evaluation — 201
Solution Evaluation Student Exercises — 205
8.1 Measure Solution Performance — 207
8.2 Analyze Solution Performance — 210
8.3 Assess Solution Limitations — 213
8.4 Assess Enterprise Limitations — 216
8.5 Recommend Actions to Increase Solution Value — 219
8.6 Solution Evaluation Pop-up Quiz — 223

# 9. UNDERLYING COMPETENCIES — 225

Overview — 225
What You Will Learn — 225
9.1 Analytical Thinking and Problem Solving — 226
9.2 Behavioral Characteristics — 230
9.3 Business Knowledge — 235
9.4 Communication Skills — 238
9.5 Interaction Skills — 241
9.6 Tools and Technology — 244

# 10. TECHNIQUES — 247

Techniques Usage by Knowledge Area — 247
Techniques — 249
Techniques Pop-up Quiz — 320

# Table of Student Exercises

| | |
|---|---|
| 1.9 BUSINESS ANALYSIS AND THE BA PROFESSION STUDENT EXERCISES | 13 |
| 2.6 BUSINESS ANALYSIS KEY CONCEPTS STUDENT EXERCISES | 27 |
| 3 BUSINESS ANALYSIS PLANNING AND MONITORING STUDENT EXERCISES | 41 |
| 4 ELICITATION AND COLLABORATION STUDENT EXERCISES | 71 |
| 5 REQUIREMENTS LIFE CYCLE MANAGEMENT STUDENT EXERCISES | 99 |
| 5.1.9 TRACE REQUIREMENTS STUDENT EXERCISES | 105 |
| 5.2.9 MAINTAIN REQUIREMENTS STUDENT EXERCISES | 110 |
| 5.3.9 PRIORITIZE REQUIREMENTS STUDENT EXERCISES | 115 |
| 5.4.9 ASSESS REQUIREMENTS CHANGES STUDENT EXERCISES | 120 |
| 5.5.9 APPROVE REQUIREMENTS STUDENT EXERCISES | 124 |
| 6 STRATEGY ANALYSIS STUDENT EXERCISES | 135 |
| 6.1.9 ANALYZE CURRENT STATE STUDENT EXERCISES | 143 |
| 6.2.9 DEFINE FUTURE STATE STUDENT EXERCISES | 149 |
| 7 REQUIREMENTS ANALYSIS AND DESIGN DEFINITION STUDENT EXERCISES | 167 |
| 7.1.9 SPECIFY AND MODEL REQUIREMENTS STUDENT EXERCISES | 173 |
| 7.2.9 VERIFY REQUIREMENTS STUDENT EXERCISES | 179 |
| 8 SOLUTION EVALUATION STUDENT EXERCISES | 205 |

# Table of Practice Quiz Questions

| | | |
|---|---|---|
| 1.10 | BUSINESS ANALYSIS AND THE BA PROFESSION POP-UP QUIZ | 15 |
| 2.7 | BUSINESS ANALYSIS KEY CONCEPTS POP-UP QUIZ | 37 |
| 3.6 | BUSINESS ANALYSIS PLANNING AND MONITORING POP-UP QUIZ | 63 |
| 4.6 | ELICITATION AND COLLABORATION POP-UP QUIZ | 89 |
| 5.6 | REQUIREMENTS LIFE CYCLE MANAGEMENT POP-UP QUIZ | 125 |
| 6.5 | STRATEGY ANALYSIS POP-UP QUIZ | 159 |
| 7.7 | REQUIREMENTS ANALYSIS AND DESIGN DEFINITION POP-UP QUIZ | 195 |
| 8.6 | SOLUTION EVALUATION POP-UP QUIZ | 223 |
| 10 | TECHNIQUES POP-UP QUIZ | 320 |

# Introduction and Overview

## Overview

This Introduction and Overview chapter provides basic information on which the remaining chapters in this study guide can build. It describes and defines business analysis and the role of the business analyst, as well as the function of the International Institute of Business Analysis (IIBA®), *A Guide to the Business Analysis Body of Knowledge® (BABOK® Guide),* and the Entry Certificate in Business Analysis™ (ECBA™) designation. On this foundation you can build knowledge about the Business Analysis Core Concept Model™ (BACCM™) and key concepts of business analysis (chapter 2), knowledge areas of business analysis (Chapters 3 through 8), underlying competencies for business analysts (Chapter 9), techniques that business analysts typically use (Chapter 10) and how perspectives can change the approach to business analysis activities (Chapter 11). Be sure to learn the content of these chapters well so that you have a strong foundation on which to build your knowledge of business analysis.

## What You Will Learn

When you are finished with this chapter, you will know:
1. The purpose, structure and audience for this ECBA™ Certification Study Guide.
2. A basic understanding of business analysis and the role of the business analyst.
3. The role and function of IIBA® and its ECBA™ certificate.
4. The purpose, structure and knowledge areas of the *BABOK® Guide*.
5. Key tips and tactics to help pass the ECBA™ exam.

## 1.1  Introduction to this ECBA™ Certification Study Guide

### 1.1.1  Purpose of this ECBA™ Certification Study Guide

This study guide was published to assist those business analysis professionals who wish to understand the content of the *A Guide to the Business Analysis Body of Knowledge® v3 (BABOK® Guide)* or to obtain the IIBA® Entry Certificate in Business Analysis™ (ECBA™) designation. This study guide will guide students through the material of the *BABOK® Guide* and provide explanatory material to help students understand the content in a more meaningful manner.

This study guide emphasizes chapters 1 (Introduction to the Business Analysis Profession) and 2 (Key Concepts) more than CBAP® and CCBA® study guides on the market because this is a major emphasis on the ECBA™ exam and not the CBAP or CCBA exams. Likewise, this study guide de-emphasizes Chapters 6 (Strategy Analysis) and Chapter 8 (Solution Evaluation) because they are not major concepts on the ECBA exam. These business analysis areas of work are typically areas business analysis professionals venture into later in their careers after some experience in the field is obtained by the individual.

It is intended that students use this study guide in conjunction with the *BABOK® Guide*. By reading the sections of the *BABOK Guide* and this study guide together, at the same time, you will be able to understand the role of the Business Analyst better and have a deeper understanding of the tasks, activities, and techniques they perform within an business organization; and the value they provide to the organization. It also puts you in a better position to pass the ECBA™ Certification exam.

### 1.1.2 Structure of this ECBA™ Certification Study Guide

The structure of this study guide follows the structure of the *BABOK® Guide* (see Section 1.3.2). As mentioned above this guide is intended to be used with the *BABOK Guide.* The chapters of this study guide have the same chapter numbers as in the *BABOK Guide.* As much as possible, even the sections within the chapters are the same as in the *BABOK Guide*, to make it easier for them to be used together. Additional sections are added in Chapter 1 of this study guide to explain the purpose, structure and audience of this study guide and the IIBA® Entry Certificate in Business Analysis™ (ECBA™) exam. There are also sections added in the remaining chapters to give students practice is demonstrating the knowledge gained from that chapter. This guide also contains pinned notes, diagrams and tables to emphasize important concepts within the chapter; pay particular attention to anything that is emphasized in a note, diagram or table.

### 1.1.3 Target Audience for this ECBA™ Certification Study Guide

As stated earlier this study guide is targeted for professionals seeking to understand the *BABOK® Guide* content or obtain the IIBA® Entry Certificate in Business Analysis™ (ECBA™). This audience primarily consists of professional who are:

- ✓ Business Analysis Professionals working in business, government and non-profit organizations
- ✓ Business Analysis Consultants
- ✓ Managers of Business Analysis Professionals
- ✓ Business professionals that work alongside Business Analysts who wish to understand the role better
- ✓ Professionals wishing to enter the business analysis role, or who just wish to understand it better

## 1.2 Overview of IIBA® and the BABOK® Guide

International Institute of Business Analysis™ (IIBA®) was formed to promote the advancement of the business analysis profession. Part of the IIBA mission is to document and maintain standards for business analysis, and to recognize its practitioners through certification and other recognition programs.

IIBA was founded in Toronto, Canada in October 2003 as a non-profit organization dedicated to creating awareness and recognition of business analysis professionals and the value that business analysis can provide to organizations. One aspect of the IIBA vision is to build its image and identity as the major professional association for business analysis (BA) professionals. IIBA also focuses on identifying BA skills and competencies, and certifying practitioners based on those skills and competencies.

IIBA's original stated mission was to "Develop and maintain standards for the practice of business analysis and for the certification of its practitioners." Today, its stated core purpose is "To unite a community of professionals to create better business outcomes." As of this writing, the organization has 29,000+ members, 300+ corporate members, and 120+ chapters world-wide. IIBA has quickly developed into the professional association for the advancement of the business analysis profession.

The Entry Certificate in Business Analysis™ (ECBA™) program was established to identify and certify qualified and knowledgeable business analyst practitioners new to the profession, perform business analysis only as part of their job or manage business analysis professionals but don't typically engage in business analysis activities. It is the first tier of a three-tier internationally acknowledged certification program. The ECBA exam is based on *A Guide to the Business Analysis Body of Knowledge®* (referred to as *BABOK®* or the *BABOK® Guide* in this study guide). This chapter provides an overview of the IIBA, the *BABOK Guide* and ECBA exam, and several strategies and tips to prepare for and pass the exam.

## 1.3 Introduction to the *BABOK® Guide*

### 1.3.1 Purpose of the *BABOK® Guide*

IIBA® created the *BABOK® Guide* to be the globally recognized standard for the practice of business analysis. It describes business analysis knowledge areas, tasks, underlying competencies, techniques and perspectives on how to approach business analysis activities to advance change within the organization. IIBA utilized hundreds, if not thousands, of business analysis practitioners from the global community so that it defines world-wide generally accepted practices of business analysis. The *BABOK Guide* is now in its third edition, showing IIBA's commitment to keeping the standard up-to-date with current global generally accepted practices.

The primary purpose of the *BABOK® Guide* is to define the profession of business analysis and provide a set of commonly accepted practices. It helps practitioners discuss and define the skills necessary to effectively perform business analysis work. The *BABOK Guide* also helps people who work with and employ business analysts to understand the skills and knowledge they should expect from a skilled practitioner.

> BABOK is a "set of commonly accepted practices" for performing business analysis.

Business analysis is a broad profession in which business analysts might perform work for many different types of initiatives across an enterprise. Practitioners may employ different competencies, knowledge, skills, terminology, and attitudes that they use when performing business analysis tasks. The *BABOK® Guide* is a common framework for all perspectives, describing business analysis tasks that are performed to properly analyze a change or evaluate the necessity for a change. Tasks may vary in form, order, or importance for individual business analysts or for various initiatives.

The six knowledge areas of the *BABOK® Guide* (Business Analysis Planning and Monitoring, Elicitation and Collaboration, Requirements Life Cycle Management, Strategy Analysis, Requirements Analysis and Design Definition (RADD), and Solution Evaluation) describe the practice of business analysis as it is applied within the boundaries of a project or throughout enterprise evolution and continuous improvement. The following image shows how three of the knowledge areas support the delivery of business value before, during, and after the life cycle of a project.

**Figure 1.3.1.1: Business Analysis Beyond Projects**

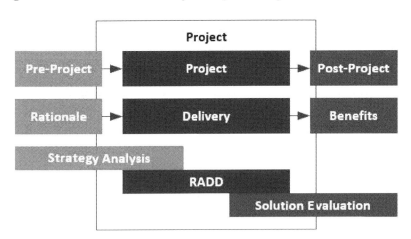

Strategy Analysis, RADD and Solution Evaluation support business analysis before, during and after a project.

© 2015 International Institute of Business Analysis

## 1.3.2 Structure of the *BABOK® Guide*

The core content of the *BABOK® Guide* is composed of business analysis tasks organized into six knowledge areas. Knowledge areas are a collection of logically (but not sequentially) related tasks. These tasks describe specific activities that accomplish the purpose of their associated knowledge area.

**Knowledge Areas (KA):**

- Business Analysis Planning and Monitoring (BAPM)
- Elicitation and Collaboration (EC)
- Requirements Life Cycle Management (RLCM)
- Strategy Analysis (SA)
- Requirements Analysis and Design Definition (RADD)
- Solution Evaluation (SE)

| Mnemonic to remember BABOK® Knowledge Areas |
| --- |
| P = BA Planning and Monitoring |
| L = Req Life Cycle Management |
| E = Elicitation and Collaboration |
| A = Req Analysis and Design Definition |
| S = Strategy Analysis |
| E = Solution Evaluation |

The Business Analysis Key Concepts, Underlying Competencies, Techniques, and Perspectives sections form the extended content in the *BABOK® Guide* that helps guide business analysts to better perform business analysis tasks.

- **Business Analysis Key Concepts**: define the key terms needed to understand all other content, concepts, and ideas within the *BABOK® Guide*.
- **Underlying Competencies**: provide a description of the behaviors, characteristics, knowledge, and personal qualities that support the effective practice of business analysis.
- **Techniques**: describes how business analysts perform business analysis tasks. The techniques described in the *BABOK® Guide* are intended to cover the most common and widespread techniques practiced within the business analysis community.
- **Perspectives**: describe various views of business analysis. Perspectives help business analysts working from various points of view to better perform business analysis tasks, given the context of the initiative.

### 1.3.2.1 Introduction (INTRO) and Key Concepts (KC)

The Introduction (Chapter 1) and Business Analysis Key Concepts (Chapter 2) chapters gives you an introduction to the business analysis profession and provides a basic understanding of the central ideas necessary for understanding that profession.

These chapters consist of:
- Purpose and Structure of the *BABOK® Guide*
- Definition of Business Analysis
- Describe who is a Business Analyst
- Business Analysis Core Concept Model™ (BACCM™)
- Key Terms
- Requirements Classification Schema
- Stakeholders
- Requirements and Design

### 1.3.2.2 Knowledge Areas (KA)

Knowledge areas represent areas of specific business analysis expertise that encompass several tasks. The following gives you a preview of each knowledge area.

**Business Analysis Planning and Monitoring (BAPM)**

This knowledge area includes tasks that deal with organizing the business analysis work, including coordinating efforts between business analyst(s) and stakeholders, throughout the initiative. Tasks in this knowledge area produce business analysis planning outputs, called approaches, which are used as inputs or guidelines and tools to tasks in the other knowledge areas. This knowledge area also includes tasks for assessing the business analysis work and recommending performance improvements.

**Elicitation and Collaboration (EC)**

Describes the tasks that business analysts perform to prepare for and conduct elicitation activities and confirm the results obtained from those elicitation activities. These elicitation results can be requirements and other important information needed during the initiative, called business analysis information. It also describes the communication with stakeholders once the business analysis information is assembled and the ongoing collaboration with them throughout the initiative.

**Requirements Life Cycle Management (RLCM)**

Requirements and designs are created and then eventually retired. The RLCM knowledge area describes the tasks that business analysts perform in order to manage and maintain requirements and design information from inception until they are no longer needed (i.e., retired). These tasks describe establishing meaningful relationships between related requirements and designs, ensuring these relationships are aligned (i.e., traced), maintained, prioritized, approved and assessing, analyzing and gaining consensus on proposed changes to requirements and designs.

## Strategy Analysis (SA)

Describes the business analysis work that must be performed to collaborate with stakeholders in order to identify a need of strategic or tactical importance (the business need) and then help the organization address that need. These Strategic Analysis tasks describe the current and future states, identifies gaps between the two and develop a strategy to transition from the current state to the future state. This strategy must be aligned with higher- and lower-level strategies within the organization. Strategy analysis not only happens at the beginning when a business need is identified, but occurs as changes are requested.

## Requirements Analysis and Design Definition (RADD)

Deals with how requirements discovered during elicitation activities are structured and organized, how business analysts specify and model requirements and designs, validate and verify information, identify options for the solution (e.g., build vs. buy), and estimate the potential value that could be realized by each solution option. This knowledge area covers the incremental and iterative activities ranging from the initial concept and exploration of the need through the transformation of those needs into a particular recommended solution.

## Solution Evaluation (SE)

Describes the tasks that business analysts perform to assess the performance of and value delivered by an implemented solution, and to recommend removal of barriers or constraints that prevent the full realization of the value. In other words, at any point during development or after implementation, the business analyst may compare the value delivered by the solution to its expected value, determine what barriers are limiting its ability to achieve expected value, and recommend ways to increase its value.

The following diagram shows a general relationship between the knowledge areas.

**Figure 1.3.2.1: Relationship between Knowledge Areas**

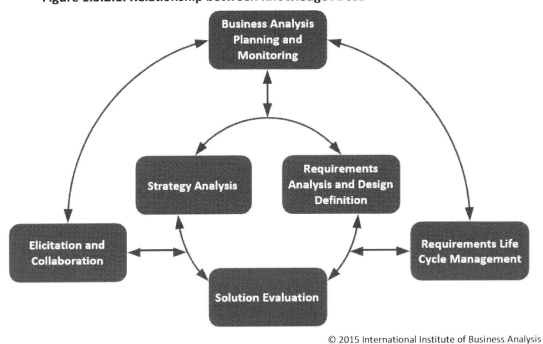

© 2015 International Institute of Business Analysis

**Tasks**

Tasks within these knowledge areas are a discrete piece of work that may be performed formally or informally as part of business analysis. The definition of a given task is universally applicable to business analysis efforts, independent of the initiative type. Business analysts perform tasks from all knowledge areas sequentially, iteratively, or simultaneously; there is no prescribed process or order in which these tasks are performed. Tasks may be performed in any order, as long as the necessary inputs to a task are present. There is a graphic at the beginning of each task that describes all of the following components of the task:

- **Purpose:** The goal of performing the task and the value it creates .
- **Description:** A summary that explains in greater detail what the task is, why it is performed, and what it should accomplish.
- **Inputs:** List of items information consumed or transformed to produce an output, and must be present for a task to begin.
- **Elements:** key concepts that are needed to understand how to perform the task.
- **Guidelines and Tools:** Tools and resources needed in completing the task. A guideline provides instructions or descriptions on performing the task. A tool is something used to undertake a task, but is not transformed or consumed in the performance of the task. This is the difference between a guideline and an input to the task.
- **Techniques:** List of techniques that can be used to perform the business analysis task.
- **Stakeholders:** List of stakeholders who are likely to participate in the performance of the task or who will be affected by it.
- **Outputs:** Describes the results produced by performing the task. Outputs are created, transformed, or changed in state as a result of the successful completion of a task.

### 1.3.2.3 Underlying Competencies (UC)

Underlying competencies reflect knowledge, skills, behaviors, characteristics, and personal qualities needed to successfully perform the tasks within each knowledge area. These underlying competencies are not unique to the business analysis profession. However, successful execution of tasks and techniques is often dependent on proficiency in one or more underlying competencies. Categories include analytical thinking and problem-solving, behavioral characteristics, business knowledge, communication skills, interaction skills, and tools and technology. Each Underlying Competency (UC) includes purpose, definition and effectiveness measures.

### 1.3.2.4 Techniques (TECH)

Techniques provide additional information on ways that business analysis tasks are performed. The 50 techniques listed in the BABOK is not exhaustive, but represent the commonly used techniques by business analysts. Techniques may be used in conjunction with one another to accomplish a particular task. Business analysts are encouraged to modify existing techniques or create new ones to best meet their goals and the situation. Make sure you are familiar with all of the techniques at a high level. For optimal studying, concentrate on the techniques that are used most frequently. Each Technique includes:

- Purpose
- Description
- Elements
- Usage Considerations

### 1.3.2.5 Perspectives (PER)

The main body of the *BABOK®* is generic and applies business analysis work to all types of initiatives in all contexts (i.e., in all business environments). Perspectives provide focus to tasks and techniques used with a specific context. The perspectives included in the *BABOK® Guide* are:

- Agile
- Business Intelligence
- Information Technology
- Business Architecture
- Business Process Management

> Perspectives are not covered on any of the IIBA core certification exams. You will not find the answer to any question on the exam in Chapter 11.

This is not an exhaustive list of all perspectives in which business analysis work can be performed, they represent the common perspectives. As noted above, perspectives are not covered on any IIBA exam, including the ECBA™ exam, therefore, we do not cover it in this study guide.

## 1.4 What is Business Analysis?

Business analysis is the practice of enabling change in an enterprise by defining needs and recommending solutions that deliver value to stakeholders. This means that business analysis helps organizations by:

- Analyze business needs
- Identifying problems and opportunities (i.e., current state)
- Articulate the rationale for change
- Collaborate with stakeholders to derive solution options to solve the business need
- Recommend the solution that will deliver the greatest value to the organization
- Develop and provide clarity to the solution design (i.e., future state) throughout the development process
- Assess the effectiveness of the solution against the expected value (i.e., solution evaluation)

The focus of business analysis throughout the change process is to deliver value to stakeholders. Business analysis is performed on a variety of initiatives within an enterprise. Initiatives may be strategic, tactical, or operational. Business analysis may be performed within the boundaries of a project or before and/or after the project. It can be used to understand the current state, to define the future state, and to determine the activities required to move from the current to the future state.

## 1.5 Who is a Business Analyst?

Simply put, a business analyst (BA) is any person who performs business analysis tasks within the organization, no matter their job title or organizational role. Anyone who works with stakeholders to define business needs, elicit information and design solutions to meet those business needs is a business analyst. Some individuals within organizations do this work as part of their duties, but perform other work such as testing or project management. During the time they are performing tasks defined in the *BABOK® Guide*, they are considered a business analyst.

Business analysts are responsible for discovering, synthesizing, and analyzing information from a variety of sources within an enterprise, including tools, processes, documentation, and stakeholders. The business analyst is responsible for eliciting the actual needs of stakeholders—which frequently involves investigating and clarifying their expressed desires—in order to determine underlying issues and causes.

Chapter 1 Introduction

Business analysts play a role in aligning the designed and delivered solutions with the needs of stakeholders. The activities that business analysts perform include:
- understanding enterprise problems and goals,
- analyzing needs and solutions,
- devising strategies,
- driving change, and
- facilitating stakeholder collaboration.

## 1.6 About the ECBA™ Exam

As of this writing, the IIBA® certification program is a multi-level competency-based program that supports lifelong business analysis career progression. The Entry Certificate in Business Analysis™ (ECBA™) designation is the first tier of that multi-level program designed to recognize those new to the business analysis profession and may not yet have experience in the field.

**Figure 1.6.1: IIBA® Multi-level Certification Program**

**Level 1**
Individuals entering the BA field.

**Level 2**
Recognizes BA professionals who have 2-3 years of BA experience.

**Level 3**
Recognizes BA professionals who lead and have over 5 years of BA experience.

© 2019 International Institute of Business Analysis

### 1.6.1 ECBA™ Eligibility

As of this writing, to qualify for the ECBA™ designation, you must:
1. Complete a minimum of 21 Professional Development (PD) Hours within the last four years,
2. Agree to the IIBA Code of Conduct, and
3. Agree to the IIBA Terms and Conditions.

For the ECBA™ designation, professional development can consist of any of the following activities:
- Classroom and online courses (e.g. EEP endorsed courses)
- Webinars - live or recorded (e.g. IIBA Webinars)
- Conference track sessions, tutorials, keynotes & workshops
- Chapter events (i.e. presentations, study groups, workshops, conference days)
- Self-directed learning (i.e. reading/reviewing the BABOK® Guide v3.0)

Notice that there is no business analysis experience requirement for the ECBA™ certificate. Please see the IIBA® website (https://iiba.org) for more information on ECBA Eligibility requirements.

## 1.6.2 ECBA™ Exam Blueprint

As of this writing, the ECBA exam has 50 multiple choice knowledge-based questions and must be completed in one hour. The questions are divided up as follows:

**Table 1.6.2.1: ECBA™ Exam Blueprint**

| Domain / Knowledge Area | % of questions on exam | # of questions on exam |
|---|---|---|
| Business Analysis and the BA Profession, Key Concepts, Underlying Competencies and Techniques | 25% | 12 |
| Business Analysis Planning and Monitoring | 5% | 3 |
| Elicitation and Collaboration | 20% | 10 |
| Requirements Life Cycle Management | 20% | 10 |
| Strategy Analysis | 5% | 2 |
| Requirements Analysis and Design Definition | 24% | 12 |
| Solution Evaluation | 1% | 1 |
| Totals | 100% | 50 |

## 1.6.3 The Value of the ECBA™ Certificate

**Stand out in a crowd!**

ECBA covers foundational knowledge on business analysis according to the *BABOK® Guide*. Putting that credential behind your name and on your resume (CV) showcases to your current employer, perspective employers and the community in general that you have the core knowledge and competencies in the hi-demand field of business analysis; even if you have no work experience in the field.

Obtaining the ECBA™ designation can possibly help you:
- Get your foot in the door in some organizations, even those that typically hire only experienced business analysts.
- Validate your business analysis knowledge and skillset.
- Increase your salary by as much as 8%.
- Build your peer network.
- Obtain promotions faster and more often.
- Get better job opportunities.

## 1.7 ECBA™ Application Process

You must apply for and have that application approved by IIBA® before you can schedule and sit for the ECBA™ exam. You must be eligible, have completed all eligibility requirements, prior to applying for the ECBA. This includes having completed your 21 professional development (PD) hours. If you are taking a 3-day class to obtain the 21 PD hours, you can not apply for the ECBA on the first or second day of class because you have not completed 21 PD hours yet. You can apply on the third day of the class as you now have the required number of professional development hours. Get a "certificate of completion" to prove you took the class, it will be useful if your ECBA application gets audited by IIBA.

Chapter 1 Introduction

Follow this 6-step process to apply for the ECBA™ Certificate. Below is the current IIBA certification application process as of the publication date of this study guide. Visit the IIBA website (https://www.iiba.org) for the most current process.

1. **Step 1: Enter your ECBA™ application into your My.IIBA Portal**

   Professional Development (PD) Hours must be entered into your account on the IIBA portal so that they will be included in your application. These will be logged in the My PD Hours section under the Certification tab in the IIBA portal.

2. **Step 2: Pay the Application Fee**

   In order to view your application in the IIBA portal, you must pay the application fee. Note that this application fee is non-refundable and non-transferable. Once the application fee is paid you will be able to see your application and the goals for each area of the application.

3. **Step 3: Submit your ECBA™ Application**

   Complete any missing information on the application, including your personal information. Once all requirements (goals) are met, you will be able to submit the application. In order to complete the submission of your application, you will need to agree to the *Terms and Conditions* and the *Code of Conduct*.

4. **Step 4: Pay the Exam Fee**

   After you submit your application, you will be notified via email if your application is Approved or Approved Pending Audit. Once approved, you will have one year from that date to take the exam. It is your responsibility to make sure that this time period does not lapse without taking the exam. Otherwise you will have to re-apply for the ECBA™. You will have to pay the exam fee before you will be permitted to schedule your exam.

5. **Step 5: Schedule Your Exam**

   You can schedule your ECBA™ exam for anytime. The ECBA exam is an online monitored exam, so you will be able to take it during business hours (like other exams) or nights and weekends. You will not have to go to a testing location to sit for the exam; you can take the exam from your home or any place you find yourself at the time of your test. It just needs to be a quiet place where you will not be interrupted. You supply the computer on which you take the exam. The IIBA website (https://www.iiba.org/certification/exam-preparation/) has system requirements for the computer.

6. **Step 6: Sit for the Exam**

   On the day of your exam, you must be available to login and take your exam at the assigned time, unless you reschedule the exam at least 24 hours prior to the original exam time. Remember they will have a monitor scheduled to monitor you taking the exam, so be considerate of them. You may login up to 15 minutes prior to your assigned exam time. If you login more than 15 minutes after your assigned exam time you will be marked as missing your exam and you will have to reschedule it. You will forfeit your exam fee for missing your appointment time. Once you login and begin your exam, plan on an hour to complete the exam.

You will have to verify your identity before you can begin your exam. Please have your driver's license or other government issued picture ID ready to show the exam monitor.

## 1.8 General Exam Taking Tips

We recommend some key test taking tactics and tips to help relieve test anxiety and improve your testing performance:

- **Online Monitored.** If you take the exam as an online monitored exam, here are some guidelines and expectations for you:
    - ✓ You can take it from anywhere you may be; however, it must be a quiet place and nobody can enter the room while you take the exam.
    - ✓ You supply the computer on which you take the exam.
    - ✓ You will have to show state issued picture ID to verify your identity.
    - ✓ You will have to show the person monitoring your exam a 360-degree view of the room and desktop around your computer; nothing can be on it.
    - ✓ You will not be allowed to have food or drink during the exam.
    - ✓ Make sure you use the restroom before you begin your exam.
    - ✓ You will not be allowed to have paper or a calculator on the desktop; however, you won't need them.
    - ✓ You will share your desktop and webcam with the person monitoring your exam.
    - ✓ You will not be allowed to have any other applications or websites open during the exam. The person monitoring your exam may ask you to open your task manager to verify all applications, except one web browser on which you are taking the exam, are shut down.

- **Rest.** Get a good night's sleep the night before taking the exam. Part of successful test taking involves problem solving and logical thinking. A well-rested mind and body will help the brain function at top performance.

- **Read every word.** Read every word of the question, then read every word of all four answer options. Once you understand the question and the answer options, answer the question.

- **Look for words that change the meaning of the question.** Words such as "not" or "except" completely change the meaning of the question. Skipping over these words when you read the question will cause you to answer it incorrectly.

- **Be careful of "Select the BEST answer".** This usually means that more than one of the answer options is technically correct. You must find the one that is most correct; making the question just that much more difficult to answer.

- **Answer every question.** You have 1 hour to answer 50 questions. If you leave a question unanswered it is wrong. If you answer it, you have a 25% chance of getting it correct. So, if you get down to those last 5 to 10 minutes and have questions left to answer, just go through and answer all remaining unanswered questions with something (e.g., answer them all 'B').

Chapter 1 Introduction

- ➤ **Take your exam in rounds.** Getting the questions you know the answer to out of the way leaves more time for the questions you have to reason through to the answer. The exam gives you the ability to flag questions for review so you can revisit it later. Use this feature. We suggest taking your exam in rounds as follow.
    - o **Round 1:** Spend less than one minute per question. Read the question (every word) and read the four answer options. If this is material straight from the *BABOK®* and you know the answer without thinking answer it. If not, don't answer it, flag it for review and move on.
    - o **Round 2:** Review the "marked for review" questions from round 1, spend 2 to 3 minutes per question. You now know about how many questions you have answered and how much time you have left, so you can pace yourself through the rest of the rounds. You can utilize deductive reasoning and process of elimination to come to the answer. Eliminate answer options that you know are wrong. Can you determine the correct answer? If so, answer it, remove the "mark for review" and move on. If not, leave the "mark for review" and move on…you can answer this next round.
    - o **Round 3:** Review the "marked for review" questions remaining from the first 2 rounds. Spend 5 to 10 minutes. Continue to use deductive reasoning and process of elimination to derive the answer. Work though any problem to solve it and derive the answer. Answer the question if you can.
    - o **Keep an eye on your time.** As stated above in *Answer every question*, when you get down to that last 5 to 10 minutes, go though and answer all remaining unanswered questions as fast as possible.
- ➤ **Don't change your answers.** Especially if take your exam in rounds as described above, don't go back and change answers. In the first round you answered the questions that you absolutely knew the answer without thinking. If you change those answers, you most likely are changing a correct answer to an incorrect answer.
- ➤ **Don't rush.** There are no points for finishing first, or early. Bragging rights about the time it took you to complete the exam will not help if you do not pass. It is far more important to pass the exam than brag to your friends about how little time it took you to finish it. Take your time to read every word of the question and answer options. Answer every question. It is far more important to answer the questions with the correct answer than finish before [insert friend's name here].

## 1.9  Student Exercises

1. List the names of all the BABOK Knowledge Areas in the blanks below and the mnemonic tip to help you remember them.

| Knowledge Area | Mnemonic |
|---|---|
|  |  |
|  |  |
|  |  |
|  |  |
|  |  |
|  |  |

2. Provide the definition of the word or phrase on the left in the space provided.

| Name | Definition |
|---|---|
| Business Analysis | |
| Business Analyst | |
| Task | |
| Underlying Competency | |
| Technique | |
| Perspective | |

## Answers to Student Exercises

1. List the names of all the BABOK Knowledge Areas in the blanks below and the mnemonic tip to help you remember them.

| Knowledge Area | Mnemonic |
|---|---|
| Business Analysis Planning and Monitoring | P |
| Requirements Life Cycle Management | L |
| Elicitation and Collaboration | E |
| Requirements Analysis and Design Definition | A |
| Strategy Analysis | S |
| Solution Evaluation | E |

2. Provide the definition of the word or phrase on the left in the space provided.

| Name | Definition |
|---|---|
| Business Analysis | The practice of enabling change in an enterprise by defining needs and recommending solutions that deliver value to stakeholders. |
| Business Analyst | Any person who performs business analysis tasks. |
| Task | Discrete piece of work that may be performed formally or informally as part of business analysis. |
| Underlying Competency | Knowledge, skills, behaviors, characteristics, and personal qualities that help one successfully perform the role of the business analyst. |
| Technique | Provides additional information on ways that a task may be performed. |
| Perspective | Provides focus to tasks and techniques specific to the context of the initiative. |

## 1.10 Business Analysis and the BA Profession Pop-up Quiz

1. Business Analysis is:
   a. Enabling change by defining business need and recommending solutions.
   b. Delivering value to stakeholders.
   c. List of tasks and techniques performed by business analysts.
   d. The process of collaborating with stakeholders to improve a business process.

2. Which of the below describes the types of initiatives that business analysts are typically involved in?
   a. Business-driven, technical-driven, and operational-driven
   b. Short-term, mid-term, and long-term
   c. Strategic, tactical, and operational
   d. Strategic, tactical, and support

3. Which of the following statements is NOT a true statement about the role of the business analyst?
   a. The business analyst discovers, synthesizes and analyzes information from a variety of sources within an enterprise.
   b. The business analyst elicits business needs from stakeholders within the enterprise.
   c. The business analyst aligns the designed and delivered solutions with stakeholder needs.
   d. The business analyst selects the change initiatives that will deliver the greatest value to the enterprise.

4. Of the six knowledge areas in the BABOK, which support delivery business value before, during, and after the project?
   a. Strategy Analysis, Requirements Life Cycle Management, Solution Evaluation
   b. Strategy Analysis, Requirements Analysis and Design Definition, Solution Evaluation
   c. Business Analysis Planning and Monitoring, Elicitation and Collaboration, Solution Evaluation
   d. All six knowledge areas support delivery of business value throughout the solution life cycle.

5. What activities do business analysts engage in to aligned designed and delivered solutions to stakeholder needs?

　　a. Understanding enterprise problems and goals, analyzing needs and solutions, devising strategies, driving change, and facilitating stakeholder collaboration.

　　b. Understanding business needs, elicit, analyze, and synthesize information from stakeholders, design solutions, driving change, and evaluate solution effectiveness.

　　c. Understanding enterprise problems and goals, elicit, analyze, and synthesize information from stakeholders, devising strategies, and facilitating stakeholder collaboration.

　　d. Understanding organizational goals, analyzing needs and solutions, devising strategies, design solutions, and evaluate solution effectiveness.

6. Which of the following are job titles that perform business analysis within an organization?

　　a. Business analyst, business systems analyst, process analyst, and systems analyst.

　　b. Enterprise analyst, business analyst, and process analyst.

　　c. Product Owner and product manager.

　　d. Job titles aren't important; anyone who performs business analysis tasks is considered a business analyst.

7. How can business analysis be used within the organization?

　　a. It can be used to understand the current state, assess risks, and develop a change strategy.

　　b. It can be used to understand the current state, define the future state, and determine the activities required to move from the current state to the future state.

　　c. It can be used to understand the future state and develop a plan to move to that future state.

　　d. It can be performed within the boundaries of a project only.

8. What does *A Guide to the Business Analysis Body of Knowledge® (BABOK® Guide)* contain?

　　a. Best practices for performing business analysis within an organization.

　　b. The standards and methodologies for performing business analysis.

　　c. Commonly accepted practices for performing business analysis within an organization.

　　d. All the tasks and techniques for performing business analysis.

9. Which of the following statements is NOT true about a task in the *BABOK® Guide*?

   a. A task is a discrete piece of work performed as part of business analysis.

   b. The definition of the task changes with the initiative type in which the business analyst is engaged.

   c. The performance of the task should create value for the organization or its stakeholders.

   d. Tasks may be performed in any order, as long as the necessary inputs to a task are present.


10. Which of the following statements is true about knowledge areas?

    a. They provide best practices and methodologies for completing business analysis work.

    b. They subdivide business analysis tasks and methodologies into work which correlates to phases of a project.

    c. They make up the business analysis life cycle.

    d. They represent areas of specific business analysis expertise that encompass several tasks.

ECBA™ Certification Study Guide

## Answers to Pop-up Quiz

| Question | Answer | Description |
|---|---|---|
| 1 | A | BABOK section 1.2. Business analysis is the practice of enabling change in an enterprise by defining needs and recommending solutions that deliver value to stakeholders. |
| 2 | C | BABOK section 1.2. Business analysis is performed on a variety of initiatives within an enterprise. Initiatives may be strategic, tactical, or operational. |
| 3 | D | BABOK section 1.3. Business analysts are responsible for discovering, synthesizing, and analyzing information from a variety of sources within an enterprise, including tools, processes, documentation, and stakeholders. The business analyst is responsible for eliciting the actual needs of stakeholders... Business analysts play a role in aligning the designed and delivered solutions with the needs of stakeholders. |
| 4 | B | BABOK figure 1.1.1. The following image shows how three of the knowledge areas support the delivery of business value before, during, and after the life cycle of a project. |
| 5 | A | BABOK section 1.3. Business analysts play a role in aligning the designed and delivered solutions with the needs of stakeholders. The activities that business analysts perform include understanding enterprise problems and goals, analyzing needs and solutions, devising strategies, driving change, and facilitating stakeholder collaboration. |
| 6 | D | BABOK section 1.3. A business analyst is any person who performs business analysis tasks described in the *BABOK® Guide*, no matter their job title or organizational role. |
| 7 | B | BABOK section 1.2. It can be used to understand the current state, to define the future state, and to determine the activities required to move from the current to the future state. |
| 8 | C | BABOK section 1.1. The primary purpose of the *BABOK® Guide* is to define the profession of business analysis and provide a set of commonly accepted practices. |
| 9 | B | BABOK section 1.4.3. The definition of a given task is universally applicable to business analysis efforts, independent of the initiative type. |
| 10 | D | BABOK section 1.4.2. Knowledge areas represent areas of specific business analysis expertise that encompass several tasks. |

# Business Analysis Key Concepts

## Overview

Business Analysis Key Concepts provides a foundation for all other content, concepts, and ideas within the practice of business analysis. It provides those new to the business analysis role with a basic understanding of the central ideas necessary for understanding and employing the basic business analysis concepts, competencies and techniques in their daily business analysis practice.

## What You Will Learn

When you are finished with this chapter, you will know:

- The Business Analysis Core Concept Model™ (BACCM™)
- Basic key terms for business analysis practitioners
- The requirements classification schema
- Who your stakeholders are
- How to distinguish requirements and designs

## 2.1 The Business Analysis Core Concept Model™

The *Business Analysis Core Concept Model™* (*BACCM™*) is a conceptual model of what business analysis is and the fundamental ideas that should be considered when determining your approach to business analysis activities. It is composed of six terms that have a common meaning to all business analysts and helps BAs discuss both business analysis and its relationships with common terminology. These six concepts transcend industries, levels of an organization, initiatives, methodologies and global perspectives.

These concepts are fundamental to the practice of business analysis. They are equal in importance and significance. This means there is no place that is best to begin or end, you can begin with any of the concepts. The concepts are interrelated; a change in any concept will have an effect on the other five concepts.

> Each concept is equal in importance and significance to the others.

These concepts are applied differently within the context of each of the knowledge areas; therefore, you will see it in the beginning of each knowledge area chapter in the *BABOK® Guide* with an explanation of how it is used and applied in that particular knowledge area. This study guide will help you understand those concepts and their application in the knowledge areas.

### Figure 2.1.1: The Business Analysis Core Concept Model™ (BACCM™)

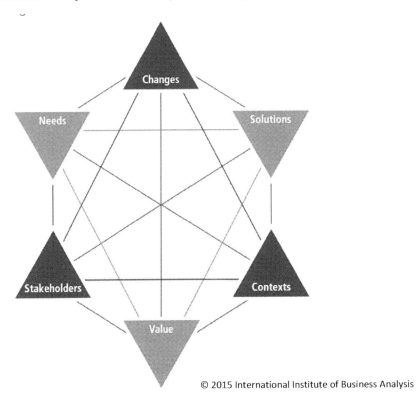

© 2015 International Institute of Business Analysis

### Table 2.1.1: The six core concepts of the BACCM™

| Core Concept | Description |
|---|---|
| **Change** | The act of transformation in response to a need. |
| | Change works to improve the performance of an enterprise. These improvements are deliberate and controlled through business analysis activities. |
| **Need** | A problem or opportunity to be addressed. |
| | Needs can cause changes by motivating stakeholders to act. Changes can also cause needs by eroding or enhancing the value delivered by existing solutions. |
| **Solution** | A specific way of satisfying one or more needs in a context. |
| | A solution satisfies a need by resolving a problem faced by stakeholders or enabling stakeholders to take advantage of an opportunity. |
| **Stakeholder** | A group or individual with a relationship to the change, the need, or the solution. |
| | Stakeholders are often defined in terms of interest in, impact on, and influence over the change. Stakeholders are grouped based on their relationship to the needs, changes, and solutions. |

Chapter 2 Business Analysis Key Concepts

| Core Concept | Description |
|---|---|
| Value | The worth, importance, or usefulness of something to a stakeholder within a context. |
| | Value can be seen as potential or realized returns, gains, and improvements. It is also possible to have a decrease in value in the form of losses, risks, and costs. |
| | Value can be tangible or intangible. Tangible value is directly measurable. Tangible value often has a significant monetary component. Intangible value is measured indirectly. Intangible value often has a significant motivational component, such as a company's reputation or employee morale. |
| | In some cases, value can be assessed in absolute terms, but in many cases is assessed in relative terms: one solution option is more valuable than another from the perspective of a given set of stakeholders. |
| Concept | The circumstances that influence, are influenced by, and provide understanding of the change. |
| | Changes occur within a context. The context is everything relevant to the change that is within the environment.<br>Context may include attitudes, behaviors, beliefs, competitors, culture, demographics, goals, governments, infrastructure, languages, losses, processes, products, projects, sales, seasons, terminology, technology, weather, and any other element meeting the definition. |

> **Memory Trick**
>
> We deliver **V**alue from a **S**olution to a **N**eed of the **S**takeholders in **C**ontext of a **C**hange.

## 2.2 Key Terms

One of the challenges that all business analysis practitioners feel during their career is the challenge of terminology. Words and phrases (terms) mean different things to different people. This can be further exacerbated by geographic or cultural barriers. This was a challenge for the framers of the *BABOK® Guide* as well. IIBA® sought to define the generally accepted terms below as they are used within the profession.

As you prepare to sit for your certification exam, remember that the exam will test you on your understanding of the terminology from the BABOK®., whether you call that concept by another name or not. So be sure to use (and think) in terminology of the BABOK as you prepare for the exam.

> Please see a more complete list of key terms in the Glossary in Appendix A in the BABOK.

**Table 2.2.1: Definition of Business Analysis Key Terms**

| Term | Definition |
| --- | --- |
| **Business Analysis** | The practice of enabling change in an enterprise by defining needs and recommending solutions that deliver value to stakeholders. |
| **Business Analysis Information** | Business analysis information refers to the broad and diverse sets of information that business analysts analyze, transform, and report. It is information of any kind—at any level of detail—that is used as an input to, or is an output of, business analysis work. Examples of business analysis information include elicitation results, requirements, designs, solution options, solution scope, and change strategy.<br><br>Talk about an ambiguous term. For a profession that brings clarity to ambiguity, it is interesting to have a concept with such a broad definition. Again, whether you like this term or not, it may be on your exam; so understand its meaning. |
| **Business Analyst** | Any person within the organization that performs business analysis tasks, no matter their job title. |
| **Design** | A usable representation of a solution. Design focuses on understanding how value might be realized by a solution if it is built. |
| **Domain** | The sphere of knowledge that defines a set of common requirements, terminology, and functionality for any program or initiative solving a problem. |
| **Enterprise** | A system of one or more organizations and the solutions they use to pursue a shared set of common goals. These solutions (also referred to as organizational capabilities) can be processes, tools or information. For the purpose of business analysis, enterprise boundaries can be defined relative to the change and need not be constrained by the boundaries of a legal entity, organization, or organizational unit. An enterprise may include any number of business, government, or any other type of organization. |
| **Organization** | An autonomous group of people under the management of a single individual or board, that works towards common goals and objectives. |
| **Plan** | A proposal for doing or achieving something. Plans describe a set of events, the dependencies among the events, the expected sequence, the schedule, the results or outcomes, the materials and resources needed, and the stakeholders involved. |
| **Requirement** | A usable representation of a need. Requirements focus on understanding what kind of value could be delivered if a requirement is fulfilled. |

Chapter 2 Business Analysis Key Concepts

| Term | Definition |
|---|---|
| **Risk** | The effect of uncertainty on the value of a change, a solution, or the enterprise. This effect can be either positive or negative.<br><br>Business analysts collaborate with other stakeholders to identify, assess, and prioritize risks, and to deal with those risks. Different ways to deal with a risk include:<br><ul><li>Reducing the likelihood that an event causing uncertainty occurs.</li><li>Mitigating the impact (consequences) of the risk.</li><li>Removing the source of the risk.</li><li>Avoiding the risk altogether by deciding not to start or continue with an activity that leads to the risk.</li><li>Sharing the risk with other parties.</li><li>Accepting a risk that might have a low probability of occurring or low impact on the change.</li><li>Increasing the risk to deal with an opportunity.</li></ul> |
| **Stakeholder** | An individual or group who are likely to participate in the execution of that task or who will be affected by it. |

## 2.3 Requirements Classification Schema

The *BABOK® Guide* defines multiple types, or levels, of requirements. These requirements types are defined at different times in the initiative life cycle, and can involve different stakeholders. They are at different levels of abstraction, going from an abstract level of context to a more concrete level as you go down the schema.

It is not enough to understand the concept of a requirement, or what some of your stakeholders may call "business requirements"; there are four types of requirements, one of which is subdivided into two categories.

**Table 2.3.1: Definition of requirement types**

| Requirement Type | Definition |
|---|---|
| **Business Requirements** | Statements of goals, objectives, and outcomes that describe why a change has been initiated. They can apply to the whole of an enterprise, a business area, or a specific initiative. |
| **Stakeholder Requirements** | Describe the needs of stakeholders that must be met in order to achieve the business requirements. They may serve as a bridge between business and solution requirements. |
| **Solution Requirements** | Describe the capabilities and qualities of a solution that meets the stakeholder requirements. They provide the appropriate |

| Requirement Type | Definition |
|---|---|
| | level of detail to allow for the development and implementation of the solution. |
| • Functional Requirements | Describe the capabilities that a solution must have in terms of the behavior and information that the solution will manage. |
| • Non-functional Requirements | Describe conditions under which a solution must remain effective or qualities that a solution must have. |
| Transition Requirements | Describe the capabilities that the solution must have and the conditions the solution must meet to facilitate transition from the current state to the future state, but which are not needed once the change is complete. They are differentiated from other requirements types because they are of a temporary nature. Transition requirements address topics such as data conversion, training, and business continuity. |

> **Mnemonic**
>
> "BSSFNT"
> You should always write in a good "BusineSS FoNT"
>
> B = Business
> S = Stakeholder
> S = Solution
> F = Functional
> N = Non-functional
> T = Transition

## 2.4 Stakeholders

A stakeholder is an individual or group that a business analyst is likely to interact with directly or indirectly in the execution of a task or who will be affected by it. Each task in the BABOK® contains a list of stakeholders who are likely to participate or be affected by that task. These lists are not intended to be an exhaustive list of all possible stakeholder classifications. Also, be aware that a single individual may fill more than one role.

Table 2.4.1: Definition of Stakeholder roles

| Stakeholder Role | Definition |
|---|---|
| Business Analyst | Responsible and accountable for business analysis activities. In some cases, may also be responsible for performing activities that fall under another stakeholder role, such as the project manager or tester. |
| Customer | Consumer of products or services produced by the enterprise and may have contractual or moral rights that the enterprise is obliged to meet. |
| Domain Subject Matter Expert | Any individual with in-depth knowledge of a topic relevant to the business need or solution scope, typically end users fill this role. |

| Stakeholder Role | Definition |
|---|---|
| End User | Stakeholders who directly interact with the solution. |
| Implementation Subject Matter Expert | Any stakeholder who has specialized knowledge regarding the implementation of one or more solution components. |
| Operational Support | Responsible for the day-to-day management and maintenance of a system or product. |
| Project Manager | Responsible for managing the work required to deliver a solution that meets a business need, and for ensuring that the project's objectives are met while balancing the project factors including scope, budget, schedule, resources, quality, and risk. |
| Regulator | Responsible for the definition and enforcement of standards |
| Sponsor | Responsible for initiating the effort to define a business need and develop a solution that meets that need. They authorize the work to be performed, and control the budget and scope for the initiative. Alternate roles are executive and project sponsor. |
| Supplier | A stakeholder outside the boundary of the organization who provide products or services to the organization and may have contractual or moral rights and obligations to do so. |
| Tester | Responsible for determining how to verify that the solution meets the requirements and ensure that it meets applicable quality standards. An alternate role is quality assurance analyst. |

## 2.5 Requirements and Designs

We have always recognized eliciting, analyzing, validating, and managing requirements as key activities of business analysis. However, it is important to recognize that business analysts are also responsible for the definition of design, at some level, in an initiative. The level of responsibility for design varies based on the perspective within which a business analyst is working.

Requirements are focused on the need; designs are focused on the solution. The distinction between requirements and designs is not always clear. The same techniques are used to elicit, model, and analyze both. A requirement leads to a design which in turn may drive the discovery and analysis of more requirements. The shift in focus is often subtle. Some of the tasks in the *BABOK® Guide* may refer to requirements, but the intent is to include designs as well.

**NOTES:**

*Use this page to write notes concerning this chapter that you want to remember and will help you pass the ECBA™ exam.*

## 2.6 Student Exercises

1. Match the definition on the right with the BACCM core concept on the left:

    1. Change  ___
    2. Need  ___
    3. Solution  ___
    4. Stakeholder  ___
    5. Context  ___
    6. Value  ___

    a. A group or individual with a relationship to the change, the need, or the solution.
    b. The worth, importance, or usefulness of something to a stakeholder within a context.
    c. The act of transformation in response to a need.
    d. A specific way of satisfying one or more needs in a context.
    e. A problem or opportunity to be addressed.
    f. The circumstances that influence, are influenced by, and provide understanding of the change.

    **BONUS:** What is the Mnemonic phrase to help you remember the six BACCM™ core concepts?

    _____

2. List the types of requirements defined in the *BABOK® Guide* in the blanks below, and the mnemonic letter to help you remember them.

| Requirement Type | Mnemonic Letter |
|---|---|
|  |  |
|  |  |
|  |  |
|  |  |
|  |  |
|  |  |

**BONUS:** What is the Mnemonic phrase to help you remember the requirements schema?

_____

3. Use the word that the definition below defines to complete the crossword puzzle.

**ACROSS**

1. A usable representation of a solution.

2. The effect of uncertainty on the value of a change, a solution, or the enterprise.

3. A proposal for doing or achieving something.

4. A usable representation of a need.

5. An individual or group who are likely to participate in the execution of that task or who will be affected by it.

**DOWN**

1. The practice of enabling change in an enterprise by defining needs and recommending solutions that deliver value to stakeholders.

2. A system of one or more organizations and the solutions they use to pursue a shared set of common goals.

Chapter 2 Business Analysis Key Concepts

## Answers to Student Exercises

1. Match the definition on the right with the BACCM core concept on the left:

   1. Change  _C_
   2. Need  _E_
   3. Solution  _D_
   4. Stakeholder  _A_
   5. Context  _F_
   6. Value  _B_

   a. A group or individual with a relationship to the change, the need, or the solution.
   b. The worth, importance, or usefulness of something to a stakeholder within a context.
   c. The act of transformation in response to a need.
   d. A specific way of satisfying one or more needs in a context.
   e. A problem or opportunity to be addressed.
   f. The circumstances that influence, are influenced by, and provide understanding of the change.

   **BONUS:** What is the Mnemonic phrase to help you remember the six BACCM™ core concepts?

   _We deliver Value from a Solution to a Need of the Stakeholders in Context of a Change_

2. List the types of requirements defined in the *BABOK® Guide* in the blanks below, and the mnemonic letter to help you remember them.

   | Requirement Type | Mnemonic Letter |
   | --- | --- |
   | Business Requirements | B |
   | Stakeholder Requirements | S |
   | Solution Requirements | S |
   | Functional Requirements | F |
   | Non-Functional Requirements | N |
   | Transition Requirements | T |

   **BONUS:** What is the Mnemonic phrase to help you remember the requirements schema?

   _Business Font_

ECBA™ Certification Study Guide

3. Use the word that the definition below defines to complete the crossword puzzle.

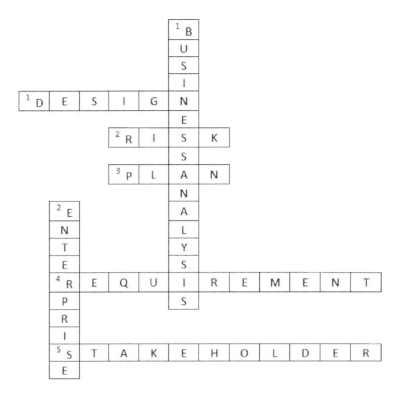

**ACROSS**

1. A usable representation of a solution.   DESIGN

2. The effect of uncertainty on the value of a change, a solution, or the enterprise.   RISK

3. A proposal for doing or achieving something.   PLAN

4. A usable representation of a need.   REQUIREMENT

5. An individual or group who are likely to participate in the execution of that task or who will be affected by it.   STAKEHOLDER

**DOWN**

1. The practice of enabling change in an enterprise by defining needs and recommending solutions that deliver value to stakeholders.   BUSINESS ANALYSIS

2. A system of one or more organizations and the solutions they use to pursue a shared set of common goals.   ENTERPRISE

## 2.7 Business Analysis Key Concepts Pop-up Quiz

1. What is the Business Analysis Core Concept Model™ (BACCM™)?

    a. A conceptual framework for business analysis composed of six terms that have a common meaning to all business analysts.

    b. A business analysis methodology composed of six terms called core concepts.

    c. A discrete framework for business analysis composed of six terms that have a common meaning to all business analysts.

    d. A mindset required to perform business analysis tasks and effectively collaborate with stakeholders within an organization.

2. What are the names of the six core concepts of the Business Analysis Core Concept Model™ (BACCM™)?

    a. Change, Necessity, Product Owner, Solution, Context, and Value.

    b. Change, Need, Stakeholder, Solution, Context, and Value.

    c. Concept, Necessity, Sponsor, Solution, Value, and Change.

    d. Necessity, Stakeholder, Sponsor, Solution, Value, and Concept.

3. Which of the following is the definition in the BABOK® of the core concept "Need"?

    a. Something a stakeholder, or group of stakeholders, desire to have in the solution.

    b. Same thing as a requirement.

    c. A perceived gap between business goals and the current state environment.

    d. A problem or opportunity to be addressed.

4. How does the BABOK® define "requirement"?

    a. A usable representation of a need.

    b. An expectation of the stakeholders.

    c. A proposal of doing or achieving something.

    d. A usable representation of a solution.

5. The business analyst is defining requirements for an initiative that are statements of goals, objectives and outcomes that describe why a change is needed. What classification of requirements is the business analyst defining?

    a. Stakeholder requirements

    b. Transition requirements

    c. Business requirements

    d. Solution requirements

6. Which stakeholder needs to have in-depth knowledge of a topic relevant to the business need or solution scope?

    a. Implementation Subject Matter Expert

    b. Sponsor

    c. Tester

    d. Domain Subject Matter Expert

7. The business analyst has a requirement to develop business strategy, goals, and objectives for a new business; what kind of design should the business analyst develop to help communicate this requirement?

    a. A process model.

    b. A business capability model.

    c. A prototype of a dashboard.

    d. A context model.

8. The business analyst is working on documenting needs concerned with data conversion for an initiative. Which type of requirements is the business analyst documenting?

    a. Non-functional requirements

    b. Solution requirements

    c. Transition requirements

    d. Stakeholder requirements

9. Which stakeholder is responsible for the definition and enforcement of standards?

   a. Regulator

   b. Project Manager

   c. Tester

   d. Sponsor

10. Some information can be viewed as a requirement or a design; what focus can help clarify what is a requirement and what is a design?

    a. Requirements focus on the solution; design focus on the need.

    b. Requirements focus on the need; design focus on the solution.

    c. They both focus on the need.

    d. They both focus on the solution.

## Answers to Pop-up Quiz

| Question | Answer | Description |
|---|---|---|
| 1 | A | BABOK section 2.1. The *Business Analysis Core Concept Model™* (*BACCM™*) is a conceptual framework for business analysis. It is composed of six terms that have a common meaning to all business analysts and helps them discuss both business analysis and its relationships with common terminology. |
| 2 | B | BABOK section 2.1. The six core concepts in the *BACCM* are: Change, Need, Solution, Stakeholder, Value, and Context. |
| 3 | D | BABOK table 2.1.1: Need - A problem or opportunity to be addressed. |
| 4 | A | BABOK section 2.2. A requirement is a usable representation of a need. |
| 5 | C | BABOK section 2.3. Business requirements: statements of goals, objectives, and outcomes that describe why a change has been initiated. |
| 6 | D | BABOK section 2.4.3. A domain subject matter expert is any individual with in-depth knowledge of a topic relevant to the business need or solution scope. |
| 7 | B | BABOK table 2.5.1. |
| 8 | C | BABOK section 2.3. Transition requirements: describe the capabilities that the solution must have and the conditions the solution must meet to facilitate transition from the current state to the future state, but which are not needed once the change is complete. Transition requirements address topics such as data conversion, training, and business continuity. |
| 9 | A | BABOK section 2.4.8. Regulators are responsible for the definition and enforcement of standards. |
| 10 | B | BABOK section 2.5. Requirements are focused on the need; designs are focused on the solution. |

# Business Analysis Planning and Monitoring

## Overview

The Business Analysis Planning and Monitoring (BAPM) knowledge area is about planning the work of the business analyst with stakeholders during an initiative, monitoring actual performance, and identifying how that performance can be improved. A business analyst typically works along with stakeholders to plan, estimate, and manage business analysis effort during a given initiative. The business analyst(s) use the inputs, and guidelines and tools, performs the tasks to produce the outputs of this knowledge area. The business analysis work begins prior to the initiative, works throughout the initiative and can continue after the initiative concludes. These tasks produce outputs that are used as key guidelines for the other tasks throughout the *BABOK® Guide*.

**Goal:** Business Analysis Planning and Monitoring tasks organize and coordinate the efforts of business analysts and stakeholders. This includes planning the business analysis effort, monitoring the results, and identifying how business analysis work can be improved.

Since BAPM is only 5% of the ECBA™ exam blueprint, you will notice that we have reduced our coverage of this knowledge area. Even though there will only be two or three questions on the exam from this knowledge area, a good understanding of this light coverage will help you get those questions right.

## What You Will Learn

When you are finished with this chapter, you will know:

- How to define Business Analysis Planning and Monitoring.
- The goal of Business Analysis Planning and Monitoring.
- The five tasks contained in Business Analysis Planning and Monitoring:
    1. Plan Business Analysis Approach
    2. Plan Stakeholder Engagement
    3. Plan Business Analysis Governance
    4. Plan Business Analysis Information Management
    5. Identify Business Analysis Performance Improvements
- The major areas of emphasis in BAPM include determining the overall approach to the effort, planning how to engage stakeholders, ensuring a process for decision-making, planning the approach to accessing and storing the results from the business analysis work, and recommending ways to improve performance of the business analysis work.

Important learnings in Business Analysis Planning and Monitoring Knowledge Area:

1. Many of the tasks in the knowledge area include the word "plan"; however, the output from these tasks are not called "plans". The BABOK® refers to these outputs as "approaches".
2. There is no Business Analysis Planning and Monitoring task for planning the actual tasks and techniques the business analyst(s) will use during the initiative. These may be considered in the Prepare for Elicitation (4.1) task in the Elicitation and Collaboration knowledge area. Plan Business Analysis Approach task is where business analysis activities are identified.
3. There is no task for estimating how long each task will take; however, estimation is a technique that is *used to determine how long it may take to perform business analysis activities* in BABOK® section 3.1.6. Be prepared to understand the many estimation techniques.
4. In this, and most, knowledge area, projects are referred to as "initiatives" or "the change", but rarely called projects. They are referred to as projects when discussing the project manager in the list of stakeholders, but rarely elsewhere.

**Figure 3.0.1: Business Analysis Planning and Monitoring Input/Task/Output Diagram**

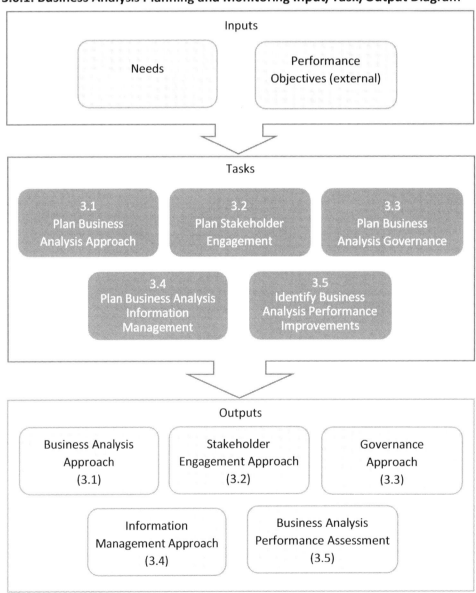

Chapter 3 Business Analysis Planning and Monitoring

## The BACCM™ in Business Analysis Planning and Monitoring

The following model describes the usage and application of each of the core concepts within the context of Business Analysis Planning and Monitoring.

**Figure 3.0.2: Core Concepts application In Business Analysis Planning and Monitoring**

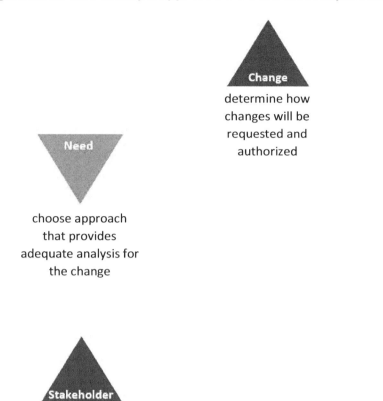

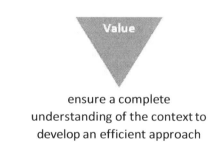

ECBA™ Certification Study Guide

## Tasks in Business Analysis Planning and Monitoring

There are five tasks in the Business Analysis Planning and Monitoring Knowledge Area:

1. Plan Business Analysis Approach
2. Plan Stakeholder Engagement
3. Plan Business Analysis Governance
4. Plan Business Analysis Information Management
5. Identify Business Analysis Performance Improvement

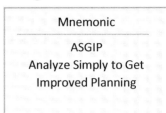

A detailed summary of the Inputs, Tasks, Techniques, Stakeholders and Outputs (ITTSO) in the Business Analysis Planning and Monitoring Knowledge Area begins on the next page.

# Chapter 3 Business Analysis Planning and Monitoring

## Detailed ITTSO Table

The following table summarizes the Inputs, Tasks, Techniques, Stakeholders and Outputs (ITTSO) in the Business Analysis Planning and Monitoring Knowledge Area.

Table 3.0.1: Inputs, Tasks, Techniques, Stakeholders and Outputs Summary

| ITTSO Summary for Business Analysis Planning and Monitoring | | | | | |
|---|---|---|---|---|---|
| **Inputs** | **Tasks** | **M\*** | **Techniques** | **Stakeholders** | **Outputs** |
| • Needs | 3.1 Plan Business Analysis Approach | A | 10.5 Brainstorming<br>10.7 Business Cases<br>10.18 Document Analysis<br>10.19 Estimation<br>10.20 Financial Analysis<br>10.22 Functional Decomposition<br>10.25 Interviews<br>10.26 Item Tracking<br>10.27 Lessons Learned<br>10.35 Process Modeling<br>10.37 Reviews<br>10.38 Risk Analysis and Management<br>10.41 Scope Modeling<br>10.45 Survey and Questionnaire<br>10.50 Workshops | • Domain SME<br>• Project Manager<br>• Regulator<br>• Sponsor | • Business Analysis Approach (3.1) |
| • Needs<br>• Business Analysis Approach (3.1) | 3.2 Plan Stakeholder Engagement | S | 10.5 Brainstorming<br>10.9 Business Rules Analysis<br>10.18 Document Analysis<br>10.25 Interviews<br>10.27 Lessons Learned<br>10.29 Mind Mapping<br>10.32 Organizational Modeling<br>10.35 Process Modeling<br>10.38 Risk Analysis and Management<br>10.41 Scope Modeling<br>10.43 Stakeholder List, Map or Personas<br>10.45 Survey and Questionnaire<br>10.50 Workshops | • Customers<br>• Domain SME<br>• End User<br>• Project Manager<br>• Regulator<br>• Sponsor<br>• Supplier | Stakeholder Engagement Approach (3.2) |

| | | | | | |
|---|---|---|---|---|---|
| • Business Analysis Approach (3.1)<br>• Stakeholder Engagement Approach (3.2) | 3.3 Plan Business Analysis Governance | G | 10.5 Brainstorming<br>10.18 Document Analysis<br>10.25 Interviews<br>10.26 Item Tracking<br>10.27 Lessons Learned<br>10.32 Organizational Modeling<br>10.33 Process Modeling<br>10.37 Reviews<br>10.45 Survey and Questionnaire<br>10.50 Workshops | • Domain SME<br>• Project Manager<br>• Regulator<br>• Sponsor | Governance Approach (3.3) |
| • Business Analysis Approach (3.1)<br>• Stakeholder Engagement Approach (3.2)<br>• Governance Approach (3.3) | 3.4 Plan Business Analysis Information Management | I | 10.5 Brainstorming<br>10.25 Interviews<br>10.26 Item Tracking<br>10.27 Lessons Learned<br>10.29 Mind Mapping<br>10.35 Process Modeling<br>10.45 Survey and Questionnaire<br>10.50 Workshops | • Domain SME<br>• Regulator<br>• Sponsor | Information Management Approach (3.4) |
| • Business Analysis Approach (3.1)<br>• Performance Objectives (external) | 3.5 Identify Business Analysis Performance Improvement | P | 10.5 Brainstorming<br>10.25 Interviews<br>10.26 Item Tracking<br>10.27 Lessons Learned<br>10.28 Metrics and KPIs<br>10.31 Observation<br>10.34 Process Analysis<br>10.35 Process Modeling<br>10.37 Reviews<br>10.38 Risk Analysis and Management<br>10.40 Root Cause Analysis<br>10.45 Survey and Questionnaire<br>10.50 Workshops | • Domain SME<br>• Regulator<br>• Sponsor | Business Analysis Performance Assessment (3.5) |

\* Mnemonic = ASGIP

# Chapter 3 Business Analysis Planning and Monitoring

## Business Analysis Planning and Monitoring Student Exercises

**Exercise 1:** Fill in the blanks to complete the Business Analysis Planning and Monitoring task name, then enter the Mnemonic letter used in this chapter to help remember the tasks in this knowledge area.

| BAPM Tasks | Mnemonic Letter |
|---|---|
| Plan Business Analysis _____ | |
| Plan _____ Engagement | |
| Plan Business Analysis _____ | |
| Plan Business Analysis _____ Management | |
| Identify Business Analysis _____ Improvements | |

**Bonus:** Enter below the phrase used in this chapter to help remember the tasks in Business Analysis Planning and Monitoring knowledge area.

_____

**Exercise 2:** For each stakeholder indicate which task they are involved in by putting an 'X' in the appropriate column under the stakeholder. Some stakeholders may not be involved in any tasks while some stakeholders may be involved in multiple tasks.

| Stakeholder / Task | All Stakeholders | Any Stakeholders | Customers | Domain SME | End User | Implementation SME | Operational Support | Project Manager | Regulator | Sponsor | Supplier | Tester |
|---|---|---|---|---|---|---|---|---|---|---|---|---|
| 3.1 Plan BA Approach | | | | | | | | | | | | |
| 3.2 Plan Stakeholder Engagement | | | | | | | | | | | | |
| 3.3 Plan BA Governance | | | | | | | | | | | | |
| 3.4 Plan BA Information Management | | | | | | | | | | | | |
| 3.5 Identify BA Performance Improvements | | | | | | | | | | | | |

## Answers to Student Exercises

**Exercise 1:** Fill in the blanks to complete the Business Analysis Planning and Monitoring task name, then enter the Mnemonic letter used in this chapter to help remember the tasks in this knowledge area.

| BAPM Tasks | Mnemonic Letter |
|---|---|
| Plan Business Analysis _Approach_ | A |
| Plan _Stakeholder_ Engagement | S |
| Plan Business Analysis _Governance_ | G |
| Plan Business Analysis _Information_ Management | I |
| Identify Business Analysis _Performance_ Improvements | P |

**Bonus:** Enter below the phrase used in this chapter to help remember the tasks in Business Analysis Planning and Monitoring knowledge area.

_Analyze Simply to Get Improved Planning_

**Exercise 2:** For each stakeholder indicate which task they are involved in by putting an 'X' in the appropriate column under the stakeholder. Some stakeholders may not be involved in any tasks while some stakeholders may be involved in multiple tasks.

| Task \ Stakeholder | All Stakeholders | Any Stakeholders | Customers | Domain SME | End User | Implementation SME | Operational Support | Project Manager | Regulator | Sponsor | Supplier | Tester |
|---|---|---|---|---|---|---|---|---|---|---|---|---|
| 3.1 Plan BA Approach | | | | X | | | | X | X | X | | |
| 3.2 Plan Stakeholder Engagement | | | X | X | X | | | X | X | X | X | |
| 3.3 Plan BA Governance | | | | X | | | | X | X | X | | |
| 3.4 Plan BA Information Management | | | | X | | | | | X | X | | |
| 3.5 Identify BA Performance Improvements | | | | X | | | | | X | X | | |

## 3.1 Plan Business Analysis Approach

**Figure 3.1.1: Plan Business Analysis Approach Input/Task/Output Diagram**

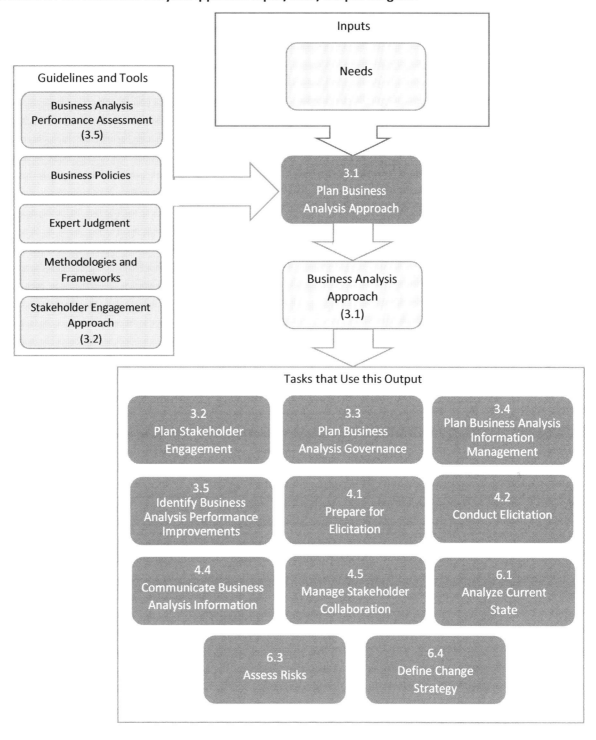

### 3.1.1 Purpose

Define an appropriate method to conduct business analysis activities.

### 3.1.2 Description

Business Analyst(s) work with stakeholders to determine business needs and develop solution options to solve those business needs during an initiative. Before business analysis activities for an initiative can begin business analyst(s) need to determine their overall approach to business analysis activities during the initiative. This includes coordinating work among the business analysts when you have more than one working on an initiative, which is common in larger organizations.

The output (Business Analysis Approach) from this task will define how and when business analysis tasks will be performed, techniques used, stakeholders involved in each task, and deliverables produced from each task. The business analysis approach should align to the overall goals of the change, coordinate the business analysis tasks with the activities and deliverables of the overall change, manage risks, and leverage techniques and tools that have historically worked well in similar change initiatives.

The initial business analysis approach may be determined at the beginning of the change initiative; however, this approach may change as the initiative progresses and the business analyst(s) learns more about the context of the change and its stakeholders.

### 3.1.3 Inputs

- **Needs**: the problem or opportunity faced by the organization.

### 3.1.4 Elements

#### 3.1.4.1 Planning Approach

Planning occurs somewhere along a continuum between predictive and adaptive approaches. Predictive approaches focus on minimizing upfront uncertainty and ensuring that the solution is defined before implementation begins in order to maximize control and minimize risk. Adaptive approaches focus on rapid delivery of business value in short iterations in return for acceptance of a higher degree of uncertainty regarding the overall delivery of the solution. Different approaches may be used within the same initiative.

Regardless of the approach, planning is an essential task to ensure value is delivered to an enterprise. Planning typically occurs more than once on a given initiative as plans are updated to address changing business conditions and newly raised issues. The business analysis approach should describe how plans will be altered if changes are required.

#### 3.1.4.2 Formality and Level of Detail of Business Analysis Deliverables

Predictive approaches typically call for formal documentation. Information is captured at various levels of detail. The specific content and format of business analysis information can vary depending on the organizational methodologies, processes, and templates in use.

Adaptive approaches define requirements and designs through team interaction and gathering feedback on a working solution. Additional business analysis documentation may be created at the discretion of the team, and generally consists of models developed to enhance the team's understanding of a specific problem.

Chapter 3 Business Analysis Planning and Monitoring

Other considerations that may affect the approach include:
- the change is complex and high risk,
- the organization is in, or interacts with, heavily regulated industries,
- contracts or agreements necessitate formality,
- stakeholders are geographically distributed,
- resources are outsourced,
- staff turnover is high and/or team members may be inexperienced,
- requirements must be formally signed off, and
- business analysis information must be maintained long-term or handed over for use on future initiatives.

### 3.1.4.3 Business Analysis Activities

A business analysis approach describes the types of activities that the business analyst(s) will perform.

Integrating business analysis activities in the business analysis approach includes:
- identifying the activities required to complete each deliverable and then breaking each activity into tasks,
- dividing the work into iterations, identifying the deliverables for each iteration, and then identifying the associated activities and tasks, or
- using a previous similar initiative as an outline and applying the detailed tasks and activities unique to the current initiative.

### 3.1.4.4 Timing of Business Analysis Work

Business analysts determine when the business analysis tasks need to be performed and if the level of effort will need to vary over time.

The timing of business analysis activities can also be affected by the availability of resources, priority of the initiative, other concurrent initiatives, or constraints such as contract terms or regulatory deadlines.

### 3.1.4.5 Complexity and Risk

The complexity and size of the change and the overall risk of the effort to the organization are considered when determining the business analysis approach. As complexity and risk increase or decrease, the nature and scope of business analysis work can be altered.

The approach may also be altered based on the number of stakeholders or business analysis resources involved in the initiative. As the number of stakeholders increases, the approach may be adjusted to include additional process steps to better manage the business analysis work.

Other factors that can impact complexity include size of the change, number of business areas or systems affected, geographic and cultural considerations, technological complexities, and any risks that could impede the business analysis effort.

Factors that can impact the risk level of an effort include experience level and domain knowledge of the BA; experience level, attitudes, and competing priorities of stakeholders; any pre-selected framework, methodology, tools, and/or techniques imposed by organizational policies and practices, and cultural norms of the organization.

#### 3.1.4.6 Acceptance

The business analysis approach is reviewed and agreed upon by key stakeholders. Some organizations have more structured processes than others, and may require stakeholder sign-off. Stakeholders also play a role in reviewing and accepting changes to the approach.

### 3.1.5 Guidelines and Tools

| Guideline or Tool | How Utilized in this Task |
|---|---|
| **Business Analysis Performance Assessment (3.5)** | provides results of previous assessments that should be reviewed and incorporated into all planning approaches. |
| **Business Policies** | define the limits within which decisions must be made. They may be described by regulations, contracts, agreements, deals, warranties, certifications, or other legal obligations. These policies can influence the business analysis approach. |
| **Expert Judgment** | used to determine the optimal business analysis approach. Expertise may be provided from a wide range of sources including stakeholders on the initiative, organizational Centers of Excellence, consultants, or associations and industry groups. Prior experiences of the business analyst and other stakeholders should be considered when selecting or modifying an approach. |
| **Methodologies and Frameworks** | shape the approach that will be used by providing methods, techniques, procedures, working concepts, and rules. They may need to be tailored to better meet the needs of the specific business challenge. |
| **Stakeholder Engagement Approach (3.2)** | understanding the stakeholders and their concerns and interests may influence decisions made when determining the business analysis approach. |

### 3.1.6 Techniques

| Technique | How Utilized in this Task |
|---|---|
| **10.5 Brainstorming** | used to identify possible business analysis activities, techniques, risks and other relevant items to help build the business analysis approach. |
| **10.7 Business Cases** | used to understand whether elements of the problem or opportunity are especially time-sensitive, high-value, or whether there is any particular uncertainty around elements of the possible need or solution. |
| **10.18 Document Analysis** | used to review existing organizational assets that might assist in planning the approach. |
| **10.19 Estimation** | used to determine how long it may take to perform business analysis activities. |
| **10.20 Financial Analysis** | used to assess how different approaches (and the supported delivery options) affect the value delivered. |

Chapter 3 Business Analysis Planning and Monitoring

| Technique | How Utilized in this Task |
|---|---|
| 10.22 Functional Decomposition | used to break down complex business analysis processes or approaches into more feasible components. |
| 10.25 Interviews | used to help build the plan with an individual or small group. |
| 10.26 Item Tracking | used to track any issues raised during planning activities with stakeholders. Can also track risk related items raised during discussions when building the approach. |
| 10.27 Lessons Learned | used to identify an enterprise's previous experience (both successes and challenges) with planning business analysis approach. |
| 10.35 Process Modeling | used to define and document the business analysis approach. |
| 10.37 Reviews | used to validate the selected business analysis approach with stakeholders. |
| 10.38 Risk Analysis and Management | used to assess risks in order to select the proper business analysis approach. |
| 10.41 Scope Modeling | used to determine the boundaries of the solution as an input to planning and to estimating. |
| 10.45 Survey and Questionnaire | used to identify possible business analysis activities, techniques, risks and other relevant items to help build the business analysis approach. |
| 10.50 Workshops | used to help build the plan in a team setting. |

## 3.1.7 Stakeholders

| Stakeholder | How Involved in this Task |
|---|---|
| Domain Subject Matter Expert | can be a source of risk when their involvement is required and availability is lacking. The approach taken may depend on availability and level of their involvement with the initiative. |
| Project Manager | determines that the approach is realistic for the overall schedule and timelines. The business analysis approach must be compatible with other project activities. |
| Regulator | may be needed to provide approval for aspects of the business analysis approach or decisions made in tailoring the process, especially in organizations where the business analysis process is audited. |
| Sponsor | can provide needs and objectives for the approach and ensures that organizational policies are followed. The selected approach may depend on availability and involvement with the initiative. |

## 3.1.8 Outputs

- **Business Analysis Approach (3.1)**: identifies activities that will be performed across an initiative including who will perform the activities, the timing and sequencing of the work, the deliverables that will be produced and techniques that may be utilized.

## 3.2 Plan Stakeholder Engagement

**Figure 3.2.1: Plan Stakeholder Engagement Input/Task/Output Diagram**

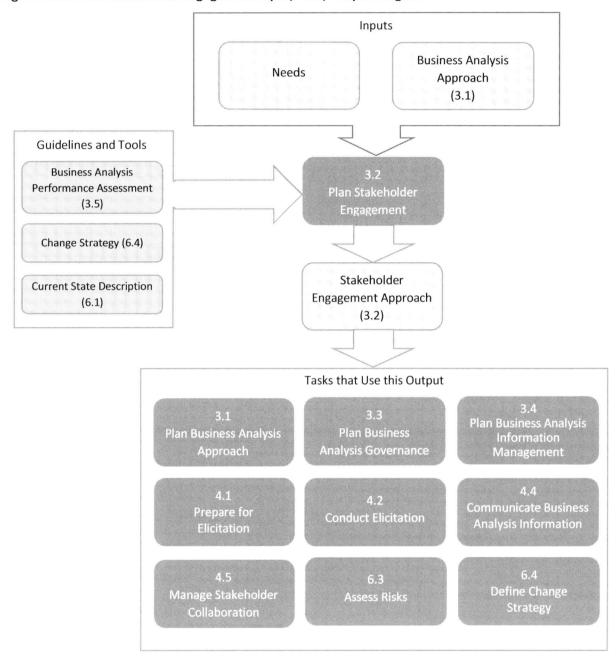

### 3.2.1 Purpose

Plan an approach for establishing and maintaining effective working relationships with the stakeholders.

## 3.2.2 Description

Business Analysts collaborate closely with stakeholders throughout an initiative. Prior to that work beginning, business analysts must determine their approach to that work with stakeholders.

Plan Stakeholder Engagement involves conducting a thorough analysis to identify all of the involved stakeholders and analyze their characteristics. The results of the analysis are then utilized to define the best collaboration and communication approaches for the initiative and to appropriately plan for stakeholder risks.

When planning for stakeholder engagement, the degree of complexity can increase disproportionately as the number of stakeholders involved in the activities increases. This is important because new or different techniques for the collaboration with stakeholders may be required when the engagement moves from collaborating with a few stakeholders into dozens, hundreds, or even thousands of people.

## 3.2.3 Inputs

- **Needs**: understanding the business need and the parts of the enterprise that it affects helps in the identification of stakeholders. The need may evolve as stakeholder analysis is performed.
- **Business Analysis Approach (3.1)**: incorporating the overall business analysis approach into the stakeholder analysis, collaboration, and communication approaches is necessary to ensure consistency across the approaches.

## 3.2.4 Elements

### 3.2.4.1 Perform Stakeholder Analysis

A thorough and detailed stakeholder list ensures that stakeholders are not overlooked. Understanding who the stakeholders are, the impact of proposed changes on them, and the influence they may have on the change is vital to the success of the initiative in meeting stakeholder expectations. If stakeholders are not identified, the business analyst may miss uncovering critical needs. Stakeholder needs uncovered late will often require a revision to business analysis and/or development tasks. This can result in increased costs and decreased stakeholder satisfaction.

How business analysts perform stakeholder analysis can vary between projects, methodologies, and organizations. Business analysts need to consider stakeholder roles, attitudes, decision making authority, and level of influence when developing their stakeholder approach.

### 3.2.4.2 Define Stakeholder Collaboration

Ensuring effective collaboration with stakeholders is essential for maintaining their engagement in business analysis activities. Collaboration can be a spontaneous event. However, much collaboration is deliberate and planned. The business analyst may plan different collaboration approaches for internal and external stakeholders. Some considerations when planning collaboration include timing and frequency of collaboration, location, available tools, delivery method such as in-person or virtual, and preferences of the stakeholders.

As factors change, the approach can be revisited, and adapted to ensure ongoing engagement of stakeholders.

### 3.2.4.3 Stakeholder Communication Needs

The business analyst evaluates what needs to be communicated, what is the appropriate delivery method (written or verbal), who the appropriate audience is, when communication should occur, frequency of communication, geographic location of stakeholders who will receive communications, level of detail appropriate for the communication and stakeholder, and level of formality of communications.

## 3.2.5 Guidelines and Tools

| Guideline or Tool | How Utilized in this Task |
| --- | --- |
| Business Analysis Performance Assessment (3.5) | provides results of previous assessments that should be reviewed and incorporated into all planning approaches. |
| Change Strategy (6.4) | used for improved assessment of stakeholder impact and the development of more effective stakeholder engagement strategies. |
| Current State Description (6.1) | provides the context within which the work needs to be completed. This information will lead to more effective stakeholder analysis and better understanding of the impact of the desired change. |

## 3.2.6 Techniques

| Technique | How Utilized in this Task |
| --- | --- |
| 10.5 Brainstorming | used to produce the stakeholder list and identify stakeholder roles and responsibilities. |
| 10.9 Business Rules Analysis | used to identify stakeholders who were the source of the business rules. |
| 10.18 Document Analysis | used to review existing organizational assets that might assist in planning stakeholder engagement. |
| 10.25 Interviews | used to interact with specific stakeholders to gain more information or knowledge about stakeholder groups. |
| 10.27 Lessons Learned | used to identify an enterprise's previous experience (both successes and challenges) with planning stakeholder engagement. |
| 10.29 Mind Mapping | used to identify potential stakeholders and help understand the relationships between them. |
| 10.32 Organizational Modeling | used to determine if the organizational units or people listed have any unique needs and interests that should be considered. Organizational models describe the roles and functions in the organization and the ways in which stakeholders interact which can help to identify stakeholders who will be affected by a change. |
| 10.35 Process Modeling | used to categorize stakeholders by the systems that support their business processes. |

Chapter 3 Business Analysis Planning and Monitoring

| Technique | How Utilized in this Task |
|---|---|
| 10.38 Risk Analysis and Management | used to identify risks to the initiative resulting from stakeholder attitudes or the inability of key stakeholders to participate in the initiative. |
| 10.41 Scope Modeling | used to develop scope models to show stakeholders that fall outside the scope of the solution but still interact with it in some way. |
| 10.43 Stakeholder List, Map or Personas | used to depict the relationship of stakeholders to the solution and to one another. |
| 10.45 Survey and Questionnaire | used to identify shared characteristics of a stakeholder group. |
| 10.50 Workshops | used to interact with groups of stakeholders to gain more information about stakeholder groups. |

### 3.2.7 Stakeholders

| Stakeholder | How Involved in this Task |
|---|---|
| **Customers** | a source of external stakeholders. |
| **Domain Subject Matter Expert** | may help to identify stakeholders and may themselves be identified to fulfill one or more roles on the initiative. |
| **End User** | a source of internal stakeholders. |
| **Project Manager** | may be able to identify and recommend stakeholders. Responsibility for stakeholder identification and management may be shared with the business analyst. |
| **Regulator** | may require that specific stakeholder representatives or groups be involved in the business analysis activities. |
| **Sponsor** | may request that specific stakeholders be involved in the business analysis activities. |
| **Supplier** | a source of external stakeholders. |

### 3.2.8 Outputs

- **Stakeholder Engagement Approach (3.2)**: contains a list of the stakeholders, their characteristics which were analyzed, and a listing of roles and responsibilities for the change. It also identifies the collaboration and communication approaches the business analyst will utilize during the initiative.

## 3.3 Plan Business Analysis Governance

**Figure 3.3.1: Plan Business Analysis Governance Input/Task/Output Diagram**

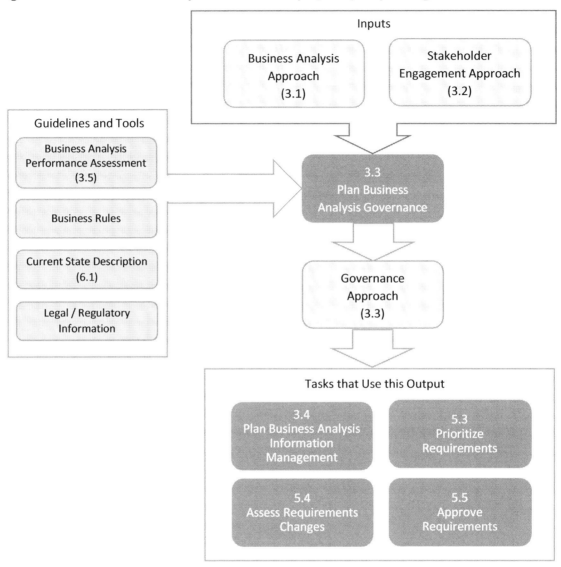

### 3.3.1 Purpose

Define how decisions are made about requirements and designs, including reviews, change control, approvals, and prioritization.

### 3.3.2 Description

A governance process identifies the decision makers, process, and information required for decisions to be made. A governance process describes how approvals and prioritization decisions are made for requirements and designs.

Governance approach identify how business analysis work will be approached and prioritized, what the process for proposing a change to business analysis information is, who has the authority and responsibility to propose changes and who should be involved in the change discussions, who has responsibility for analyzing change requests, who has the authority to approve changes, and how changes will be documented and communicated.

Chapter 3 Business Analysis Planning and Monitoring

## 3.3.3 Inputs

- **Business Analysis Approach (3.1)**: incorporating the overall business analysis approach into the governance approach is necessary to ensure consistency across the approaches.
- **Stakeholder Engagement Approach (3.2)**: identifying stakeholders and understanding their communication and collaboration needs is useful in determining their participation in the governance approach. The engagement approach may be updated based on the completion of the governance approach.

## 3.3.4 Elements

### 3.3.4.1 Decision Making

A stakeholder may serve in various roles in the decision-making process such as participant in decision-making discussions, SME lending experience and knowledge to the decision-making process, reviewer, and approver.

The decision-making process defines the escalation path when teams cannot reach consensus.

### 3.3.4.2 Change Control Process

The change control process defines:

- **The process for requesting changes**: specify which requirements and designs the change control process covers and determine whether it applies to all changes or only to specific changes. This process details the steps for proposing a change, when changes can be proposed, who can propose changes and how change requests are communicated.
- **The elements of the change request**: identify the information to be included in a change request. Possible components to consider on a change request are cost and time estimates, benefits, risks, priority, and course(s) of action.
- **How changes will be prioritized**: the priority of the proposed change is established relative to other competing interests within the current initiative.
- **How changes will be documented**: configuration management and traceability standards establish product baselines and version control practices that identify which baseline is affected by the change.
- **How changes will be communicated**: how proposed changes, changes under review, and approved, declined, or deferred changes will be communicated to stakeholders.
- **Who will perform the impact analysis**: specify who is responsible for performing the impact analysis for proposed changes.
- **Who will authorize changes**: include a designation of who can approve changes.

### 3.3.4.3 Plan Prioritization Approach

Timelines, expected value, dependencies, resource constraints, adopted methodologies, and other factors influence how requirements and designs are prioritized. When planning the prioritization process, determine the formality and rigor of the prioritization process, participants who will be involved in prioritization, process for deciding how prioritization will occur, including techniques used, and criteria to be used for prioritization.

#### 3.3.4.4 Plan for Approvals

An approval formalizes the agreement between all stakeholders that the content and presentation of the requirements and designs are accurate, adequate, and contain sufficient detail to allow for continued progress to be made.

The timing and frequency of approvals are dependent on the size and complexity of the change and associated risks. The business analyst must determine the type of requirements and designs to be approved, the timing, process, and who will approve them.

When planning the appropriate approval process, business analysts consider the organizational culture and the type of information being approved.

### 3.3.5 Guidelines and Tools

| Guideline or Tool | How Utilized in this Task |
|---|---|
| **Business Analysis Performance Assessment (3.5)** | provides results of previous assessments that should be reviewed and incorporated into all planning approaches. |
| **Business Policies** | define the limits within which decisions must be made. They may be described by regulations, contracts, agreements, warranties, certifications or other legal obligations. |
| **Current State Description (6.1)** | provides the context within which the work needs to be completed. This information can help drive how to make better decisions. |
| **Legal/Regulatory Information** | describes legislative rules or regulations that must be followed, and can be used to help develop a framework that ensures sound business decision making. |

### 3.3.6 Techniques

| Technique | How Utilized in this Task |
|---|---|
| **10.5 Brainstorming** | used to generate an initial list of potential stakeholder names who may need approval roles in the defined governance process. |
| **10.18 Document Analysis** | used to evaluate existing governance processes or templates. |
| **10.25 Interviews** | used to identify possible decision-making, change control, approval, or prioritization approaches and participants with an individual or small group. |
| **10.26 Item Tracking** | used to track any issues that arise when planning a governance approach. |
| **10.27 Lessons Learned** | used to find if past initiatives have identified valuable experiences with governance that can be leveraged on current or future initiatives. |
| **10.32 Organizational Modeling** | used to understand roles/responsibilities within the organization in an effort to define a governance approach that involves the right stakeholders. |
| **10.35 Process Modeling** | used to document the process or method for governing business analysis. |

Chapter 3 Business Analysis Planning and Monitoring

| Technique | How Utilized in this Task |
|---|---|
| 10.37 Reviews | used to review the proposed governance plan with key stakeholders. |
| 10.45 Survey and Questionnaire | used to identify possible decision-making, change control, approval, or prioritization approaches and participants. |
| 10.50 Workshops | used to identify possible decision-making, change control, approval, or prioritization approaches and participants within a team setting. |

### 3.3.7 Stakeholders

| Stakeholder | How Involved in this Task |
|---|---|
| **Domain Subject Matter Expert** | may be a possible source of a requested change or may be identified as needing to be involved in change discussions. |
| **Project Manager** | works with the business analyst to ensure that overall project governance aligns with the business analysis governance approach. |
| **Regulator** | may impose rules or regulations that need to be considered when determining the business analysis governance plan. May also be a possible source of a requested change. |
| **Sponsor** | can impose their own requirements for how business analysis information should be managed. Participates in change discussions and approves proposed changes. |

### 3.3.8 Outputs

- **Governance Approach (3.3)**: identifies the stakeholders who will have the responsibility and authority to make decisions about business analysis work including who will be responsible for setting priorities and who will approve changes to business analysis information. It also defines the requirements and design change process.

## 3.4 Plan Business Analysis Information Management

### 3.4.1 Purpose

Develop an approach for how business analysis information will be stored and accessed.

### 3.4.2 Description

Business analysis information is comprised of all the information business analysts elicit, create, compile, and disseminate in the course of performing business analysis, including models, scope statements, stakeholder concerns, elicitation results, requirements, designs, solution options, user stories, prototypes, etc.

Information management entails identifying how information should be organized, the level of detail at which information should be captured, any relationships between the information, how information may be used across multiple initiatives and throughout the enterprise, how information should be accessed and stored, and characteristics about the information that must be maintained.

**Figure 3.4.1: Plan Business Analysis Information Management Input/Task/Output Diagram**

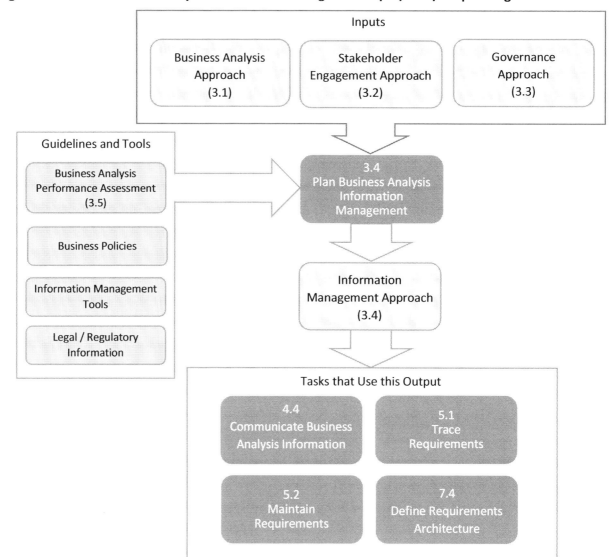

### 3.4.3 Inputs

- **Business Analysis Approach (3.1)**: incorporating the overall business analysis approach into the information management approach is necessary to ensure consistency across the approaches.

- **Governance Approach (3.2)**: defines how business analysts manage changes to requirements and designs, how decisions and approvals for business analysis deliverables will be made, and how priorities will be set.

- **Stakeholder Engagement Approach (3.3)**: identifying stakeholders and understanding their communication and collaboration needs is useful in determining their specific information management needs.

Chapter 3 Business Analysis Planning and Monitoring

### 3.4.4 Elements

#### 3.4.4.1 Organization of Business Analysis Information

Business analysts are responsible for organizing business analysis information in a manner that allows for efficient access and use.

The business analyst determines how best to structure and organize the business analysis information at the start of an initiative. This involves taking into consideration the type and amount of information to be collected, the stakeholder's access and usage needs, and the size and complexity of the change.

#### 3.4.4.2 Level of Abstraction

Level of abstraction describes the breadth and depth of the information being provided. In determining how much detail each stakeholder may require as the initiative evolves, consideration is given to the needs of the stakeholders, the complexity of what is being explained, and the importance of the change. Rather than present the same information to all stakeholders, business analysts should present information with appropriate breadth and level of detail based on each stakeholder's role.

#### 3.4.4.3 Plan Traceability Approach

The traceability approach is based on the complexity of the domain, the number of views of requirements that will be produced, any requirement-related risks, organizational standards, applicable regulatory requirements, and an understanding of the costs and benefits involved with tracing. Business analysts plan to ensure the approach is at a level of detail to add value without excessive overhead.

#### 3.4.4.4 Plan for Requirements Reuse

Reusing requirements can save an organization time, effort, and cost. To make requirements useful beyond the current change, business analysts plan ahead for requirements reuse by identifying how best to structure, store, and access requirements so they are usable and accessible for future business analysis efforts. In order for requirements to be reused they must be clearly named, defined, and stored in a repository that is available to other business analysts.

#### 3.4.4.5 Storage and Access

Storage decisions depend on many factors such as who must access the information, how often they need to access it, and what conditions must be present for access. Organizational standards and tool availability also influence storage and access decisions. The business analysis approach defines how various tools will be used on the initiative and how the information will be captured and stored within those tools. The repository may need to store information other than requirements and designs. It should be able to indicate the status of any stored information, and allow for modification of that information over time.

#### 3.4.4.6 Requirements Attributes

Requirements attributes provide information about requirements, and aid in the ongoing management of the requirements throughout the change. The information documented by the attributes helps the team efficiently and effectively make trade-offs between requirements, identify stakeholders affected by potential changes, and understand the effect of a proposed change.

Some commonly used requirements attributes include:
- **Absolute reference**: provides a unique identifier. The reference is not altered or reused if the requirement is moved, changed, or deleted.
- **Author**: provides the name of the person who needs to be consulted should the requirement later be found to be ambiguous, unclear, or in conflict.
- **Complexity**: indicates how difficult the requirement will be to implement.
- **Ownership**: indicates the individual or group that needs the requirement or will be the business owner after the solution is implemented.
- **Priority**: indicates relative importance of requirements. Priority can refer to the relative value of a requirement or to the sequence in which it will be implemented.
- **Risks**: identifies uncertain events that may impact requirements.
- **Source**: identifies the origin of the requirement. The source is often consulted if the requirement changes or if more information regarding the requirement or the need that drove the requirement has to be obtained.
- **Stability**: indicates the maturity of the requirement.
- **Status**: indicates the state of the requirement, whether it is proposed, accepted, verified, postponed, cancelled, or implemented.
- **Urgency**: indicates how soon the requirement is needed. It is usually only necessary to specify this separately from the priority when a deadline exists for implementation.

## 3.4.5 Guidelines and Tools

| Guideline or Tool | How Utilized in this Task |
|---|---|
| **Business Analysis Performance Assessment (3.5)** | provides results of previous assessments that should be reviewed and incorporated into all planning approaches. |
| **Business Policies** | define the limits within which decisions must be made. They may be described by regulations, contracts, agreements, warranties, certifications, or other legal obligations. |
| **Information Management Tools** | each organization uses some tools to store, retrieve, and share business analysis information. These may be as simple as a whiteboard, or as complex as a global wiki or robust requirements management tool. |
| **Legal/Regulatory Information** | describes legislative rules or regulations that must be followed, and helps determine how business analysis information will be managed. |

## 3.4.6 Techniques

| Technique | How Utilized in this Task |
|---|---|
| 10.5 Brainstorming | used to help stakeholders uncover their business analysis information management needs. |
| 10.25 Interviews | used to help specific stakeholders uncover their business analysis information management needs. |
| 10.26 Item Tracking | used to track issues with current information management processes. |
| 10.27 Lessons Learned | used to create a source of information for analyzing approaches for efficiently managing business analysis information. |
| 10.29 Mind Mapping | used to identify and categorize the kinds of information that need to be managed. |
| 10.35 Process Modeling | used to document the process or method for managing business analysis information. |
| 10.45 Survey and Questionnaire | used to ask stakeholders to provide input into defining business analysis information management. |
| 10.50 Workshops | used to uncover business analysis information management needs in a group setting. |

## 3.4.7 Stakeholders

| Stakeholder | How Involved in this Task |
|---|---|
| **Domain Subject Matter Expert** | may need to access and work with business analysis information, and will be interested in a more specific view of business analysis information which relates to their area of expertise. |
| **Regulator** | may define rules and processes related to information management. |
| **Sponsor** | reviews, comments on, and approves business analysis information. |

## 3.4.8 Outputs

- **Information Management Approach (3.4)**: includes the defined approach for how business analysis information will be stored, accessed, and utilized during the change and after the change is complete.

## 3.5 Identify Business Analysis Performance Improvements

### 3.5.1 Purpose

Assess business analysis work and to plan to improve processes where required.

ECBA™ Certification Study Guide

**Figure 3.5.1: Identify Business Analysis Performance Improvements Input/Task/Output Diagram**

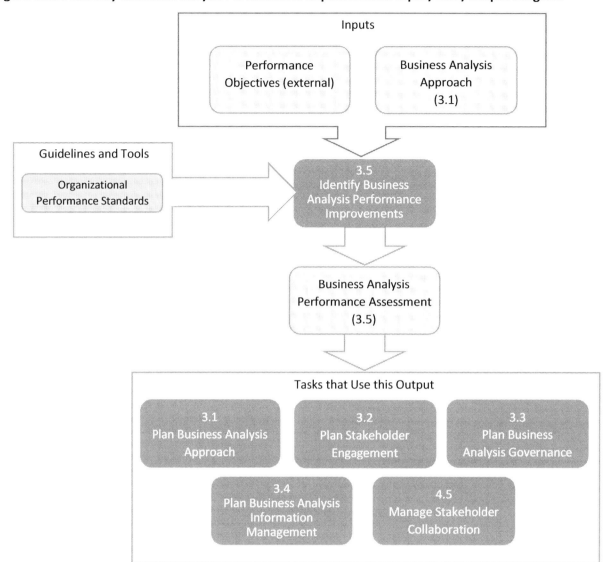

### 3.5.2 Description

To monitor and improve performance, it is necessary to establish the performance measures, conduct the performance analysis, report on the results of that analysis, and identify any necessary improvement actions that can be taken.

### 3.5.3 Inputs

- **Business Analysis Approach (3.1)**: identifies business analysis deliverables that will be produced, activities that will need to be performed (including when they will be performed and who will be performing them), and techniques that will be used.
- **Performance Objectives (external)**: describe the desired performance outcomes that an enterprise or organization is hoping to achieve.

Chapter 3 Business Analysis Planning and Monitoring

## 3.5.4 Elements

### 3.5.4.1 Performance Analysis

Effective business analysis work depends on the context of a particular organization or initiative. Reports on business analysis performance can be informal and verbal, or they may include formal documentation. It can be tailored to meet the needs of the reviewers.

### 3.5.4.2 Assessment Measures

If current measures exist, the business analyst may leverage them or determine new measures. The business analyst may also elicit assessment measures from stakeholders. Appropriate performance measures enable the business analyst to determine when problems are occurring that may affect the performance of business analysis or identify opportunities for improvement. Measures may be both quantitative and qualitative.

All performance metrics will encourage certain behaviors and discourage others. Poorly chosen metrics may drive behavior that is detrimental to the enterprise as a whole.

### 3.5.4.3 Analyze Results

The business analysis process and deliverables are compared against the set of defined measures. The analysis may be performed on the business analysis process, the resources involved, and the deliverables. Performance may be determined from the point of view of the stakeholders who are the recipients of the business analysis work, personnel managers, or Centers of Excellence within the organization.

### 3.5.4.4 Recommend Actions for Improvement

Once the analysis of performance results is complete, the business analyst engages the appropriate stakeholders to identify preventative, corrective and/or improvement for future business analysis work.

## 3.5.5 Guidelines and Tools

| Guideline or Tool | How Utilized in this Task |
| --- | --- |
| Organizational Performance Standards | may include performance metrics or expectations for business analysis work mandated by the organization. |

## 3.5.6 Techniques

| Technique | How Utilized in this Task |
| --- | --- |
| 10.5 Brainstorming | used to generate ideas for improvement opportunities. |
| 10.25 Interviews | used to gather assessments of business analysis performance. |
| 10.26 Item Tracking | used to track issues that occur during the performance of business analysis for later resolution. |
| 10.27 Lessons Learned | used to identify recommended changes to business analysis processes, deliverables, templates, and other organizational process assets that can be incorporated into the current initiative and future work. |

| Technique | How Utilized in this Task |
|---|---|
| **10.28 Metrics and KPIs** | used to determine what metrics are appropriate for assessing business analysis performance and how they may be tracked. |
| **10.31 Observation** | used to witness business analysis performance. |
| **10.34 Process Analysis** | used to analyze existing business analysis processes and identify opportunities for improvement. |
| **10.35 Process Modeling** | used to define business analysis processes and understand how to improve those processes to reduce problems from hand-offs, improve cycle times, or alter how business analysis work is performed to support improvements in downstream processes. |
| **10.37 Reviews** | used to identify changes to business analysis processes and deliverables that can be incorporated into future work. |
| **10.38 Risk Analysis and Management** | used to identify and manage potential conditions or events that may impact business analysis performance. |
| **10.40 Root Cause Analysis** | used to help identify the underlying cause of failures or difficulties in accomplishing business analysis work. |
| **10.45 Survey and Questionnaire** | used to gather feedback from stakeholders about their satisfaction with business analysis activities and deliverables. |
| **10.50 Workshops** | used to gather assessments of business analysis performance and generate ideas for improvement opportunities. |

### 3.5.7 Stakeholders

| Stakeholder | How Involved in this Task |
|---|---|
| **Domain Subject Matter Experts** | should be informed about the business analysis activities in order to set expectations regarding their involvement in the work and to elicit their feedback regarding possible improvements to the approach. |
| **Project Manager** | is accountable for the success of a project and must be kept informed of the current status of work. They are consulted before changes are implemented to assess the impact on the project. They may also deliver reports on business analysis performance to the sponsor and other stakeholders. |
| **Sponsor** | may require reports on business analysis performance to address problems as they are identified. A manager of business analysts may also sponsor initiatives to improve the performance of business analysis activities. |

### 3.5.8 Outputs

- **Business Analysis Performance Assessment (3.5)**: includes a comparison of planned versus actual performance, identifying the root cause of variances from the expected performance, proposed approaches to address issues, and other findings to help understand the performance of business analysis processes.

## 3.6 Business Analysis Planning and Monitoring Pop-up Quiz

1. Fill in the blanks, many planning approaches fit somewhere along the continuum between _____ and _____ approaches.

    a. plan-driven, change-driven

    b. predictive, value-driven

    c. predictive, adaptive

    d. event-driven, date-driven

2. Throughout an initiative you perform analysis to ensure that business analysis activities continue to produce sufficient value to the stakeholders. Which business analysis core concept you are applying to your initiative?

    a. Need

    b. Value

    c. Change

    d. Context

3. In which output artifact will the business analysis activities done throughout the initiative, including who will do them, and timing and sequencing of the work be identified?

    a. Stakeholder Engagement Approach

    b. Business Analysis Information Management Approach

    c. Governance Approach

    d. Business Analysis Approach

## Answers to Pop-up Quiz

| Question | Answer | Description |
|---|---|---|
| 1 | C | BABOK section 3.1.4.1. Many planning methods fit somewhere along a continuum between predictive and adaptive approaches. |
| 2 | B | BABOK table 3.0.1. Value: conduct performance analysis to ensure business analysis activities continue to produce sufficient value for the stakeholders. |
| 3 | D | BABOK section 3.1.8. **Business Analysis Approach**: identifies the business analysis approach and activities that will be performed across an initiative including who will perform the activities, the timing and sequencing of the work. |

# Elicitation and Collaboration

## Overview

Elicitation and Collaboration is concerned with drawing out requirements and other business analysis information from stakeholders. It is the main path to discovering requirements and design information, and might involve talking directly with stakeholders, researching topics, experimenting, or simply being handed information. This includes communication of the requirements and information to, and collaboration with, stakeholders. Elicitation is not a single point-in-time activity, but happens throughout the initiative. Collaboration is the act of two or more people working together towards a common goal.

**Definition:** Elicitation means to draw forth or bring out information.

**Goal:** Tasks in the Elicitation and Collaboration Knowledge Area are design to collaborate with stakeholders to draw information out from them, including requirements and other business analysis information, ensure the timeliness and accuracy of the information and communicate it out to the appropriate stakeholders; all to continue progression toward the goals and objectives of the change initiative.

## What You Will Learn

When you are finished with this chapter, you will know:
- How business analysts elicit and collaborate with stakeholders toward the objective of their initiative
- The five tasks in the Elicitation and Collaboration Knowledge Area
    1. Prepare for Elicitation
    2. Conduct Elicitation
    3. Confirm Elicitation Results
    4. Communicate Business Analysis Information
    5. Manage Stakeholder Collaboration
- A greater understanding of the role of the business analyst in a change initiative

Important learnings in Elicitation and Collaboration Knowledge Area:
1. Elicitation activities are ongoing activities during the change initiative.
2. Elicitation activities can be planned or unplanned activities. Both types of activities may be used during a given initiative.
3. Elicitation activities can take any number of forms, including discussions, research, experimenting, or just being handed information.
4. Elicitation and Collaboration with stakeholders is a major part of many business analysts job, and is a major topic of the ECBA™ exam.

**Figure 4.0.1: Elicitation and Collaboration Input/Task/Output Diagram**

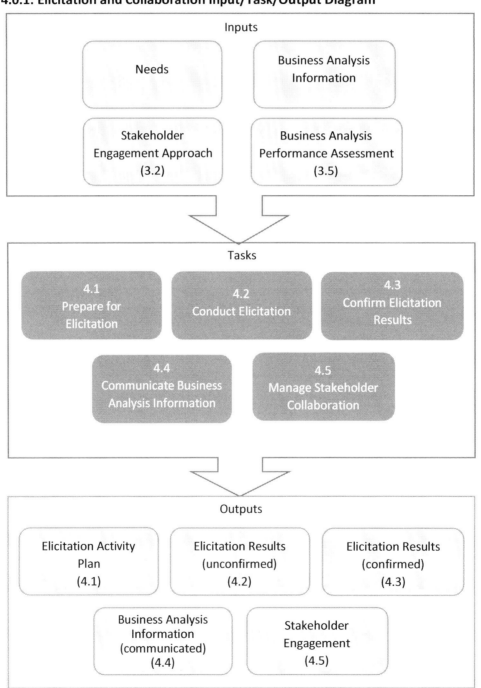

Chapter 3 Business Analysis Planning and Monitoring

## The BACCM™ in Elicitation and Collaboration

The following model describes the usage and application of each of the core concepts within the context of Elicitation and Collaboration.

**Figure 4.0.2: Core Concepts application In Elicitation and Collaboration**

fully identify the characteristics of the change and stakeholder concerns to determine appropriate activities

elicit, confirm, and communicate needs and information iteratively and incrementally

elicit, confirm, and communicate characteristics of proposed solutions

manage collaboration with stakeholders

use a variety of elicitation techniques to identify the context of the change

assess the value of information provided through elicitation and confirm that value

## Tasks in Elicitation and Collaboration

There are five tasks in the Elicitation and Collaboration Area:

1. Prepare for Elicitation
2. Conduct Elicitation
3. Confirm Elicitation Results
4. Communicate Business Analysis Information
5. Manage Stakeholder Collaboration

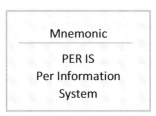

| Mnemonic |
| --- |
| PER IS |
| Per Information System |

A detailed summary of the Inputs, Tasks, Techniques, Stakeholders and Outputs (ITTSO) in the Elicitation and Collaboration Knowledge Area begins on the next page.

# Chapter 3 Business Analysis Planning and Monitoring

## Detailed ITTSO Table

The following table summarizes the Inputs, Tasks, Techniques, Stakeholders and Outputs in the Elicitation and Collaboration Knowledge Area.

**Table 4.0.1: Inputs, Tasks, Techniques, Stakeholders and Outputs Summary**

| ITTSO Summary for Elicitation and Collaboration | | | | | |
|---|---|---|---|---|---|
| **Inputs** | **Tasks** | **M*** | **Techniques** | **Stakeholders** | **Outputs** |
| • Needs<br>• Stakeholder Engagement Approach (3.2) | 4.1 Prepare for Elicitation | P | 10.5 Brainstorming<br>10.14 Data Mining<br>10.18 Document Analysis<br>10.19 Estimation<br>10.25 Interviews<br>10.29 Mind Mapping<br>10.38 Risk Analysis and Management<br>10.43 Stakeholder List, Map and Personas | • Domain SME<br>• Project Manager<br>• Sponsor | • Elicitation Activity Plan (4.1) |
| • Elicitation Activity Plan (4.1) | 4.2 Conduct Elicitation | E | 10.4 Benchmarking and Market Analysis<br>10.5 Brainstorming<br>10.9 Business Rules Analysis<br>10.10 Collaborative Games<br>10.11 Concept Modeling<br>10.14 Data Mining<br>10.15 Data Modeling<br>10.18 Document Analysis<br>10.21 Focus Groups<br>10.24 Interface Analysis<br>10.25 Interviews<br>10.29 Mind Mapping<br>10.31 Observation<br>10.34 Process Analysis<br>10.35 Process Modeling<br>10.36 Prototyping<br>10.45 Survey and Questionnaire<br>10.50 Workshops | • Any Stakeholder<br>• Customer<br>• Domain SME<br>• End User<br>• Implementation SME<br>• Sponsor | Elicitation Results (unconfirmed) (4.2) |

| | | | | | |
|---|---|---|---|---|---|
| • Elicitation Results (unconfirmed) (4.2) | 4.3 Confirm Elicitation Results | R | 10.18 Document Analysis<br>10.25 Interviews<br>10.37 Reviews<br>10.50 Workshops | • Any Stakeholder<br>• Domain SME | Elicitation Results (confirmed) (4.3) |
| • Business Analysis Information<br>• Stakeholder Engagement Approach (3.2) | 4.4 Communicate Business Analysis Information | I | 10.25 Interviews<br>10.37 Reviews<br>10.50 Workshops | • Any Stakeholder<br>• Customer<br>• Domain SME<br>• End User<br>• Implementation SME<br>• Tester | Business Analysis Information (communicated) (4.4) |
| • Stakeholder Engagement Approach (3.2)<br>• Business Analysis Performance Assessment (3.5) | 4.5 Manage Stakeholder Collaboration | S | 10.10 Collaborative Games<br>10.27 Lessons Learned<br>10.38 Risk Analysis and Management<br>10.43 Stakeholder List, Map and Personas | • All Stakeholders | Stakeholder Engagement (4.5) |

\* Mnemonic = PER IS

# Elicitation and Collaboration Student Exercises

**Exercise 1:** Fill in the blanks to complete the Elicitation and Collaboration task name, then enter the Mnemonic letter used in this chapter to help remember the tasks in this knowledge area.

| EC Tasks | Mnemonic Letter |
|---|---|
| _____ for Elicitation | |
| Conduct _____ | |
| Confirm Elicitation _____ | |
| Communicate Business Analysis _____ | |
| Manage _____ Collaboration | |

**Bonus:** Enter below the phrase used in this chapter to help remember the tasks in Elicitation and Collaboration knowledge area.

_____

**Exercise 2:** For each stakeholder indicate which task they are involved in by putting an 'X' in the appropriate column under the stakeholder. Some stakeholders may not be involved in any tasks while some stakeholders may be involved in multiple tasks.

| Task \ Stakeholder | All Stakeholders | Any Stakeholders | Customers | Domain SME | End User | Implementation SME | Operational Support | Project Manager | Regulator | Sponsor | Supplier | Tester |
|---|---|---|---|---|---|---|---|---|---|---|---|---|
| 4.1 Prepare for Elicitation | | | | | | | | | | | | |
| 4.2 Conduct Elicitation | | | | | | | | | | | | |
| 4.3 Confirm Elicitation Results | | | | | | | | | | | | |
| 4.4 Communicate Business Analysis Information | | | | | | | | | | | | |
| 4.5 Manage Stakeholder Collaboration | | | | | | | | | | | | |

## Answers to Student Exercises

**Exercise 1:** Fill in the blanks to complete the Elicitation and Collaboration task name, then enter the Mnemonic letter used in this chapter to help remember the tasks in this knowledge area.

| EC Tasks | Mnemonic Letter |
|---|---|
| _Prepare_ for Elicitation | P |
| Conduct _Elicitation_ | E |
| Confirm Elicitation _Results_ | R |
| Communicate Business Analysis _Information_ | I |
| Manage _Stakeholder_ Collaboration | S |

**Bonus:** Enter below the phrase used in this chapter to help remember the tasks in Elicitation and Collaboration knowledge area.

_Per Information Systems_

**Exercise 2:** For each stakeholder indicate which task they are involved in by putting an 'X' in the appropriate column under the stakeholder. Some stakeholders may not be involved in any tasks while some stakeholders may be involved in multiple tasks.

| Task \ Stakeholder | All Stakeholders | Any Stakeholders | Customers | Domain SME | End User | Implementation SME | Operational Support | Project Manager | Regulator | Sponsor | Supplier | Tester |
|---|---|---|---|---|---|---|---|---|---|---|---|---|
| 4.1 Prepare for Elicitation | | | | X | | | | X | | X | | |
| 4.2 Conduct Elicitation | | X | X | X | X | X | | | | X | | |
| 4.3 Confirm Elicitation Results | | X | | X | | | | | | | | |
| 4.4 Communicate Business Analysis Information | | X | X | X | X | X | | | | | | X |
| 4.5 Manage Stakeholder Collaboration | | X | | | | | | | | | | |

## 4.1 Prepare for Elicitation

**Figure 4.1.1: Prepare for Elicitation Input/Task/Output Diagram**

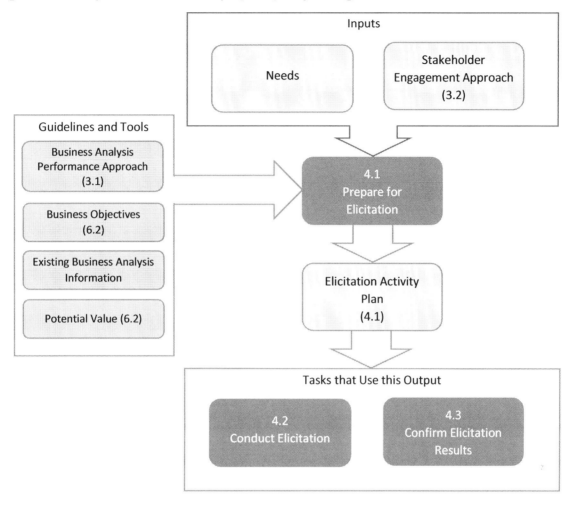

### 4.1.1 Purpose

Understand the scope of the elicitation activity, select appropriate techniques, and plan for (or procure) appropriate supporting materials and resources.

### 4.1.2 Description

Business analysts prepare for elicitation by defining the desired outcomes of the activity, considering the stakeholders involved and the goals of the initiative. This includes determining which work products will be produced using the elicitation results, deciding which techniques are best suited to produce those results, establishing the elicitation logistics, identifying any supporting materials needed, and understanding circumstances to foster collaboration during an elicitation activity.

### 4.1.3 Inputs

- **Needs**: guides the preparation in terms of the scope and purpose of elicitation activities.
- **Stakeholder Engagement Approach (3.2)**: understanding stakeholders' communication and collaboration needs helps prepare appropriate and effective elicitation events.

### 4.1.4 Elements

#### 4.1.4.1 Understanding the Scope of Elicitation

To decide how to approach your elicitation activities and decide on techniques to use, you must first have to understand what information you are trying to draw out of your stakeholders. Scope puts boundaries on the type of information you are seeking, and therefore, on the activities and techniques you will employ in this effort. This allows you to keep activities and discussions of stakeholders on point or within the scope of discovery. Having a good understanding of the scope of your discovery also allows you to determine when you are done.

#### 4.1.4.2 Select Elicitation Techniques

Business analysts use multiple techniques to elicit information from stakeholders. These techniques may be used in combination, meaning using multiple techniques at one time. Business analysts need to consider several things when determining which techniques to use, including on cost and time constraints, types of business analysis information sources and their access, the culture of the organization, desired outcomes, and needs, availability and location of the stakeholders.

> *Using the right technique, at the right time is extremely important to the success of the elicitation activity.*

#### 4.1.4.3 Setup Logistics

Now that you have decided on the type of information you are eliciting and the techniques you will use, now you have to prepare for the actual elicitation activity. Things to consider are goal of elicitation, participants, schedule resources (room and tools), location, and communication methods.

#### 4.1.4.4 Secure Supporting Material

Supporting material can be categorized in two categories:

Data or information includes historical data from systems, material concerning the change initiative (scope, schedule, etc.), business analysis models, or material about the organization and the environment in which it operates (organization charts, department procedures, goals and objectives, market analysis, etc.)

Office material can include projectors, whiteboards and markers, easels and paper, post-it notes, and other such office supplies to help conduct the elicitation activity.

#### 4.1.4.5 Prepare Stakeholders

Preparing stakeholders involves educating them on how elicitation techniques work. It may be the first time that stakeholders have been involved in a particular business analysis technique, so a little explanation on what is expected of them will increase the success of the activity. People who don't understand the activity or what is expected from it, may choose to be passive or avoid (not show up) the activity all together. They may also have a lot of questions and have great confusion about what is going on.

> *Preparing stakeholders is about gaining their buy-in for the activity.*

## 4.1.5 Guidelines and Tools

| Guideline or Tool | How Utilized in this Task |
| --- | --- |
| **Business Analysis Approach (3.1)** | sets the general strategy to be used to guide the business analysis work. This includes the general methodology, types of stakeholders and how they should be involved, list of stakeholders, timing of the work, expected format and level of detail of elicitation results, and identified challenges and uncertainties. |
| **Business Objectives (6.2)** | describe the desired direction needed to achieve the future state. They can be used to plan and prepare elicitation events, and to develop supporting materials. |
| **Existing Business Analysis Information** | may provide a better understanding of the goals of the elicitation activity, and aid in preparing for elicitation. |
| **Potential Value (6.2)** | describes the value to be realized by implementing the proposed future state, and can be used to shape elicitation events. |

## 4.1.6 Techniques

| Technique | How Utilized in this Task |
| --- | --- |
| **10.5 Brainstorming** | used to collaboratively identify and reach consensus about which sources of business analysis information should be consulted and which elicitation techniques might be most effective. |
| **10.14 Data Mining** | used to identify information or patterns that require further investigation. |
| **10.18 Document Analysis** | used to identify and assess candidate sources of supporting materials. |
| **10.19 Estimation** | used to estimate the time and effort required for the elicitation and the associated cost. |
| **10.25 Interviews** | used to identify concerns about the planned elicitation, and can be used to seek authority to proceed with specific options. |
| **10.29 Mind Mapping** | used to collaboratively identify and reach consensus about which sources of business analysis information should be consulted and which elicitation techniques might be most effective. |
| **10.38 Risk Analysis and Management** | used to identify, assess, and manage conditions or situations that could disrupt the elicitation, or affect the quality and validity of the elicitation results. The plans for the elicitation should be adjusted to avoid, transfer, or mitigate the most serious risks. |
| **10.43 Stakeholder List, Map and Personas** | used to determine who should be consulted while preparing for the elicitation, who should participate in the event, and the appropriate roles for each stakeholder. |

### 4.1.7 Stakeholders

| Stakeholder | How Involved in this Task |
|---|---|
| **Domain Subject Matter Expert** | provides supporting materials as well as guidance about which other sources of business analysis information to consult. May also help to arrange research, experiments, and facilitated elicitation. |
| **Project Manager** | ensures that the appropriate people and resources are available to conduct the elicitation. |
| **Sponsor** | has the authority to approve or deny a planned elicitation event, and to authorize and require the participation of specific stakeholders. |

### 4.1.8 Outputs

- **Elicitation Activity Plan (4.1)**: used for each elicitation activity. It includes logistics, scope of the elicitation activity, selected techniques, and supporting materials.

## 4.2 Conduct Elicitation

**Figure 4.2.1: Conduct Elicitation Input/Task/Output Diagram**

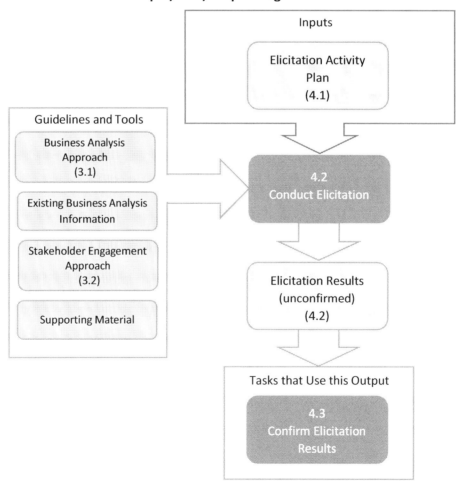

### 4.2.1 Purpose

Draw out, explore, and identify information relevant to the change.

### 4.2.2 Description

There are three common types of elicitation:

- **Collaborative**: involves direct interaction with stakeholders, and relies on their experiences, expertise, and judgment.
- **Research**: involves systematically discovering and studying information from materials or sources that are not directly known by stakeholders involved in the change. Stakeholders might still participate in the research. Research can include data analysis of historical data to identify trends or past results.
- **Experiments**: involves identifying information that could not be known without some sort of controlled test. Some information cannot be drawn from people or documents—because it is unknown. Experiments can help discover this kind of information. Experiments include observational studies, proofs of concept, and prototypes.

### 4.2.3 Inputs

- **Elicitation Activity Plan (4.1)**: includes the planned elicitation activities and techniques, activity logistics (for example, date, time, location, resources, agenda), scope of the elicitation activity, and available sources of background information.

### 4.2.4 Elements

#### 4.2.4.1 Guide Elicitation Activities

Effective planning for elicitation helps business analysts understand the type of information that is being sought and at what level of detail. This knowledge will help the business analyst to guide and facilitate elicitation activity to keep it on track toward that goal.

#### 4.2.4.2 Capture Elicitation Outcomes

It is important to capture the outcomes of your elicitation activities so that information is not lost. Capturing outcomes may be iterative, or done all at once. It may be in parallel or in sequence with the actual elicitation activity. Storing this outcome, which is usually information from the stakeholders, for later reference is important as the initiative moves forward.

### 4.2.5 Guidelines and Tools

| Guideline or Tool | How Utilized in this Task |
|---|---|
| **Business Analysis Approach (3.1)** | influences how each elicitation activity is performed, as it identifies the types of outputs that will be needed based on the approach. |
| **Existing Business Analysis Information** | may guide the questions posed during elicitation and the approach used to draw out information from various stakeholders. |

| Guideline or Tool | How Utilized in this Task |
|---|---|
| **Stakeholder Engagement Approach (3.2)** | provides collaboration and communication approaches that might be effective during elicitation. |
| **Supporting Materials** | includes any materials to prepare both the business analyst and participants before elicitation, as well as any information, tools, or equipment to be used during the elicitation. |

### 4.2.6 Techniques

| Technique | How Utilized in this Task |
|---|---|
| **10.4 Benchmarking and Market Analysis** | used as a source of business analysis information by comparing a specific process, system, product, service, or structure with some external baseline. Market analysis is used to determine what customers want and what competitors provide. |
| **10.5 Brainstorming** | used to generate many ideas from a group of stakeholders in a short period, and to organize and prioritize those ideas. |
| **10.9 Business Rules Analysis** | used to identify the rules that govern decisions in an organization and that define, constrain, or enable organizational operations. |
| **10.10 Collaborative Games** | used to develop a better understanding of a problem or to stimulate creative solutions. |
| **10.11 Concept Modeling** | used to identify key terms and ideas of importance and define the relationships between them. |
| **10.14 Data Mining** | used to identify relevant information and patterns. |
| **10.15 Data Modeling** | used to understand entity relationships during elicitation. |
| **10.18 Document Analysis** | used to review existing systems, contracts, business procedures and policies, standards, and regulations. |
| **10.21 Focus Groups** | used to identify and understand ideas and attitudes from a group. |
| **10.24 Interface Analysis** | used to understand the interaction, and characteristics of that interaction, between two entities, such as two systems, two organizations, or two people or roles. |
| **10.25 Interviews** | used to ask questions of stakeholders to uncover needs, identify problems, or discover opportunities. |
| **10.29 Mind Mapping** | used to generate many ideas from a group of stakeholders in a short period, and to organize and prioritize those ideas. |
| **10.31 Observation** | used to gain insight about how work is currently done, possibly in different locations and in different circumstances. |
| **10.34 Process Analysis** | used to understand current processes and to identify opportunities for improvement in those processes. |

| Technique | How Utilized in this Task |
|---|---|
| 10.35 Process Modeling | used to elicit processes with stakeholders during elicitation activities. |
| 10.36 Prototyping | used to elicit and validate stakeholders' needs through an iterative process that creates a model of requirements or designs. |
| 10.45 Survey and Questionnaire | used to elicit business analysis information, including information about customers, products, work practices, and attitudes, from a group of people in a structured way and in a relatively short period of time. |
| 10.50 Workshops | used to elicit business analysis information, including information about customers, products, work practices, and attitudes, from a group of people in a collaborative, facilitated way. |

### 4.2.7 Stakeholders

| Stakeholder | How Involved in this Task |
|---|---|
| Customer | will provide valuable business analysis information during elicitation. |
| Domain Subject Matter Expert | has expertise in some aspect of the situation and can provide the required business analysis information. Often guides and assists the business analyst in identifying appropriate research sources, and may help to arrange research, experiments, and facilitated elicitation. |
| End User | the user of existing and future solutions, who should participate in elicitation. |
| Implementation Subject Matter Expert | designs and implements a solution and provides specialist expertise, and can participate in elicitation by asking clarifying questions and offering alternatives. |
| Sponsor | authorizes and ensures that the stakeholders necessary to participate in elicitation are involved. |
| Any Stakeholder | could have relevant knowledge or experience to participate in elicitation activities. |

### 4.2.8 Outputs

- **Elicitation Results (unconfirmed) (4.2)**: captured information in a format that is specific to the elicitation activity.

## 4.3 Confirm Elicitation Results

### 4.3.1 Purpose

Check the information gathered during an elicitation session for accuracy and consistency with other information.

**Figure 4.3.1: Confirm Elicitation Results Input/Task/Output Diagram**

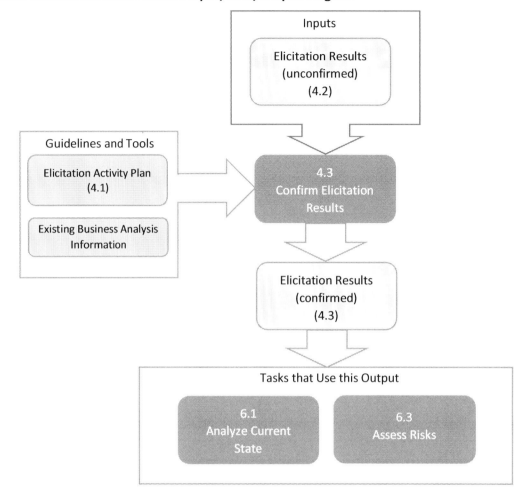

### 4.3.2 Description

Elicited information is confirmed to identify any problems and resolve them before resources are committed to using the information. This review may discover errors, omissions, conflicts, and ambiguity.

The elicitation results can be compared against their source and other elicitation results to ensure consistency. If information is not correct, the business analyst determines what is correct, which can require more elicitation. Committing resources to business analysis activities based on unconfirmed elicitation results may mean stakeholder expectations are not met. If the results are inconsistent, additional elicitation might need to be conducted to resolve the discrepancies.

Confirming the elicitation results requires less effort than occurs during analysis.

### 4.3.3 Inputs

- **Elicitation Results (unconfirmed) (4.2)**: capture information in a format specific to the elicitation activity.

## 4.3.4 Elements

### 4.3.4.1 Compare Elicitation Results Against Source Information

The business analyst may lead follow-up meetings where stakeholders correct the elicitation results. Stakeholders may also confirm the elicitation results independently.

### 4.3.4.2 Compare Elicitation Results Against Other Elicitation Results

Business analysts compare elicitation results collected from multiple activities to confirm that the information is consistent and accurately represented. As comparisons are drawn, business analysts identify variations in results and resolve them in collaboration with stakeholders. Comparisons may also be made with historical data to confirm more recent elicitation results.

## 4.3.5 Guidelines and Tools

| Guideline or Tool | How Utilized in this Task |
| --- | --- |
| Elicitation Activity Plan (4.1) | used to guide which alternative sources and which elicitation results are to be compared. |
| Existing Business Analysis Information | can be used to confirm the results of elicitation activities or to develop additional questions to draw out more detailed information. |

## 4.3.6 Techniques

| Technique | How Utilized in this Task |
| --- | --- |
| 10.18 Document Analysis | used to confirm elicitation results against source information or other existing documents. |
| 10.25 Interviews | used to confirm the business analysis information and to confirm that the integration of that information is correct. |
| 10.37 Reviews | used to confirm elicitation results. Such reviews could be informal or formal depending on the risks of not having correct, useful, and relevant information. |
| 10.50 Workshops | used to conduct reviews of the drafted elicitation results using any level of formality. A predetermined agenda, scripts, or scenario text may be used to walk through the elicitation results, and feedback is requested from the participants and recorded. |

### 4.3.7 Stakeholders

| Stakeholder | How Involved in this Task |
|---|---|
| **Domain Subject Matter Experts** | people with substantial knowledge, experience, or expertise about the business analysis information being elicited, or about the change or the solution, help to confirm that elicitation results are correct, and can help to identify omissions, inconsistencies and conflicts in elicitation results. They can also confirm that the right business analysis information has been elicited. |
| **Any stakeholder** | all types of stakeholders may need to participate in confirming elicitation results. |

### 4.3.8 Outputs

- **Elicitation Results (confirmed) (4.3)**: integrated output that the business analyst and other stakeholders agree correctly reflects captured information and confirms that it is relevant and useful as an input to further work.

## 4.4 Communicate Business Analysis Information

**Figure 4.4.1: Communicate Business Analysis Information Input/Task/Output Diagram**

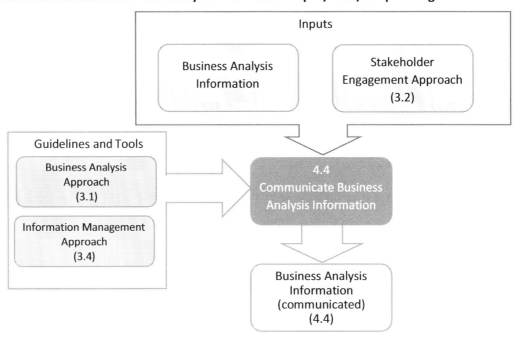

### 4.4.1 Purpose

Ensure stakeholders have a shared understanding of business analysis information.

## 4.4.2 Description

Communication is a central part of the business analysis, and this task is dedicated to it. Because of the importance of communication, you are likely to see questions on it on the exam. The important thing to understand about communication is to communicate the right information, to the right stakeholders, in the right format, at the right time to help ensure shared understanding of that business analysis information. Communicate the information in language, tone, and style that is appropriate to the audience.

> *Communicate the right information in the right format at the right time.*

Communication of business analysis information is bi-directional and iterative. It involves determining the recipients, content, purpose, context, and expected outcomes. Communicating information does not simply involve pushing information out and assuming it was received and understood. Business analysts engage stakeholders to ensure they understand the information and gain agreement.

> *Business analysts ensure shared understanding of information communicated.*

## 4.4.3 Inputs

- **Business Analysis Information**: any kind of information at any level of detail that is used as an input or output of business analysis work. Business analysis information becomes an input for this task when the need is discovered to communicate the information to additional stakeholders.
- **Stakeholder Engagement Approach (3.2)**: describes stakeholder groups, roles, and general needs regarding communication of business analysis information.

## 4.4.4 Elements

### 4.4.4.1 Determining Objectives and Format of Communication

The BABOK® referred to information that the business analyst wishes to communicate as a business analysis information package. Reasons a business analyst would prepare a business analysis information package include (but not limited to):

- communication of requirements and designs to stakeholders,
- early assessment of quality and planning,
- evaluation of possible alternatives,
- formal reviews and approvals,
- inputs to solution design,
- conformance to contractual and regulatory obligations, and
- maintenance for reuse.

> *The primary goal of developing a package is to convey information clearly and in usable format for continuing change activities.*

Possible forms of business analysis information packages include formal, informal and presentations. Consideration is given to the best way to combine and present the materials to convey a cohesive and effective message.

#### 4.4.4.2 Communicate Business Analysis Package

The purpose of communicating the business analysis package is to provide stakeholders with the appropriate level of detail about the change so they can understand the information it contains. Stakeholders are given the opportunity to review the package, ask questions about the information, and raise any concerns they may have.

Selecting the appropriate communication platform is important. Common communication platforms include:

- **Group collaboration**: used to communicate the package to a group of relevant stakeholders at the same time. It allows immediate discussion about the information and related issues.
- **Individual collaboration**: used to communicate the package to a single stakeholder at a time. It can be used to gain individual understanding of the information when a group setting is not feasible, most productive, or going to yield the best results.
- **E-mail or other non-verbal methods**: used to communicate the package when there is a high maturity level of information that will need little or no verbal explanation to support it.

### 4.4.5 Guidelines and Tools

| Guideline or Tool | How Utilized in this Task |
|---|---|
| **Business Analysis Approach (3.1)** | describes how the various types of information will be disseminated rather than what will be disseminated. It describes the level of detail and formality required, frequency of the communications, and how communications could be affected by the number and geographic dispersion of stakeholders. |
| **Information Management Approach (3.4)** | helps determine how business analysis information will be packaged and communicated to stakeholders. |

### 4.4.6 Techniques

| Technique | How Utilized in this Task |
|---|---|
| **10.25 Interviews** | used to individually communicate information to stakeholders. |
| **10.37 Reviews** | used to provide stakeholders with an opportunity to express feedback, request required adjustments, understand required responses and actions, and agree or provide approvals. Reviews can be used during group or individual collaboration. |
| **10.50 Workshops** | used to provide stakeholders with an opportunity to express feedback and to understand required adjustments, responses, and actions. They are also useful for gaining consensus and providing approvals. Typically used during group collaboration. |

## Chapter 3 Business Analysis Planning and Monitoring

### 4.4.7 Stakeholders

| Stakeholder | How Involved in this Task |
|---|---|
| Customer | needs to be communicated with frequently so they are aware of relevant business analysis information. |
| Domain Subject Matter Expert | needs to understand the business analysis information as part of confirming and validating it throughout the change initiative. |
| End User | needs to be communicated with frequently so they are aware of relevant business analysis information. |
| Implementation Subject Matter Expert | needs to be aware of and understand the business analysis information, particularly requirements and designs, for implementation purposes. |
| Tester | needs to be aware of and understand the business analysis information, particularly requirements and designs for testing purposes. |
| Any Stakeholder | all types of stakeholders will likely need to be communicated with at some point during the change initiative. |

### 4.4.8 Outputs

- **Business Analysis Information (communicated) (4.4)**: business analysis information is considered communicated when the target stakeholders have reached an understanding of its content and implications.

## 4.5 Manage Stakeholder Collaboration

### Figure 4.5.1: Manage Stakeholder Collaboration Input/Task/Output Diagram

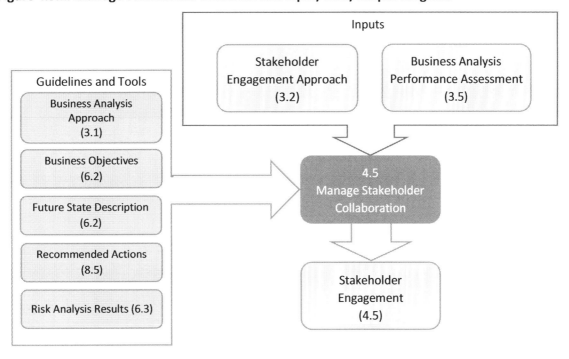

### 4.5.1 Purpose

Encourage stakeholders to work towards a common goal.

### 4.5.2 Description

Along with communication, collaboration is an important part of effective business analysis. The goal of collaboration is to work effectively with stakeholders to achieve a common goal. The business analysis role lends itself to working together with stakeholders at all different levels of the organization. They will have different levels of influence and authority within the organization. The business analyst ensures that the right stakeholders participate at the right times in the appropriate roles.

> *The BA ensures that the right stakeholders participate at the right times in the appropriate roles.*

This task literally encompasses all interactions with stakeholders. Given the broad spectrum of this task there are some important points to consider in all interactions with stakeholders:

- The goal of every interaction with stakeholders is for it to be a positive experience for all involved. To capitalize on positive reactions and mitigate negative reactions of the stakeholders.
- Stakeholder collaboration begins when stakeholders are identified. New stakeholders may be identified later during the initiative. New stakeholders' role, attitudes, influence, and relationship to the initiative need to be analyzed.
- Stakeholders' role, influence, responsibilities, attitudes, and authority may change over time. The business analyst needs to be able to recognize and adapt to these changes affecting the initiative.
- The ability to collaborate with stakeholders is built on relationships with each individual stakeholder. Detrimental effects from a poor relationship with a stakeholder can have detrimental effect on the initiative. When this happens the business analyst needs to work to build a more positive, trust-based relationship with "difficult" stakeholders.

### 4.5.3 Inputs

- **Stakeholder Engagement Approach (3.2)**: describes the types of expected engagement with stakeholders and how they might need to be managed.
- **Business Analysis Performance Assessment (3.5)**: provides key information about the effectiveness of business analysis tasks being executed, including those focused on stakeholder engagement.

### 4.5.4 Elements

#### 4.5.4.1 Gain Agreement on Commitments

Stakeholders participate in business analysis activities that may require time and resource commitments. The business analyst and stakeholders identify and agree upon these commitments as early in the initiative as possible. This is about setting expectations and creating shared understanding of the desired outcomes.

#### 4.5.4.2 Monitor Stakeholder Engagement

Business analysts monitor the participation and performance of stakeholders to ensure that the right stakeholders are participating effectively, stakeholder attitudes and interest are staying constant or improving, elicitation results are confirmed in a timely manner, and agreements and commitments are maintained.

### 4.5.4.3 Collaboration

Stakeholders are more likely to support change if business analysts collaborate with them and encourage the free flow of information, ideas, and innovations. Genuine stakeholder engagement requires that all stakeholders involved feel that they are heard, their opinions matter, and their contributions are recognized. How effectively stakeholders collaborate with business analysts is based on the relationship that the business analyst has built with the stakeholders. If you have trust, you will have effective collaboration.

## 4.5.5 Guidelines and Tools

| Guideline or Tool | How Utilized in this Task |
|---|---|
| **Business Analysis Approach (3.1)** | describes the nature and level of collaboration required from each stakeholder group to perform planned business analysis activities. |
| **Business Objectives (6.2)** | describe the desired direction needed to achieve the future state. They can be used to focus diverse stakeholders on a common vision of the desired business outcomes. |
| **Future State Description (6.2)** | defines the desired future state and the expected value it delivers which can be used to focus diverse stakeholders on the common goal. |
| **Recommended Actions (8.5)** | communicating what should be done to improve the value of a solution can help to galvanize support and focus stakeholders on a common goal. |
| **Risk Analysis Results (6.3)** | stakeholder-related risks will need to be addressed to ensure stakeholder collaboration activities are successful. |

## 4.5.6 Techniques

| Technique | How Utilized in this Task |
|---|---|
| **10.10 Collaborative Games** | used to stimulate teamwork and collaboration by temporarily immersing participants in a safe and fun situation in which they can share their knowledge and experience on a given topic, identify hidden assumptions, and explore that knowledge in ways that may not occur during the course of normal interactions. |
| **10.27 Lessons Learned** | used to understand stakeholders' satisfaction or dissatisfaction, and offer them an opportunity to help improve the working relationships. |
| **10.38 Risk Analysis and Management** | used to identify and manage risks as they relate to stakeholder involvement, participation, and engagement. |
| **10.43 Stakeholder List, Map and Personas** | used to determine who is available to participate in the business analysis work, show the informal relationships between stakeholders, and understand which stakeholders should be consulted about different kinds of business analysis information. |

### 4.5.7 Stakeholders

| Stakeholder | How Involved in this Task |
|---|---|
| **All Stakeholders** | all types of stakeholders who might be involved in collaboration during change. |

### 4.5.8 Outputs

- **Stakeholder Engagement (4.5)**: willingness from stakeholders to engage in business analysis activities and interact with the business analyst when necessary.

**NOTES:**

*Use this space to write notes concerning this chapter that you want to remember and will help you pass the ECBA™ exam.*

Chapter 3 Business Analysis Planning and Monitoring

## 4.6  Elicitation and Collaboration Pop-up Quiz

1. What are the three common types of elicitation business analysts use?

   a. Collaboration, research, and experimenting.

   b. Workshops, interviews, and prototyping.

   c. Reviews, focus groups, and prototyping.

   d. Interviews, research, and being handed the information directly.

2. How would the business analysis core concept of 'Need' be applied during Elicitation and Collaboration activities?

   a. Use a variety of elicitation techniques to fully identify the characteristics of the change including concerns that stakeholders have about the change.

   b. Elicit, confirm, and communicate needs and supporting business analysis information.

   c. E licit, confirm, and communicate necessary or desired characteristics of proposed solutions.

   d. Elicit, confirm, and communicate list of stakeholders to be involved in elicitation activities.

3. Which of the following are some of the techniques for conducting elicitation activities?

   a. brainstorming, collaborative games, document analysis, focus groups, and workshops.

   b. benchmarking and market analysis, business rules analysis, decision analysis, and roles and permissions matrix.

   c. brainstorming, risk analysis and management, roles and permissions matrix, vendor assessments, and workshops.

   d. benchmarking and market analysis, business cases, business process watching, retrospectives, and vendor analysis.

4. What are the inputs for the Confirm Elicitation Results task?

   a. Business Requirements, Elicitation Activity Plan, and Existing Business Analysis Information.

   b. Elicitation Results (any state), and Existing Business Analysis Information.

   c. Stakeholder Requirements, Elicitation Results (any State), and Elicitation Activity Plan.

   d. Elicitation Results (unconfirmed).


5. What Guidelines and Tools can the business analyst utilize when Preparing for Elicitation?

   a. Needs, and Stakeholder Engagement Approach.

   b. Needs, Business Requirements, Existing Business Analysis Information, and Stakeholder Engagement Approach.

   c. Business Analysis Approach, Business Objectives, Existing Business Analysis Information, and Potential Value.

   d. Business Requirements, and Potential Value.


6. What is the purpose for doing the Communicate Business Analysis Information task?

   a. to understand the scope of the elicitation activity, select appropriate techniques, and plan for appropriate supporting materials and resources.

   b. to ensure stakeholders have a shared understanding of business analysis information.

   c. to ensure the project sponsor and project manager are informed of current business analysis activities.

   d. to ensure that organization management is aware of current status of the project.

7. Which of the following lists are the skillsets that business analysts need to gain stakeholder agreement on commitments?

    a. Facilitation, presentation, and negotiation.

    b. Problem solving, interaction, and communication.

    c. Problem solving, presentation, and tools and technology.

    d. Negotiation, communication, and conflict resolution.

8. What communication platforms may the business analyst utilize to communicate business analysis information to the stakeholders?

    a. Individual collaboration, group collaboration, and email or other non-verbal methods.

    b. Workshops, focus groups, and formal presentation.

    c. Voice phone call, video chat, and panel discussion.

    d. Written communication, verbal communication, and non-verbal communication.

## Answers to Pop-up Quiz

| Question | Answer | Description |
|---|---|---|
| 1 | A | BABOK section 4.2.2. There are three common types of elicitation: Collaborative, Research, and Experiments. |
| 2 | B | BABOK table 4.0.1. Need: elicit, confirm, and communicate needs and supporting business analysis information. |
| 3 | A | BABOK section 4.2.6. |
| 4 | D | BABOK figure 4.3.1 and section 4.3.3. |
| 5 | C | BABOK figure 4.1.1 and section 4.1.5 |
| 6 | B | BABOK section 4.4.1. The purpose of Communicate Business Analysis Information is to ensure stakeholders have a shared understanding of business analysis information. |
| 7 | D | BABOK section 4.5.4.1. There may be dialogue and negotiation regarding the terms and conditions of the commitments. Effective negotiation, communication, and conflict resolution skills are important to effective stakeholder management. |
| 8 | A | BABOK section 4.4.4.2. Selecting the appropriate communication platform is also important. Common communication platforms include: Group collaboration, Individual collaboration, and E-mail or other non-verbal methods. |

# Requirements Life Cycle Management

## Overview

The Requirements Life Cycle Management knowledge area describes how requirements and designs are managed and maintained from inception to retirement (archived, deleted, stored for re-use, etc); that is throughout their life cycle. It involves creating meaningful relationships between related requirements and designs, assessing changes to requirements and designs, and analyzing and gaining consensus on changes.

The requirements life cycle extends beyond the life cycle of a project to create a solution. It begins with the representation of a business need as a requirement, continues through the development and implementation of a solution, and ends when that solution and the requirements that represent it are retired. So, requirements live through the time of the project and while the solution is in use by the organization. When the solution is retired, the requirements and designs for that solution may be retired along with it.

**Goal:** Ensure that business, stakeholder, and solution requirements and designs are aligned to one another and that the solution implements them.

## What You Will Learn

When you are finished with this chapter, you will know:
- How to define Requirements Life Cycle Management.
- The five tasks in this knowledge area.
    1. Trace Requirements
    2. Maintain Requirements
    3. Prioritize Requirements
    4. Assess Requirements Changes
    5. Approve Requirements
- A deeper understanding of the business analysts' responsibility to manage requirements and designs throughout their life cycle.

Important learnings in Requirements Life Cycle Management Knowledge Area:
1. Elicitation activities are ongoing activities during the change initiative.
2. Elicitation activities can be planned or unplanned activities. Both types of activities may be used during a given initiative.

**Figure 5.0.1: Requirements Life Cycle Managements Input/Task/Output Diagram**

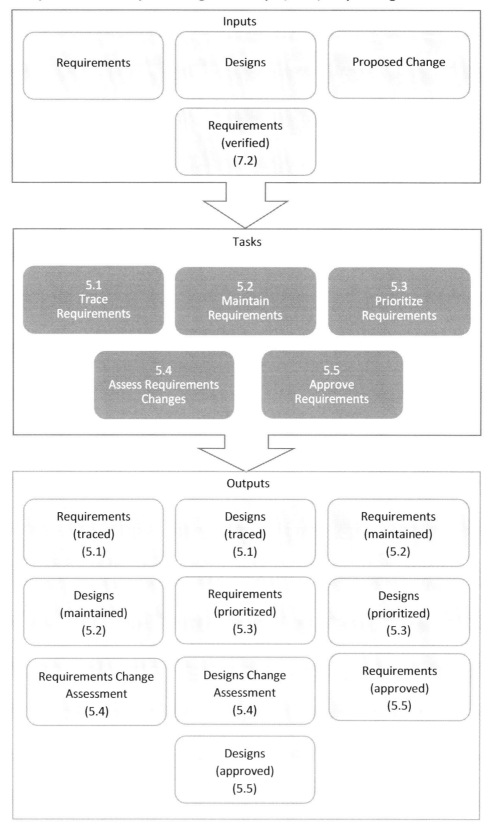

# Chapter 5 Requirements Life Cycle Management

## The BACCM™ in Requirements Life Cycle Management

The following model describes the usage and application of each of the core concepts within the context of Requirements Life Cycle Management.

**Figure 5.0.2: Core Concepts application In Requirements Life Cycle Management**

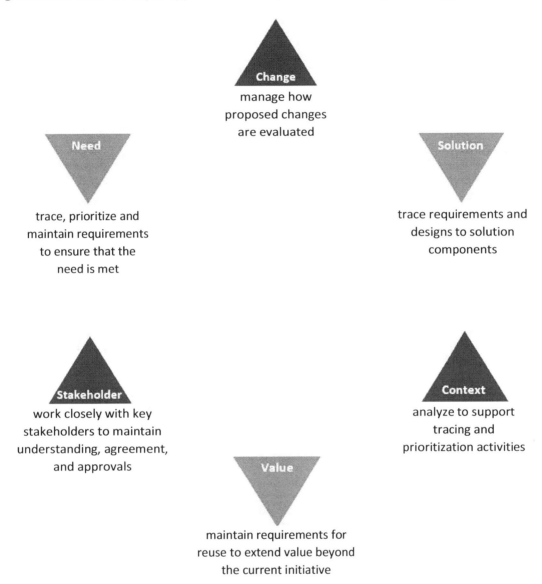

## Tasks in Requirements Life Cycle Management

There are five tasks in the Requirements Life Cycle Management Knowledge Area:

1. <u>T</u>race Requirements
2. <u>M</u>aintain Requirements
3. <u>P</u>rioritize Requirements
4. <u>A</u>ssess Requirements Changes
5. <u>A</u>pprove Requirements

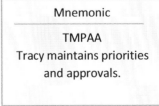

# Detailed ITTSO Table

The following table summarizes the Inputs, Tasks, Techniques, Stakeholders and Outputs in the Requirements Life Cycle Management Knowledge Area.

**Table 5.0.1: Inputs, Tasks, Techniques, Stakeholders and Outputs Summary**

| \\ | ITTSO Summary for Requirements Life Cycle Management | | | | |
|---|---|---|---|---|---|
| **Inputs** | **Tasks** | **M*** | **Techniques** | **Stakeholders** | **Outputs** |
| • Requirements<br>• Designs | 5.1 Trace Requirements | T | 10.9 Business Rules Analysis<br>10.22 Functional Decomposition<br>10.35 Process Modeling<br>10.41 Scope Modeling | • Customers<br>• Domain SME<br>• End User<br>• Implementation SME<br>• Operational Support<br>• Project Manager<br>• Sponsor<br>• Suppliers<br>• Tester | • Requirements (traced) (5.1)<br>• Designs (traced) (5.1) |
| • Requirements<br>• Designs | 5.2 Maintain Requirements | M | 10.9 Business Rules Analysis<br>10.13 Data Flow Diagrams<br>10.15 Data Modeling<br>10.18 Document Analysis<br>10.22 Functional Decomposition<br>10.35 Process Modeling<br>10.47 Use Cases and Scenarios<br>10.48 User Stories | • Domain SME<br>• Implementation SME<br>• Operational Support<br>• Regulator<br>• Tester | • Requirements (maintained) (5.2)<br>• Designs (maintained) (5.2) |
| • Requirements<br>• Designs | 5.3 Prioritize Requirements | P | 10.2 Backlog Management<br>10.7 Business Cases<br>10.16 Decision Analysis<br>10.19 Estimation<br>10.20 Financial Analysis<br>10.25 Interviews<br>10.26 Item Tracking<br>10.33 Prioritization<br>10.38 Risk Analysis and Management<br>10.50 Workshops | • Customer<br>• Domain SME<br>• End User<br>• Implementation SME<br>• Project Manager<br>• Regulator<br>• Sponsor | • Requirements (prioritized) (5.3)<br>• Designs (prioritized) (5.3) |

| | | | | | |
|---|---|---|---|---|---|
| • Requirements<br>• Designs<br>• Proposed Change | 5.4 Assess Requirements Changes | A | 10.7 Business Cases<br>10.9 Business Rules Analysis<br>10.16 Decision Analysis<br>10.20 Financial Analysis<br>10.24 Interface Analysis<br>10.25 Interviews<br>10.38 Risk Analysis and Management<br>10.50 Workshops | • Customer<br>• Domain SME<br>• End User<br>• Operational Support<br>• Project Manager<br>• Regulator<br>• Sponsor<br>• Tester | • Requirements Change Assessment (5.4)<br>• Designs Change Assessment (5.4) |
| • Requirements (verified)<br>• Designs | 5.5 Approve Requirements | A | 10.1 Acceptance and Evaluation Criteria<br>10.16 Decision Analysis<br>10.26 Item Tracking<br>10.37 Reviews<br>10.50 Workshops | • Customer<br>• Domain SME<br>• End User<br>• Operational Support<br>• Project Manager<br>• Regulator<br>• Sponsor | • Requirements (approved) (5.5)<br>• Designs (approved) (5.5) |

\* Mnemonic = TMPAA

## NOTES:

*Use this page to write notes concerning this chapter that you want to remember and will help you pass the ECBA™ exam.*

Chapter 5 Requirements Life Cycle Management

# Requirements Life Cycle Management Student Exercises

**Exercise 1:** Fill in the blanks to complete the Requirements Life Cycle Management task name, then enter the Mnemonic letter used in this chapter to help remember the tasks in this knowledge area.

| RLCM Tasks | Mnemonic Letter |
|---|---|
| _____ Requirements | |
| _____ Requirements | |
| _____ Requirements | |
| _____ Requirements Changes | |
| _____ Requirements | |

**Bonus:** Enter below the phrase used in this chapter to help remember the tasks in **Requirements Life Cycle Management** Knowledge Area.

_____

**Exercise 2:** For each stakeholder indicate which task they are involved in by putting an 'X' in the appropriate column under the stakeholder. Some stakeholders may not be involved in any tasks while some stakeholders may be involved in multiple tasks.

| Task \ Stakeholder | All Stakeholders | Any Stakeholders | Customers | Domain SME | End User | Implementation SME | Operational Support | Project Manager | Regulator | Sponsor | Supplier | Tester |
|---|---|---|---|---|---|---|---|---|---|---|---|---|
| 5.1 Trace Requirements | | | | | | | | | | | | |
| 5.2 Maintain Requirements | | | | | | | | | | | | |
| 5.3 Prioritize Requirements | | | | | | | | | | | | |
| 5.4 Assess Requirements Changes | | | | | | | | | | | | |
| 5.5 Approve Requirements | | | | | | | | | | | | |

## Answers to Student Exercises

**Exercise 1:** Fill in the blanks to complete the Requirements Life Cycle Management task name, then enter the Mnemonic letter used in this chapter to help remember the tasks in this knowledge area.

| RLCM Tasks | Mnemonic Letter |
|---|---|
| _Trace_ Requirements | T |
| _Maintain_ Requirements | M |
| _Prioritize_ Requirements | P |
| _Assess_ Requirements Changes | A |
| _Approve_ Requirements | A |

**Bonus:** Enter below the phrase used in this chapter to help remember the tasks in **Requirements Life Cycle Management** Knowledge Area.

__Tracy Maintains Priorities and Approvals__

**Exercise 2:** For each stakeholder indicate which task they are involved in by putting an 'X' in the appropriate column under the stakeholder. Some stakeholders may not be involved in any tasks while some stakeholders may be involved in multiple tasks.

| Task \ Stakeholder | All Stakeholders | Any Stakeholders | Customers | Domain SME | End User | Implementation SME | Operational Support | Project Manager | Regulator | Sponsor | Supplier | Tester |
|---|---|---|---|---|---|---|---|---|---|---|---|---|
| 5.1 Trace Requirements | | | X | X | X | X | X | X | | X | X | X |
| 5.2 Maintain Requirements | | | | X | | X | X | | X | | | X |
| 5.3 Prioritize Requirements | | | X | X | X | X | | X | X | X | | |
| 5.4 Assess Requirements Changes | | | X | X | X | | X | X | X | X | | X |
| 5.5 Approve Requirements | | | X | X | X | | X | X | X | X | | |

# Chapter 5 Requirements Life Cycle Management

## 5.1 Trace Requirements

**Figure 5.1.1: Trace Requirements Input/Task/Output Diagram**

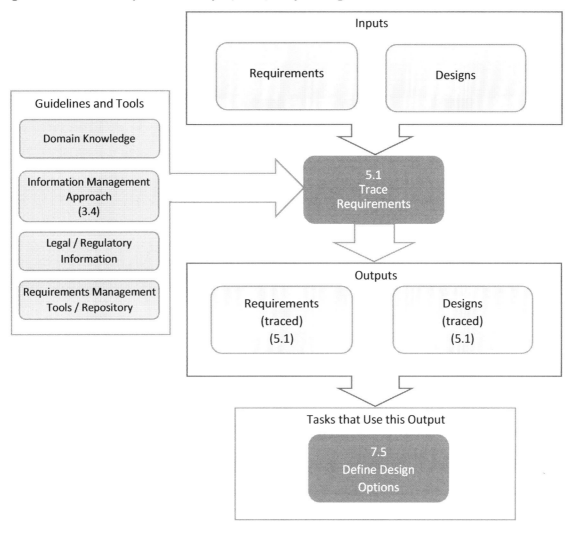

### 5.1.1 Purpose

To ensure that requirements and designs at different levels are aligned to one another, and to manage the effects of change to one level on related requirements.

### 5.1.2 Description

Through traceability you establish meaningful relationships among your requirements and designs. It identifies lineage of each requirement and design, backward and forward. This means that the business, stakeholder, solution, and transition requirements link to each other and there is consistency among all requirements. You can trace a stakeholder requirement backward to the business requirement it supports, and forward to the solution requirements that came from it. Traceability ensures that the solution conforms to the requirements and designs. It assists in scope, change, risk, cost, time, and communication management. It also is used to detect missing functionality in the solution, and functionality in the solution that is not supported by the requirements and design.

The following images show examples of visual representations of traceability for a process and for software requirements.

Figure 5.1.2.1: Process Traceability

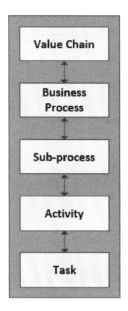

Figure 5.1.2.2: Software Requirements Traceability

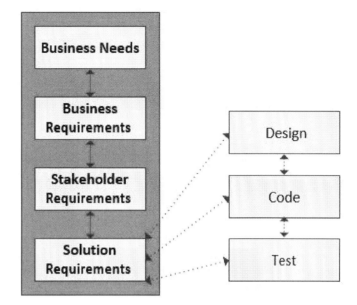

## 5.1.3 Inputs

- **Requirements**: may be traced to other requirements (including goals, objectives, business requirements, stakeholder requirements, solution requirements, and transition requirements), solution components, visuals, business rules, and other work products.
- **Designs**: may be traced to other requirements, solution components, and other work products.

## 5.1.4 Elements

### 5.1.4.1 Level of Formality

The greater the number of traceable levels and linkages, the more complex the traceability structure will be and more effort will be needed to maintain it. BAs need to ensure that each linkage created adds value.

*The complexity of requirements traceability grows with the number of requirements and amount of formality.*

### 5.1.4.2 Relationships

Requirements are related to other requirements, test cases and/or solution components. These relationships are important as many of these relationships show a dependency of one requirement on another. This may dictate the order in which requirements are implemented in the solution.

Requirements relationships include:

Table 5.1.4.1: Requirement Relationships

| Relationship | Description | Example |
|---|---|---|
| Derive | When one requirement is derived from another requirement, at a different level of abstraction. | A solution requirement derived from a stakeholder requirement. |
| Depends | When two requirements depend on each other. This relationship is divided into two categories. | |

Chapter 5 Requirements Life Cycle Management

| Relationship | Description | Example |
|---|---|---|
| Necessity | When it doesn't make sense to implement a requirement unless the related requirement is implemented. | A requirement for a new report requires another requirement for access to the database that contains the data to be reported. |
| Effort | When it is easier to implement one requirement when the related requirement is implemented. | A requirement for a new report is easier to implement if it is to be delivered in one format instead of five formats. |
| Satisfy | When a solution component satisfies a requirement. | A page or screen shows the data defined in a solution requirement. |
| Validate | When a test case validates that a requirement is fulfilled. | A test case shows the steps that will be used to validate that the solution meets the requirement. |

A quick guide to requirements relationships:

| **Relationship:** | **Think of:** |
|---|---|
| Derive | different level of abstraction |
| Necessity | Needed |
| Effort | Easier |
| Satisfy | Solution component |
| Validate | Test case |

### 5.1.4.3 Traceability Repository

Requirements traceability is documented and maintained in accordance with the methods identified by the business analysis approach. Requirements management tools can provide significant benefits when there is a need to trace a large number of requirements that may be deemed unmanageable with manual approaches.

## 5.1.5 Guidelines and Tools

| Guideline or Tool | How Utilized in this Task |
|---|---|
| **Domain Knowledge** | knowledge of and expertise in the business domain needed to support traceability. |
| **Information Management Approach (3.4)** | provides decisions from planning activities concerning the traceability approach. |
| **Legal/Regulatory Information** | describes legislative rules or regulations that must be followed. These may need to be considered when defining traceability rules. |
| **Requirements Management Tools/Repository** | used to store and manage business analysis information. The tool may be as simple as a text document or as complex as a dedicated requirements management tool. |

## 5.1.6 Techniques

| Technique | How Utilized in this Task |
|---|---|
| 10.9 Business Rules Analysis | used to trace business rules to requirements that they support, or rules that support requirements. |
| 10.22 Functional Decomposition | used to break down solution scope into smaller components for allocation, as well as to trace high-level concepts to low-level concepts. |
| 10.35 Process Modeling | used to visually show the future state process, as well as tracing requirements to the future state process. |
| 10.41 Scope Modeling | used to visually depict scope, as well as trace requirements to the area of scope the requirement supports. |

## 5.1.7 Stakeholders

| Stakeholder | How Involved in this Task |
|---|---|
| Customers | are affected by how and when requirements are implemented, and may have to be consulted about, or agree to, the traceability relationships. |
| Domain Subject Matter Expert | may have recommendations regarding the set of requirements to be linked to a solution component or to a release. |
| End User | may require specific dependency relationships that allow certain requirements to be implemented at the same time or in a specific sequence. |
| Implementation Subject Matter Expert | traceability ensures that the solution being developed meets the business need and brings awareness of dependencies between solution components during implementation. |
| Operational Support | traceability documentation provides another reference source for help desk support. |
| Project Manager | traceability supports project change and scope management. |
| Sponsor | is required to approve the various relationships. |
| Suppliers | are affected by how and when requirements are implemented. |
| Tester | needs to understand how and where requirements are implemented when creating test plans and test cases, and may trace test cases to requirements. |

## 5.1.8 Outputs

- **Requirements (traced) (5.1)**: have clearly defined relationships to other requirements, solution components, or releases, phases, or iterations, within a solution scope, such that coverage and the effects of change are clearly identifiable.
- **Designs (traced) (5.1)**: have clearly defined relationships to other requirements, solution components, or releases, phases, or iterations, within a solution scope, such that coverage and the effects of change are clearly identifiable.

## 5.1.9 Trace Requirements Student Exercises

1. Match the requirements relationship on the left with its definition on the right.

   1. Satisfy ___
   2. Derive ___
   3. Validate ___
   4. Effort ___
   5. Necessity ___

   a. when it only makes sense to implement a particular requirement if a related requirement is also implemented.
   b. relationship between a requirement and a test case or other element that can determine whether a solution fulfills the requirement.
   c. relationship between an implementation element and the requirements it is satisfying.
   d. relationship between two requirements, used when a requirement is created from another requirement.
   e. when a requirement is easier to implement if a related requirement is also implemented.


2. Match the Business Analysis Technique on the left with how it is applied to trace requirements on the right.

   1. Business Rules Analysis ___
   2. Functional Decomposition ___
   3. Process Modeling ___
   4. Scope Modeling ___

   a. used to break down solution scope into smaller components for allocation, as well as to trace high-level concepts to low-level concepts.
   b. used to visually depict scope, as well as trace requirements to the area of scope the requirement supports.
   c. used to trace business rules to requirements that they support, or rules that support requirements.
   d. used to visually show the future state process, as well as tracing requirements to the future state process.

## Answers to Student Exercises

1. Match the requirements relationship on the left with its definition on the right.

   1. Satisfy  _C_
   2. Derive  _D_
   3. Validate  _B_
   4. Effort  _E_
   5. Necessity  _A_

   a. when it only makes sense to implement a particular requirement if a related requirement is also implemented.
   b. relationship between a requirement and a test case or other element that can determine whether a solution fulfills the requirement.
   c. relationship between an implementation element and the requirements it is satisfying.
   d. relationship between two requirements, used when a requirement is created from another requirement.
   e. when a requirement is easier to implement if a related requirement is also implemented.

2. Match the Business Analysis Technique on the left with how it is applied to trace requirements on the right.

   1. Business Rules Analysis  _C_
   2. Functional Decomposition  _A_
   3. Process Modeling  _D_
   4. Scope Modeling  _B_

   a. used to break down solution scope into smaller components for allocation, as well as to trace high-level concepts to low-level concepts.
   b. used to visually depict scope, as well as trace requirements to the area of scope the requirement supports.
   c. used to trace business rules to requirements that they support, or rules that support requirements.
   d. used to visually show the future state process, as well as tracing requirements to the future state process.

## 5.2 Maintain Requirements

### Figure 5.2.1: Maintain Requirements Input/Task/Output Diagram

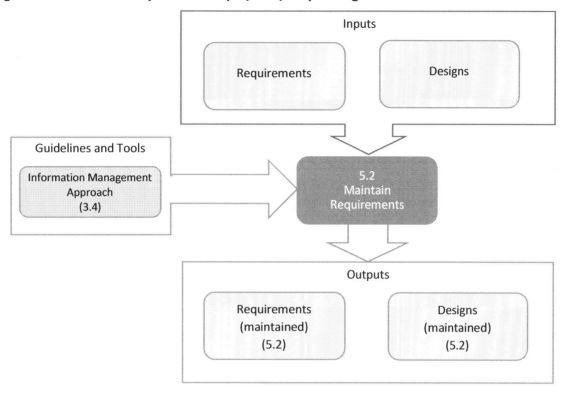

### 5.2.1 Purpose

To retain requirement accuracy and consistency throughout requirements life cycle, and to support reuse of requirements in other solutions.

### 5.2.2 Description

Maintaining requirements is concerned with ensuring that requirements remain accurate and consistent throughout the life cycle, including supporting the reuse of requirements. In order to maximize the benefits of maintaining and reusing requirements, the requirements should be:

- consistently represented,
- reviewed and approved for maintenance using a standardized process that defines proper access rights and ensures quality, and
- easily accessible and understandable.

### 5.2.3 Inputs

- **Requirements**: include goals, objectives, business requirements, stakeholder requirements, solution requirements, and transition requirements. These should be maintained throughout their life cycle.
- **Designs**: can be maintained throughout their life cycle, as needed.

### 5.2.4 Elements

#### 5.2.4.1 Maintain Requirements

Business analysts maintain requirements to ensure accuracy and consistency throughout the initiative and beyond. This includes maintaining relationships among requirements, sets of requirements, and associated business analysis information to ensure the context and original intent of the requirement is preserved. For requirements to be maintained they need to be:

- clearly named,
- clearly defined, and
- easily accessible by the stakeholders.

New requirements and business analysis information is often discovered throughout the initiative. Maintaining requirements includes integrating new requirements into the set of requirements and ensuring all requirements stay current after the change.

#### 5.2.4.2 Maintain Attributes

While eliciting requirements, business analysts elicit requirement attributes. Information such as the requirement's source, priority, and complexity aid in managing each requirement throughout the life cycle. Some attributes change as the business analyst uncovers more information and conducts further analysis. An attribute may change even though the requirement does not. See section 3.4.4.6 for a list of Requirements Attributes.

#### 5.2.4.3 Reusing Requirements

There are situations in which requirements can be reused.

Requirements at high levels of abstraction tend to be more suitable for reuse because they typically are without direct ties to a particular tool or organizational structure. Requirements can be reused:

- within the current initiative,
- within similar initiatives,
- within similar departments, and
- enterprise-wide.

### 5.2.5 Guidelines and Tools

| Guideline or Tool | How Utilized in this Task |
|---|---|
| **Information Management Approach (3.4)** | indicates how requirements will be managed for reuse. |

## 5.2.6 Techniques

| Technique | How Utilized in this Task |
|---|---|
| 10.9 Business Rules Analysis | used to identify business rules that may be similar across the enterprise in order to facilitate reuse. |
| 10.13 Data Flow Diagrams | used to identify information flow that may be similar across the enterprise in order to facilitate reuse. |
| 10.15 Data Modeling | used to identify data structure that may be similar across the enterprise in order to facilitate reuse. |
| 10.18 Document Analysis | used to analyze existing documentation about an enterprise that can serve as the basis for maintaining and reusing requirements. |
| 10.22 Functional Decomposition | used to identify requirements associated with the components and available for reuse. |
| 10.35 Process Modeling | used to identify requirements associated with the processes that may be available for reuse. |
| 10.47 Use Cases and Scenarios | used to identify a solution component that may be utilized by more than one solution. |
| 10.50 Workshops | used to identify requirements associated with the story that may be available for reuse. |

## 5.2.7 Stakeholders

| Stakeholder | How Involved in this Task |
|---|---|
| Domain Subject Matter Expert | references maintained requirements on a regular basis to ensure they are accurately reflecting stated needs. |
| Implementation Subject Matter Expert | utilizes maintained requirements when developing regression tests and conducting impact analysis for an enhancement. |
| Operational Support | maintained requirements are likely to be referenced to confirm the current state. |
| Regulator | maintained requirements are likely to be referenced to confirm compliance to standards. |
| Tester | maintained requirements are used by testers to aid in test plan and test case creation. |

## 5.2.8 Outputs

- **Requirements (maintained) (5.2)**: defined once and available for long-term usage by the organization. They may become organizational process assets or be used in future initiatives. In some cases, a requirement that was not approved or implemented may be maintained for a possible future initiative.
- **Designs (maintained) (5.2)**: may be reusable once defined. For example, as a self- contained component that can be made available for possible future use.

## 5.2.9 Maintain Requirements Student Exercises

1. Match the Business Analysis Technique on the left with how it is applied for maintaining requirements on the right.

   1. Business Rules Analysis ___
   2. Data Flow Diagrams ___
   3. Data Modeling ___
   4. Document Analysis ___
   5. Functional Decomposition ___
   6. Process Modeling ___
   7. Use Cases and Scenarios ___
   8. User Stories ___

   a. used to analyze existing documentation about an enterprise that can serve as the basis.
   b. used to identify information flow that may be similar across the enterprise in order to facilitate reuse.
   c. used to identify requirements associated with the story that may be available for reuse.
   d. used to identify requirements associated with the processes that may be available for reuse.
   e. used to identify a solution component that may be utilized by more than one solution.
   f. used to identify business rules that may be similar across the enterprise in order to facilitate reuse.
   g. used to identify data structure that may be similar across the enterprise in order to facilitate reuse.
   h. used to identify requirements associated with the components and available for reuse.

## Answers to Student Exercises

1. Match the Business Analysis Technique on the left with how it is applied for maintaining requirements on the right.

   1. Business Rules Analysis _F_
   2. Data Flow Diagrams _B_
   3. Data Modeling _G_
   4. Document Analysis _A_
   5. Functional Decomposition _H_
   6. Process Modeling _D_
   7. Use Cases and Scenarios _E_
   8. User Stories _C_

   a. used to analyze existing documentation about an enterprise that can serve as the basis.
   b. used to identify information flow that may be similar across the enterprise in order to facilitate reuse.
   c. used to identify requirements associated with the story that may be available for reuse.
   d. used to identify requirements associated with the processes that may be available for reuse.
   e. used to identify a solution component that may be utilized by more than one solution.
   f. used to identify business rules that may be similar across the enterprise in order to facilitate reuse.
   g. used to identify data structure that may be similar across the enterprise in order to facilitate reuse.
   h. used to identify requirements associated with the components and available for reuse.

## 5.3 Prioritize Requirements

**Figure 5.3.1: Prioritize Requirements Input/Task/Output Diagram**

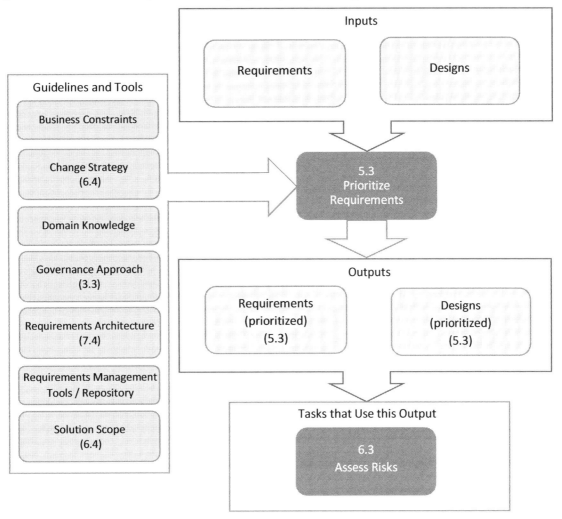

### 5.3.1 Purpose

To rank requirements in the order of relative importance.

### 5.3.2 Description

Prioritization is the act of ranking requirements to determine their relative importance to stakeholders. Priority can refer to the relative value of a requirement, or to the sequence in which it will be implemented. Prioritization is an ongoing process, with priorities changing as the context changes. Prioritization is a critical exercise that seeks to ensure the maximum value is achieved.

### 5.3.3 Inputs

- **Requirements**: any requirements in the form of text, matrices, or diagrams that are ready to prioritize.
- **Designs**: any designs in the form of text, prototypes, or diagrams that are ready to prioritize.

### 5.3.4 Elements

#### 5.3.4.1 Basis for Prioritization

Typical factors that influence prioritization include:
- **Benefit**: the advantage that accrues to stakeholders as a result of requirement implementation, as measured against the goals and objectives for the change. Benefit can be perceived differently by different stakeholders. Conflict resolution and negotiation may be employed to come to consensus on overall benefit.
- **Penalty**: the consequences that result from not implementing a given requirement. Penalty may refer to the negative consequence of not implementing a requirement that improves the experience of a customer.
- **Cost**: the effort and resources needed to implement the requirement. Cost is often used in conjunction with other criteria, such as cost-benefit analysis.
- **Risk**: the chance that the requirement cannot deliver the potential value, or cannot be met at all. This may include many factors such as the difficulty of implementing a requirement, or the chance that stakeholders will not accept a solution component. A proof of concept may be developed to establish that high risk options are possible.
- **Dependencies**: relationships between requirements where one requirement cannot be fulfilled unless the other requirement is fulfilled.
- **Time Sensitivity**: the 'best before' date of the requirement, after which the implementation of the requirement loses significant value. This includes time-to-market scenarios, in which the benefit derived will be exponentially greater if the functionality is delivered ahead of the competition. It can also refer to seasonal functionality that only has value at a specific time of year.
- **Stability**: the likelihood that the requirement will change, either because it requires further analysis or because stakeholders have not reached a consensus about it.
- **Regulatory or Policy Compliance**: requirements that must be implemented in order to meet regulatory or policy demands imposed on the organization, which may take precedence over other stakeholder interests.

#### 5.3.4.2 Challenges of Prioritization

There are a variety of challenges involved in prioritizing requirements. Stakeholders commonly need to make tradeoffs during the prioritization process. Gaining consensus on priorities requires conflict resolution skills.

#### 5.3.4.3 Continual Prioritization

Priorities may shift as the context evolves and as more information becomes available. As these changes evolve, reprioritization of requirements may become necessary. Prioritization is not a one-time-and-your-done activity, prioritization is always re-assessed as work on the initiative continues.

## 5.3.5 Guidelines and Tools

| Guideline or Tool | How Utilized in this Task |
|---|---|
| **Business Constraints** | regulatory statutes, contractual obligations and business policies that may define priorities. |
| **Change Strategy (6.4)** | provides information on costs, timelines, and value realization which are used to determine priority of requirements. |
| **Domain Knowledge** | knowledge and expertise of the business domain needed to support prioritization. |
| **Governance Approach (3.3)** | outlines the approach for prioritizing requirements. |
| **Requirements Architecture (7.4)** | utilized to understand the relationship with other requirements and work products. |
| **Requirements Management Tools/Repository** | including a requirements attribute for prioritization can help the business analyst to sort and access requirements by priority. |
| **Solution Scope (6.4)** | considered when prioritizing requirements to ensure scope is managed. |

## 5.3.6 Techniques

| Technique | How Utilized in this Task |
|---|---|
| **10.2 Backlog Management** | used to compare requirements to be prioritized. The backlog can be the location where the prioritization is maintained. |
| **10.7 Business Cases** | used to assess requirements against identified business goals and objectives to determine importance. |
| **10.16 Decision Analysis** | used to identify high-value requirements. |
| **10.19 Estimation** | used to produce estimates for the basis of prioritization. |
| **10.20 Financial Analysis** | used to assess the financial value of a set of requirements and how the timing of delivery will affect that value. |
| **10.25 Interviews** | used to gain an understanding of a single or small group of stakeholders' basis of prioritization or priorities. |
| **10.26 Item Tracking** | used to track issues raised by stakeholders during prioritization. |
| **10.33 Prioritization** | used to facilitate the process of prioritization. |
| **10.38 Risk Analysis and Management** | used to understand the risks for the basis of prioritization. |
| **10.50 Workshops** | used to gain an understanding of stakeholders' basis of prioritization or priorities in a facilitated group setting. |

### 5.3.7 Stakeholders

| Stakeholder | How Involved in this Task |
|---|---|
| **Customer** | verifies that the prioritized requirements will deliver value from a customer or end-user perspective. The customer can also negotiate to have the prioritization changed based on relative value. |
| **End User** | verifies that the prioritized requirements will deliver value from a customer or end-user perspective. |
| **Implementation Subject Matter Expert** | provides input relating to technical dependencies and can negotiate to have the prioritization changed based on technical constraints. |
| **Project Manager** | uses the prioritization as input into the project plan and into the allocation of requirements to releases. |
| **Regulator** | can verify that the prioritization is consistent with legal and regulatory constraints. |
| **Sponsor** | verifies that the prioritized requirements will deliver value from an organizational perspective. |

### 5.3.8 Outputs

- **Requirements (prioritized) (5.3)**: prioritized or ranked requirements are available for additional work, ensuring that the highest valued requirements are addressed first.
- **Designs (prioritized) (5.3)**: prioritized or ranked designs are available for additional work, ensuring that the highest valued designs are addressed first.

**NOTES:**

*Use this space to write notes concerning this chapter that you want to remember and will help you pass the ECBA™ exam.*

Chapter 5 Requirements Life Cycle Management

## 5.3.9 Prioritize Requirements Student Exercises

1. Fill in the blanks with the basis for prioritization that the sentence is describing, then look up that word in the word find puzzle.

| D | R | T | T | L | A | N | E | P | G | B | R |
|---|---|---|---|---|---|---|---|---|---|---|---|
| S | E | I | C | N | E | D | N | E | P | E | D |
| T | N | M | S | O | T | S | Y | N | E | N | R |
| A | B | E | N | E | F | I | T | A | N | E | E |
| B | E | S | R | Y | E | R | L | L | A | F | G |
| I | N | E | R | R | S | A | A | R | O | N | U |
| B | E | N | E | O | T | R | N | I | P | T | L |
| I | F | S | C | T | A | S | E | C | O | S | A |
| Y | I | I | O | A | B | R | P | K | K | W | B |
| L | N | T | S | L | I | T | S | S | N | E | S |
| A | E | I | F | U | L | I | T | Y | N | R | E |
| N | P | V | E | G | R | A | N | E | P | C | M |
| E | E | I | M | E | N | F | T | S | O | C | I |
| P | D | T | I | R | N | E | S | E | M | I | T |
| R | E | Y | T | I | L | I | B | A | T | S | N |

a. The advantage that accrues to stakeholders as a result of requirement implementation, as measured against the goals and objectives for the change. _____.

b. The effort and resources needed to implement the requirement. _____.

c. The 'best before' date of the requirement, after which the implementation of the requirement loses significant value. _____.

d. The consequences that result from not implementing a given requirement. _____.

e. Relationships between requirements where one requirement cannot be fulfilled unless the other requirement is fulfilled. _____.

f. The likelihood that the requirement will change, either because it requires further analysis or because stakeholders have not reached a consensus about it. _____.

g. The chance that the requirement cannot deliver the potential value, or cannot be met at all. _____.

h. Requirements that must be implemented in order to meet regulatory or policy demands imposed on the organization, which may take precedence over other stakeholder interests. _____.

## Answers to Student Exercises

1. Fill in the blanks with the basis for prioritization that the sentence is describing, then look up that word in the word find puzzle.

| D | R | T | T | L | A | N | E | P | G | B | R |
|---|---|---|---|---|---|---|---|---|---|---|---|
| S | E | I | C | N | E | D | N | E | P | E | D |
| T | N | M | S | O | T | S | Y | N | E | N | R |
| A | B | E | N | E | F | I | T | A | N | E | E |
| B | E | S | R | Y | E | R | L | L | A | F | G |
| I | N | E | R | R | S | A | A | R | O | N | U |
| B | E | N | E | O | T | R | N | I | P | T | L |
| I | F | S | C | T | A | S | E | C | O | S | A |
| Y | I | I | O | A | B | R | P | K | K | W | B |
| L | N | T | S | L | I | T | S | S | N | E | S |
| A | E | I | F | U | L | I | I | Y | N | R | E |
| N | P | V | E | G | R | A | N | E | P | C | M |
| E | E | I | M | E | N | F | T | S | O | C | I |
| P | D | T | I | R | N | E | S | E | M | I | T |
| R | E | Y | T | I | L | I | B | A | T | S | N |

a. The advantage that accrues to stakeholders as a result of requirement implementation, as measured against the goals and objectives for the change.  **Benefit**            .

b. The effort and resources needed to implement the requirement. **Cost**    .

c. The 'best before' date of the requirement, after which the implementation of the requirement loses significant value.  **Time Sensitivity**       .

d. The consequences that result from not implementing a given requirement.  **Penalty**         .

e. Relationships between requirements where one requirement cannot be fulfilled unless the other requirement is fulfilled.  **Dependencies**  .

f. The likelihood that the requirement will change, either because it requires further analysis or because stakeholders have not reached a consensus about it.  **Stability**  .

g. The chance that the requirement cannot deliver the potential value, or cannot be met at all.  **Risk**  .

h. Requirements that must be implemented in order to meet regulatory or policy demands imposed on the organization, which may take precedence over other stakeholder interests.  **Regulatory**  .

## 5.4 Assess Requirements Changes

**Figure 5.4.1: Assess Requirements Changes Input/Task/Output Diagram**

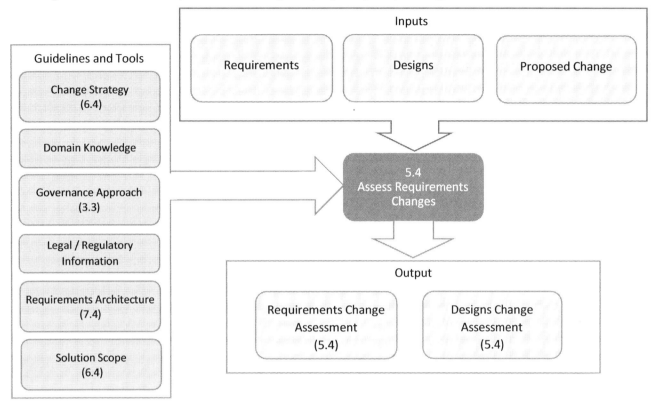

### 5.4.1 Purpose

To evaluate the implications of proposed changes to requirements and designs.

### 5.4.2 Description

Whenever new needs or possible solution changes are identified the business analyst needs to access the impact of that change on the other requirements and designs. The BA looks at whether the change introduces conflict with other requirements, increase the level of risk, delay delivery of the solution or features, and whether it can be traced back to a need. The business analysis performs an assessment to determine whether a proposed change will increase the value of the solution, and if so, what should be done.

When assessing changes, the business analyst(s) considers if the change:
- aligns with the solution scope,
- aligns with the overall strategy,
- affects value delivered to the business or stakeholder groups,
- impacts the time to deliver or the resources required to deliver the value, and
- alters any risks, opportunities, or constraints associated with the overall initiative.

### 5.4.3 Inputs

- **Proposed Change**: can be identified at any time and impact any aspect of business analysis work or deliverables completed to date. There are many triggers for a proposed change including business strategy changes, stakeholders, legal requirements, or regulatory changes.
- **Requirements**: may need to be assessed to identify the impact of a proposed modification.
- **Designs**: may need to be assessed to identify the impact of a proposed modification.

### 5.4.4 Elements

#### 5.4.4.1 Assessment Formality

Business analysts will determine the formality of the assessment process based on the information available, the apparent importance of the change, and the governance process as laid out on the Governance Approach (3.3). The level of formality depends on the approach taken as described below:

| Approach | Level of Formality |
|---|---|
| Predictive | More formal due to the impact of each change can be disruptive; the change can potentially generate a substantial reworking of tasks and activities completed in previous activities. |
| Adaptive | Less formal, while there may be reworking needed as a result of each change, adaptive approaches try to minimize the impact of changes by utilizing iterative and incremental implementation techniques. |

#### 5.4.4.2 Impact Analysis

Impact analysis is performed to evaluate the effect of a change. When a requirement changes, its relationships to other requirements or solution components needs to be reviewed. Each related requirement or component may also require a change to support the new requirement.

*Traceability is a useful tool for impact analysis in helping determine the extent of the change.*

Areas that need to be considered in impact analysis:

| Approach | Level of Formality |
|---|---|
| Benefit | the benefit that will be gained by accepting the change. |
| Cost | the total cost to implement the change including the cost to make the change, the cost of associated rework, and the opportunity costs such as the number of other features that may need to be sacrificed or deferred. |
| Impact | the number of customers or business processes affected if the change is accepted. |
| Schedule | the impact to the existing delivery commitments if the change is approved. |
| Urgency | the level of importance including the factors which drive necessity such as regulator or safety issues. |

#### 5.4.4.3 Impact Resolution

The results of the impact analysis, including agreement on resolution, is documented and communicated to the appropriate stakeholders. The final resolution and disposition of the requested change (approved, denied, deferred) is made by following the processes approved in the Governance Approach (3.3).

## 5.4.5 Guidelines and Tools

| Guideline or Tool | How Utilized in this Task |
|---|---|
| **Change Strategy (6.4)** | describes the purpose and direction for changes, establishes context for the change, and identifies the critical components for change. |
| **Domain Knowledge** | knowledge of and expertise in the business domain is needed to assess proposed requirements changes. |
| **Governance Approach (3.3)** | provides guidance regarding the change control and decision-making processes, as well as the roles of stakeholders within this process. |
| **Legal/Regulatory Information** | describes legislative rules or regulations that must be followed. These may impact requirements and must be considered when making changes. |
| **Requirements Architecture (7.4)** | requirements may be related to each other; therefore, the business analyst examines and analyzes the requirement relationships to determine which requirements will be impacted by a requested requirement change. |
| **Solution Scope (6.4)** | must be considered when assessing changes to fully understand the impact of a proposed change. |

## 5.4.6 Techniques

| Technique | How Utilized in this Task |
|---|---|
| **10.7 Business Cases** | used to justify a proposed change. |
| **10.9 Business Rules Analysis** | used to assess changes to business policies and business rules, and develop revised guidance. |
| **10.16 Decision Analysis** | used to facilitate the change assessment process. |
| **10.18 Document Analysis** | used to analyze any existing documents that facilitate an understanding of the impact of the change. |
| **10.19 Estimation** | used to determine the size of the change. |
| **10.20 Financial Analysis** | used to estimate the financial consequences of a proposed change. |
| **10.24 Interface Analysis** | used to help business analysts identify interfaces that can be affected by the change. |
| **10.25 Interviews** | used to gain an understanding of the impact on the organization or its assets from a single or small group of stakeholders. |
| **10.26 Item Tracking** | used to track any issues or conflicts discovered during impact analysis. |
| **10.38 Risk Analysis and Management** | used to determine the level of risk associated with the change. |
| **10.50 Workshops** | used to gain an understanding of the impact or to resolve changes in a group setting. |

## 5.4.7 Stakeholders

| Stakeholder | How Involved in this Task |
|---|---|
| Customer | provides feedback concerning the impact the change will have on value. |
| Domain Subject Matter Expert | has expertise in some aspect of the situation and can provide insight into how the change will impact the organization and value. |
| End User | uses the solution or is a component of the solution, and can offer information about the impact of the change on their activities. |
| Operational Support | provides information on both their ability to support the operation of the solution and their need to understand the nature of the change in the solution in order to be able to support it. |
| Project Manager | reviews the requirements change assessment to determine if additional project work is required for a successful implementation of the solution. |
| Regulator | changes are likely to be referenced by auditors to confirm compliance to standards. |
| Sponsor | accountable for the solution scope and can provide insight to be utilized when assessing change. |
| Tester | consulted for establishing impact of the proposed changes. |

## 5.4.8 Outputs

- **Requirements Change Assessment (5.4)**: the recommendation to approve, modify, or deny a proposed change to requirements.
- **Designs Change Assessment (5.4)**: the recommendation to approve, modify, or deny a proposed change to one or more design components.

## 5.4.9 Assess Requirements Changes Student Exercises

1. Match the consideration for assessing impact of requirements changes on the left to its definition on the right.

    1. Benefit \_\_\_    a. the impact to the existing delivery commitments if the change is approved.

    2. Cost \_\_\_    b. the number of customers or business processes affected if the change is accepted.

    3. Impact \_\_\_    c. the total cost to implement the change.

    4. Schedule \_\_\_    d. the level of importance including the factors which drive necessity such as regulator or safety issues.

    5. Urgency \_\_\_    e. what will be gained by accepting the change.

# Answers to Student Exercises

1. Match the consideration for assessing impact of requirements changes on the left to its definition on the right.

    1. Benefit _E_    a. the impact to the existing delivery commitments if the change is approved.

    2. Cost _C_    b. the number of customers or business processes affected if the change is accepted.

    3. Impact _B_    c. the total cost to implement the change.

    4. Schedule _A_    d. the level of importance including the factors which drive necessity such as regulator or safety issues.

    5. Urgency _D_    e. what will be gained by accepting the change.

## 5.5 Approve Requirements

**Figure 5.5.1: Approve Requirements Input/Task/Output Diagram**

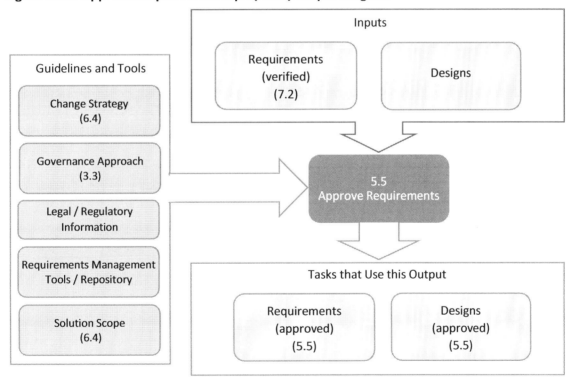

### 5.5.1 Purpose

To obtain agreement on and approval of requirements and designs for business analysis work to continue and/or solution construction to proceed.

## 5.5.2 Description

Business analysts communicate requirements, designs, and pertinent business analysis information to key stakeholders. Those key stakeholders approve, reject or defer the approval of the information. Business analyst is responsible to track, manage and communicate the approvals to all stakeholders.

*The approval process can be formal or informal*

The level of formality depends on the approach taken:

| Approach | Description |
|---|---|
| Predictive | Approvals typically happen at the end of the phase or during planned change control meetings |
| Adaptive | Approvals typically happen only when construction and implementation of a solution meeting the requirement can begin |

## 5.5.3 Inputs

- **Requirements (verified) (7.2)**: a set of requirements that have been verified to be of sufficient quality to be used as a reliable body of work for further specification and development.
- **Designs**: a set of designs that have been determined as ready to be used for further specification and development.

## 5.5.4 Elements

### 5.5.4.1 Understand Stakeholder Roles

The approval process is defined in the Business Analysis Governance Approach (3.3), including stakeholder roles and approval authorities. Business analysts must understand these roles and who has the decision-making authority. Business analysts not only has to consider stakeholders with approval authority, but those that may be able to influence these decisions.

### 5.5.4.2 Conflict and Issue Management

Business analysts typically seek consensus among the stakeholders prior to asking for sign-off. This helps raise and resolves issues and conflicts prior to any formal sign-off. Conflicts can arise from stakeholders' different interpretations of the requirements, designs and business analysis information and conflicting values placed on them.

### 5.5.4.3 Gain Consensus

Business analysts work with stakeholders with the authority to approve requirements and changes to ensure they understand and accept the requirements or changes to requirements. Business analysts review the requirements with accountable stakeholders, address their questions and concerns by providing additional information as needed, and request sign-off from the stakeholders.

### 5.5.4.4 Track and Communicate Approval

The business analyst records approval decisions, possibly in requirements maintenance and tracking tools. There may be value in maintaining an audit history of changes to requirements: what was changed, who made the change, the reason for the change, and when it was made.

## 5.5.5 Guidelines and Tools

| Guideline or Tool | How Utilized in this Task |
|---|---|
| **Change Strategy (6.4)** | provides information which assists in managing stakeholder consensus regarding the needs of all stakeholders. |
| **Governance Approach (3.3)** | identifies the stakeholders who have the authority and responsibility to approve business analysis information, and explains when such approvals will take place and how they will align to organizational policies. |
| **Legal/Regulatory Information** | describes legislative rules or regulations that must be followed. They may impact the requirements and designs approval process. |
| **Requirements Management Tools/Repository** | tool to record requirements approvals. |
| **Solution Scope (6.4)** | must be considered when approving requirements to accurately assess alignment and completeness. |

## 5.5.6 Techniques

| Technique | How Utilized in this Task |
|---|---|
| **10.1 Acceptance and Evaluation Criteria** | used to define approval criteria. |
| **10.16 Decision Analysis** | used to resolve issues and gain agreement. |
| **10.26 Item Tracking** | used to track issues identified during the agreement process. |
| **10.37 Reviews** | used to evaluate requirements. |
| **10.50 Workshops** | used to facilitate obtaining approval. |

## 5.5.7 Stakeholders

| Stakeholder | How Involved in this Task |
|---|---|
| **Customer** | may play an active role in reviewing and approving requirements and designs to ensure needs are met. |
| **Domain Subject Matter Expert** | may be involved in the review and approval of requirements and designs as defined by stakeholder roles and responsibilities designation. |
| **End User** | people who use the solution, or who are a solution component, and may be involved in the review, validation, and prioritization of requirements and designs as defined by the stakeholder roles and responsibilities designation. |
| **Operational Support** | responsible for ensuring that requirements and designs are supportable within the constraints imposed by technology standards and organizational capability plans. Operational support personnel may have a role in reviewing and approving requirements. |

| Stakeholder | How Involved in this Task |
|---|---|
| **Project Manager** | responsible for identifying and managing risks associated with solution design, development, delivery, implementation, operation and sustainment. The project manager may manage the project plan activities pertaining to review and/or approval. |
| **Regulator** | external or internal party who is responsible for providing opinions on the relationship between stated requirements and specific regulations, either formally in an audit, or informally as inputs to requirements life cycle management tasks. |
| **Sponsor** | responsible to review and approve the business case, solution or product scope, and all requirements and designs. |
| **Tester** | responsible for ensuring quality assurance standards are feasible within the business analysis information. For example, requirements have the testable characteristic. |

### 5.5.8 Outputs

- **Requirements (approved) (5.5)**: requirements which are agreed to by stakeholders and are ready for use in subsequent business analysis efforts.
- **Designs (approved) (5.5)**: designs which are agreed to by stakeholders and are ready for use in subsequent business analysis or solution development efforts.

### 5.5.9 Approve Requirements Student Exercises

1. Match the Approve Requirements element on the left with its description on the right.

   1. Understand Stakeholder Roles ___
   2. Conflict and Issue Management ___
   3. Gain Consensus ___
   4. Track and Communicate Approval ___

   a. handling varying points of views and priorities.
   b. prior to asking for approval ensure there is shared understanding of the requirements changes.
   c. record decisions and keep accurate records of current decision status.
   d. understand authority levels.

# Answers to Student Exercises

1. Match the Approve Requirements element on the left with its description on the right.

    1. Understand Stakeholder Roles  _D_
    2. Conflict and Issue Management  _A_
    3. Gain Consensus  _B_
    4. Track and Communicate Approval  _C_

    a. handling varying points of views and priorities.
    b. prior to asking for approval ensure there is shared understanding of the requirements changes.
    c. record decisions and keep accurate records of current decision status.
    d. understand authority levels.

## 5.6 Requirements Life Cycle Management Pop-up Quiz

1. What are the tasks of the Requirements Life Cycle Management knowledge area?

    a. Maintain requirements, prioritize requirements, validate requirements, verify requirements, and approve requirements.

    b. Prioritize requirements, maintain requirements, trace requirements, assess requirements changes, and approve requirements.

    c. Trace requirements, manage requirements, verify requirements, analyze requirements, and approve requirements.

    d. Trace requirements, maintain requirements, prioritize requirements, analyze requirements, and assess requirements changes.

2. Which of the following is NOT a guideline or tool for the Trace Requirements task?

    a. Legal and Regulatory Information
    b. Domain Knowledge
    c. Change Strategy
    d. Requirements Management Tool/Repository

3. Which requirement relationship describes the relationship between a requirement and the solution component that fulfills that requirement?

   a. Satisfy

   b. Depends

   c. Derive

   d. Validate

4. The business analyst is maintaining requirements attributes and dealing with how soon the requirement will be needed. Which requirement attribute is he dealing with?

   a. Satisfy

   b. Source

   c. Priority

   d. Urgency

5. The business analyst is prioritizing requirements based on how likely the requirement will change. Which basis of prioritization is she dealing with?

   a. Risk

   b. Stability

   c. Time Sensitivity

   d. Dependencies

6. Which of the following statement best describes the business analyst role in Conflict and Issue Management when attempting to get approval for requirements?

   a. The business analyst facilitates communication among stakeholders so that they have appreciation for the needs of others.

   b. The business analyst considers who should be informed or consulted about the requirements.

   c. The business analyst facilitates the approval process by addressing any questions or providing additional information when requested.

   d. The business analyst keeps accurate records of approval decisions and communicates information to stakeholders.

7. The business analyst is doing an impact analysis for a requirement change and is currently looking at the number customers or business processes that are affected. Which consideration of impact analysis is the business analyst currently looking at?

   a. Benefit

   b. Cost

   c. Impact

   d. Urgency

8. When working to approve requirements which technique would you use to define approval criteria?

   a. Decision Analysis

   b. Reviews

   c. Workshops

   d. Acceptance and Evaluation Criteria

9. When tracing requirements which requirement relationship deals with a requirement that is easier to implement if a related requirement is also implemented?

   a. Effort

   b. Derive

   c. Depends

   d. Validate

## Answers to Pop-up Quiz

| Question | Answer | Description |
|---|---|---|
| 1 | B | BABOK sections 5.1, 5.2, 5.3, 5.4, 5.5. |
| 2 | C | BABOK figure 5.1.3 and section 5.1.5 |
| 3 | A | BABOK section 5.1.4.2. Satisfy: relationship between an implementation element and the requirements it is satisfying. |
| 4 | D | BABOK section 3.4.4.6. Urgency: indicates how soon the requirement is needed. Not to be confused with Priority: indicates relative importance of requirements. |
| 5 | B | BABOK section 5.3.4.1. Stability: the likelihood that the requirement will change. Not to be confused with Risk: the chance that the requirement cannot deliver the potential value, or Time Sensitivity: the 'best before' date of the requirement, after which the implementation of the requirement loses significant value. |
| 6 | A | BABOK section 5.5.4.2. The business analyst facilitates communication between stakeholders in areas of conflict so that each group has an improved appreciation for the needs of the others. |
| 7 | C | BABOK section 5.4.4.2. Impact: the number of customers or business processes affected if the change is accepted. |
| 8 | D | BABOK section 5.5.6. Acceptance and Evaluation Criteria: used to define approval criteria. |
| 9 | A | BABOK section 5.1.4.2. Effort: when a requirement is easier to implement if a related requirement is also implemented. |

# 6 Strategy Analysis

## Overview

Strategy analysis describes how business analysts collaborate with stakeholders to move the organization from the current state to the desired future state. It includes assessing risks of a change and formulating a strategy for delivering a solution to meet the business need. Strategy defines the most effective way to apply the capabilities of an enterprise in order to reach a desired set of goals and objectives.

> *Strategy defines the most effective way to apply the capabilities of an enterprise in order to reach a desired set of goals and objectives.*

Strategies may exist for the entire enterprise, for a division, department or region, and for a product, project, or iteration. Strategy analysis aligns the higher-level and lower-level strategies to move to the future state. The need for a strategy is triggered by the identification of a need of strategic or tactical importance to the organization. Strategy analysis is an ongoing activity that assesses any changes in that need, in its context, or any new information that may indicate that an adjustment to the change strategy may be required.

Since Strategy Analysis is only 5% of the ECBA™ exam blueprint, you will notice that we have reduced our coverage of this knowledge area. Even though there will only be two or three questions on the exam from this knowledge area, a good understanding of this light coverage will help you get those questions right.

**Goal:** The goal of strategy analysis is to identify a need of strategic or tactical importance, enable the enterprise to address that need, and align the resulting strategy for the change with higher-level and lower=level strategies.

The following image illustrates the spectrum of value as business analysis activities progress from delivering potential value to actual value.

### Figure 6.0.1: Business Analysis Value Spectrum

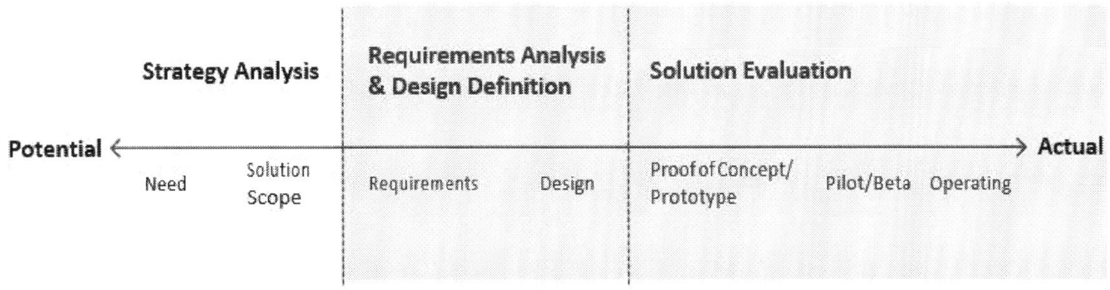

## What You Will Learn

When you are finished with this chapter, you will know:
- How to define Strategy, in BABOK® terms.
- How the business analyst conducts strategy analysis.
- How strategy analysis fits into business needs.
- The four tasks in this knowledge area:
    1. Analyze Current State
    2. Define Future State
    3. Assess Risks
    4. Define Change Strategy

Important learnings in Strategy Analysis Knowledge Area:
- Strategy Analysis is an ongoing activity.
- Strategy analysis is the strategic thinking part of business analysis, helping the organization to envision potential solutions that deliver value.

**Figure 6.0.2: Strategy Analysis Input/Task/Output Diagram**

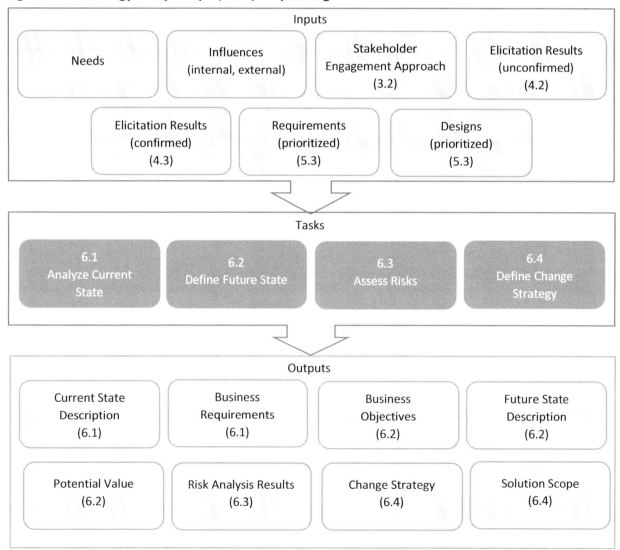

# Chapter 6 Strategy Analysis

## The BACCM™ in Strategy Analysis

The following model describes the usage and application of each of the core concepts within the context of Strategy Analysis.

**Figure 6.0.3: Core Concepts application In Strategy Analysis**

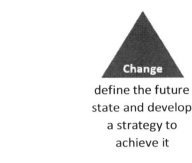

define the future state and develop a strategy to achieve it

identify needs within the current state and prioritize needs to determine the desired future state

define the scope of a solution as part of developing a change strategy

collaborate with stakeholders to understand the need and to define the future state and strategy to achieve it

consider the context of the enterprise in developing a change strategy

examine the potential value of the solution to determine if a change is justified

## Tasks in Strategy Analysis

There are four tasks in the Strategy Analysis Knowledge Area:

1. Analyze <u>C</u>urrent State
2. Define <u>F</u>uture State
3. Assess <u>R</u>isks
4. Define Change <u>S</u>trategy

| Mnemonic |
| --- |
| CFRS |
| Going from <u>C</u>urrent State to <u>F</u>uture State takes <u>R</u>isk and <u>S</u>trategy |

# Detailed ITTSO Table

The following table summarizes the Inputs, Tasks, Techniques, Stakeholders and Outputs (ITTSO) in the Strategy Analysis Knowledge Area.

Table 6.0.1: Inputs, Tasks, Techniques, Stakeholders and Outputs Summary

| ITTSO Summary for Strategy Analysis | | | | | |
|---|---|---|---|---|---|
| Inputs | Tasks | M* | Techniques | Stakeholders | Outputs |
| • Needs<br>• Elicitation Results (confirmed) (4.3) | 6.1 Analyze Current State | C | 10.4 Benchmarking and Market Analysis<br>10.6 Business Capability Analysis<br>10.7 Business Cases<br>10.8 Business Model Canvas<br>10.11 Concept Modeling<br>10.14 Data Mining<br>10.18 Document Analysis<br>10.20 Financial Analysis<br>10.21 Focus Groups<br>10.22 Functional Decomposition<br>10.25 Interviews<br>10.26 Item Tracking<br>10.27 Lessons Learned<br>10.28 Metrics and KPIs<br>10.29 Mind Mapping<br>10.31 Observation<br>10.32 Organizational Modeling<br>10.34 Process Analysis<br>10.35 Process Modeling<br>10.38 Risk Analysis and Management<br>10.40 Root Cause Analysis<br>10.41 Scope Modeling<br>10.45 Survey and Questionnaire<br>10.46 SWOT Analysis<br>10.49 Vendor Assessment<br>10.50 Workshops | • Customer<br>• Domain SME<br>• End User<br>• Implementation SME<br>• Operational Support<br>• Project Manager<br>• Regulator<br>• Supplier<br>• Sponsor | • Current State Description (6.1)<br>• Business Requirements (6.1 |

Chapter 6 Strategy Analysis

| | | | | | |
|---|---|---|---|---|---|
| • Business Requirements (6.1) | 6.2 Define Future State | F | 10.1 Acceptance and Evaluation Criteria<br>10.3 Balanced Scorecard<br>10.4 Benchmarking and Market Analysis<br>10.5 Brainstorming<br>10.6 Business Capability Analysis<br>10.7 Business Cases<br>10.8 Business Model Canvas<br>10.16 Decision Analysis<br>10.17 Decision Modeling<br>10.20 Financial Analysis<br>10.22 Functional Decomposition<br>10.25 Interviews<br>10.27 Lessons Learned<br>10.28 Metrics and KPIs<br>10.29 Mind Mapping<br>10.32 Organizational Modeling<br>10.35 Process Modeling<br>10.36 Prototyping<br>10.41 Scope Modeling<br>10.45 Survey and Questionnaire<br>10.46 SWOT Analysis<br>10.49 Vendor Assessment<br>10.50 Workshops | • Customers<br>• Domain SME<br>• End User<br>• Implementation SME<br>• Operational Support<br>• Project Manager<br>• Regulator<br>• Sponsor<br>• Supplier<br>• Supplier | • Business Objectives (6.2)<br>• Future State Descriptions (6.2)<br>• Potential Value (6.2) |
| • Elicitation Results (confirmed) (4.3)<br>• Requirements (prioritized) (5.3)<br>• Designs (prioritized) (5.3)<br>• Business Objectives (6.2)<br>• Influences | 6.3 Assess Risks | R | 10.5 Brainstorming<br>10.7 Business Cases<br>10.16 Decision Analysis<br>10.18 Document Analysis<br>10.20 Financial Analysis<br>10.25 Interviews<br>10.27 Lessons Learned<br>10.29 Mind Mapping<br>10.38 Risk Analysis and Management<br>10.40 Root Cause Analysis<br>10.45 Survey and Questionnaire<br>10.50 Workshops | • Domain SME<br>• Implementation Analysis<br>• Operational Support<br>• Project Manager<br>• Regulator<br>• Sponsor<br>• Supplier<br>• Tester | • Risk Analysis Results (6.3) |

| | | | | | |
|---|---|---|---|---|---|
| • Stakeholder Engagement Approach (3.2)<br>• Current State Description (6.1)<br>• Future State Description (6.2)<br>• Risk Analysis Results (6.3) | 6.4 Define Change Strategy | S | 10.3 Balanced Scorecard<br>10.4 Benchmarking and Market Analysis<br>10.5 Brainstorming<br>10.6 Business Capability Analysis<br>10.7 Business Cases<br>10.8 Business Model Canvas<br>10.16 Decision Analysis<br>10.19 Estimation<br>10.20 Financial Analysis<br>10.21 Focus Groups<br>10.22 Functional Decomposition<br>10.25 Interviews<br>10.27 Lessons Learned<br>10.29 Mind Mapping<br>10.32 Organizational Modeling<br>10.35 Process Modeling<br>10.41 Scope Modeling<br>10.46 SWOT Analysis<br>10.49 Vendor Assessment<br>10.50 Workshops | • Customer<br>• Domain SME<br>• End User<br>• Implementation SME<br>• Operational Support<br>• Project Manager<br>• Regulator<br>• Sponsor<br>• Supplier<br>• Tester | • Change Strategy (6.4)<br>• Solution Scope (6.4) |

\* Mnemonic = CFRS

# Chapter 6 Strategy Analysis

## Strategy Analysis Student Exercises

**Exercise 1:** Fill in the blanks to complete the Strategy Analysis task name, then enter the Mnemonic letter used in this chapter to help remember the tasks in this knowledge area.

| SA Tasks | Mnemonic Letter |
|---|---|
| Analyze _____ State | |
| Define _____ State | |
| Assess _____ | |
| Define Change _____ | |

Bonus: Enter below the phrase used in this chapter to help remember the tasks in Strategy Analysis knowledge area.

_____

**Exercise 2:** For each stakeholder indicate which task they are involved in by putting an 'X' in the appropriate column under the stakeholder. Some stakeholders may not be involved in any tasks while some stakeholders may be involved in multiple tasks.

| Stakeholder / Task | All Stakeholders | Any Stakeholders | Customers | Domain SME | End User | Implementation SME | Operational Support | Project Manager | Regulator | Sponsor | Supplier | Tester |
|---|---|---|---|---|---|---|---|---|---|---|---|---|
| 6.1 Analyze Current State | | | | | | | | | | | | |
| 6.2 Define Future State | | | | | | | | | | | | |
| 6.3 Assess Risks | | | | | | | | | | | | |
| 6.4 Define Change Strategy | | | | | | | | | | | | |

ECBA™ Certification Study Guide

# Answers to Student Exercises

**Exercise 1:** Fill in the blanks to complete the Strategy Analysis task name, then enter the Mnemonic letter used in this chapter to help remember the tasks in this knowledge area.

| SA Tasks | Mnemonic Letter |
|---|---|
| Analyze _Current_ State | C |
| Define _Future_ State | F |
| Assess _Risks_ | R |
| Define Change _Strategy_ | S |

**Bonus:** Enter below the phrase used in this chapter to help remember the tasks in Strategy Analysis knowledge area.

## Going from Current State to Future State takes Risks and Strategy

**Exercise 2:** For each stakeholder indicate which task they are involved in by putting an 'X' in the appropriate column under the stakeholder. Some stakeholders may not be involved in any tasks while some stakeholders may be involved in multiple tasks.

| Stakeholder / Task | All Stakeholders | Any Stakeholders | Customers | Domain SME | End User | Implementation SME | Operational Support | Project Manager | Regulator | Sponsor | Supplier | Tester |
|---|---|---|---|---|---|---|---|---|---|---|---|---|
| 6.1 Analyze Current State | | | X | X | X | X | X | X | X | X | X | |
| 6.2 Define Future State | | | X | X | X | X | X | X | X | X | X | |
| 6.3 Assess Risks | | | | X | | X | X | X | X | X | X | X |
| 6.4 Define Change Strategy | | | X | X | X | X | X | X | X | X | X | X |

# Chapter 6 Strategy Analysis

## 6.1 Analyze Current State

**Figure 6.1.1: Analyze Current State Input/Task/Output Diagram**

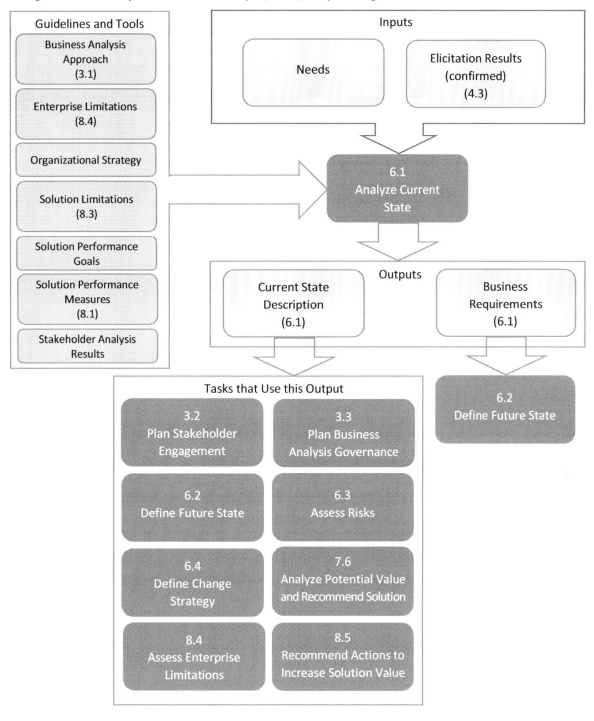

### 6.1.1 Purpose

To understand why an enterprise needs to change and what would be directly or indirectly affected by the change.

### 6.1.2 Description

The starting point for any change is an understanding of *why* the change is needed. In order to effectively navigate the organization through a change initiative, including developing a viable change strategy, you must understand the starting point. Change always occurs in a context of existing stakeholders, processes, technology, and policies which constitute the current state of the enterprise. Business analysts examine the current state in the context of the business need to understand what may influence proposed changes, and what will be affected by them. The current state is explored in just enough detail to validate the need for a change and/or the change strategy. Understanding the current state of the enterprise prior to the change is necessary to identify what will need to change to achieve a desired future state and how the effect of the change will be assessed. Creating a model of the current state might require collaboration throughout or outside the enterprise.

### 6.1.3 Inputs

- **Elicitation Results (confirmed) (4.3)**: used to define and understand the current state.
- **Needs**: the problem or opportunity faced by an enterprise or organization often launches business analysis work to better understand these needs.

### 6.1.4 Elements

#### 6.1.4.1 Business Needs

Business needs are the problems and opportunities of strategic importance faced by the enterprise. A business need may be identified at many different levels of the enterprise:

- **From the top-down**: a strategic goal that needs to be achieved.
- **From the bottom-up**: a problem with the current state of a process, function or system.
- **From middle management**: a manager needs additional information to make sound decisions or must perform additional functions to meet business objectives.
- **From external drivers**: customer demand or business competition in the marketplace.

#### 6.1.4.2 Organizational Structure and Culture

Organizational structure defines the formal relationships between people working in the enterprise. While communication channels and relationships are not limited to that structure, they are heavily influenced by it, and the reporting structure may aid or limit a potential change.

Organizational culture is the beliefs, values, and norms shared by the members of an organization. These beliefs drive the actions taken by an organization.

#### 6.1.4.3 Capabilities and Processes

Capabilities and processes describe the activities an enterprise performs. They also include the knowledge the enterprise has, the products and services it provides, the functions it supports, and the methods it uses to make decisions. Business analysts may use:

- A capability-centric view of the enterprise when looking for innovative solutions that combine existing capabilities to produce a new outcome.
- A process-centric view of the enterprise when looking for ways to improve the performance of current activities.

### 6.1.4.4 Technology and Infrastructure

Information systems used by the enterprise support people in executing processes, making decisions, and in interactions with suppliers and customers. The infrastructure describes the enterprise's environment with respect to physical components and capabilities. The infrastructure can include components such as computer hardware, physical buildings, and logistics, as well as their operation and upkeep.

### 6.1.4.5 Policies

Policies define the scope of decision making at different levels of an enterprise. They generally address routine operations rather than strategic change.

### 6.1.4.6 Business Architecture

Business analysts must understand how all of these elements of the current state fit together and support one another in order to recommend changes that will be effective. The existing business architecture typically meets an assortment of business and stakeholder needs. If those needs are not recognized or do not continue to be met by a proposed transition or future state, changes are likely to result in a loss of value.

### 6.1.4.7 Internal Assets

Business analysts identify enterprise assets used in the current state. Resources can be tangible, or intangible (such as financial resources, patents, reputation, and brand names).

### 6.1.4.8 External Influences

There are external influences on the enterprise that do not participate in a change but might present constraints, dependencies, or drivers on the current state, such as:

| External Influencer | Effect of influence |
| --- | --- |
| Industry Structure | individual industries have distinct ways in which value is created within that industry; this is a particularly important influencer if a proposed change involves entering a new industry. |
| Competitors | the nature and intensity of competitors between enterprises within an industry can be significant. The entry of a new competitor may also change the nature of the industry or increase competition. |
| Customers | the size and nature of existing and potential customer segments can provide influences such as negotiating power and a degree of price sensitivity. Alternatively, the emergence of new alternative ways that customers can meet their needs may drive the enterprise to deliver greater value. |
| Suppliers | the variety and diversity of suppliers might be an influencer, as can the power that suppliers have over their customers. |
| Political and Regulatory Environment | there is often influence from the current and potential impact of laws and regulations upon the industry. |
| Technology | the productivity enhancing potential of recent and expected technological innovations might influence the need. |

| Macroeconomic Factors | the constraints and opportunities that exist within the existing and expected macroeconomic environment (for example, trade, unemployment, or inflation) might influence the need. |

### 6.1.5 Guidelines and Tools

| Guideline or Tool | How Utilized in this Task |
|---|---|
| Business Analysis Approach (3.1) | guides how the business analyst undertakes an analysis of the current state. |
| Enterprise Limitation (8.4) | used to understand the challenges that exist within the enterprise. |
| Organizational Strategy | an organization will have a set of goals and objectives which guides operations, establishes direction, and provides a vision for the future state. This can be implicitly or explicitly stated. |
| Solution Limitation (8.3) | used to understand the current state and the challenges of existing solutions. |
| Solution Performance Goals | measure the current performance of an enterprise or solution, and serve as a baseline for setting future state goals and measuring improvement. |
| Solution Performance Measures (8.1) | describe the actual performance of existing solutions. |
| Stakeholder Analysis Results | stakeholders from across the organization will contribute to an understanding and analysis of the current state. |

### 6.1.6 Techniques

| Technique | How Utilized in this Task |
|---|---|
| 10.4 Benchmarking and Market Analysis | provides an understanding of where there are opportunities for improvement in the current state. Specific frameworks that may be useful include 5 Forces analysis, PEST, STEEP, CATWOE, and others. |
| 10.6 Business Capability Analysis | identifies gaps and prioritizes them in relation to value and risk. |
| 10.7 Business Cases | used to capture information regarding the business need and opportunity. |
| 10.8 Business Model Canvas | provides an understanding of the value proposition that the enterprise satisfies for its customers, the critical factors in delivering that value, and the resulting cost and revenue streams. |
| 10.11 Concept Modeling | used to capture key terms and concepts in the business domain and define the relationships between them. |
| 10.14 Data Mining | used to obtain information on the performance of the enterprise. |
| 10.18 Document Analysis | analyzes any existing documentation about the current state. |

# Chapter 6 Strategy Analysis

| Technique | How Utilized in this Task |
|---|---|
| 10.20 Financial Analysis | used to understand the profitability of the current state and the financial capability to deliver change. |
| 10.21 Focus Groups | solicits feedback from customers or end users about the current state. |
| 10.22 Functional Decomposition | breaks down complex systems or relationships in the current state. |
| 10.25 Interviews | facilitate dialogue with stakeholders to understand the current state and any needs evolving from the current state. |
| 10.26 Item Tracking | tracks and manages issues discovered about the current state. |
| 10.27 Lessons Learned | enables the assessment of failures and opportunities for improvement in past initiatives, which may drive a business need for process improvement. |
| 10.28 Metrics and KPIs | assesses performance of the current state of an enterprise. |
| 10.29 Mind Mapping | used to explore relevant aspects of the current state and better understand relevant factors affecting the business need. |
| 10.31 Observation | may provide opportunities for insights into needs within the current state that have not been identified previously by a stakeholder. |
| 10.32 Organizational Modeling | describes the roles, responsibilities, and reporting structures that exist within the current state organization. |
| 10.34 Process Analysis | identifies opportunities to improve the current state. |
| 10.35 Process Modeling | describes how work occurs within the current solution. |
| 10.38 Risk Analysis and Management | identifies risks to the current state. |
| 10.40 Root Cause Analysis | provides an understanding of the underlying causes of any problems in the current state in order to further clarify a need. |
| 10.41 Scope Modeling | helps define the boundaries on the current state description. |
| 10.45 Survey and Questionnaire | helps to gain an understanding of the current state from a large, varied, or disparate group of stakeholders. |
| 10.46 SWOT Analysis | evaluates the strengths, weaknesses, opportunities, and threats to the current state enterprise. |
| 10.49 Vendor Assessment | determines whether any vendors that are part of the current state are adequately meeting commitments, or if any changes are needed. |
| 10.50 Workshops | engage stakeholders to collaboratively describe the current state and their needs. |

### 6.1.7 Stakeholders

| Stakeholder | How Involved in this Task |
| --- | --- |
| **Customer** | makes use of the existing solution and might have input about issues with a current solution. |
| **Domain Subject Matter Expert** | has expertise in some aspect of the current state. |
| **End User** | directly uses a solution and might have input about issues with a current solution. |
| **Implementation Subject Matter Expert** | has expertise in some aspect of the current state. |
| **Operational Support** | directly involved in supporting the operations of the organization and provides information on their ability to support the operation of an existing solution, as well as any known issues. |
| **Project Manager** | may use information on current state as input to planning. |
| **Regulator** | can inform interpretations of relevant regulations that apply to the current state in the form of business policies, business rules, procedures, or role responsibilities. The regulator might have unique input to the operational assessment, as there might be new laws and regulations with which to comply. |
| **Sponsor** | might have context for performance of existing solutions. |
| **Supplier** | might be an external influencer of the current state. |
| **Tester** | able to provide information about issues with any existing solutions. |

### 6.1.8 Outputs

- **Current State Description (6.1)**: the context of the enterprise's scope, capabilities, resources, performance, culture, dependencies, infrastructure, external influences, and significant relationships between these elements.
- **Business Requirements (6.1)**: the problem, opportunity, or constraint which is defined based on an understanding of the current state.

**NOTES:**
*Use this space to write notes concerning this chapter that you want to remember and will help you pass the ECBA™ exam.*

### 6.1.9 Analyze Current State Student Exercises

1. Match the External Influencer on the left with its effect on the current state on the right.

**1. Industry Structure** \_\_\_     a. the nature and intensity of competitors between enterprises within an industry can be significant. The entry of a new competitor may also change the nature of the industry or increase competition.

**2. Competitors** \_\_\_     b. there is often influence from the current and potential impact of laws and regulations upon the industry.

**3. Customers** \_\_\_     c. the productivity enhancing potential of recent and expected technological innovations might influence the need.

**4. Macroeconomic Factors** \_\_\_     d. the variety and diversity of suppliers might be an influencer, as can the power that suppliers have over their customers.

**5. Political and Regulatory Environment** \_\_\_     e. individual industries have distinct ways in which value is created within that industry; this is a particularly important influencer if a proposed change involves entering a new industry.

**6. Suppliers** \_\_\_     f. the constraints and opportunities that exist within the existing and expected macroeconomic environment (for example, trade, unemployment, or inflation) might influence the need.

**7. Technology** \_\_\_     g. the size and nature of existing and potential customer segments can provide influences such as negotiating power and a degree of price sensitivity. Alternatively, the emergence of new alternative ways that customers can meet their needs may drive the enterprise to deliver greater value.

## Answers to Student Exercises

1. Match the External Influencer on the left with its effect on the current state on the right.

**1. Industry Structure** _E_     a. the nature and intensity of competitors between enterprises within an industry can be significant. The entry of a new competitor may also change the nature of the industry or increase competition.

**2. Competitors** _A_     b. there is often influence from the current and potential impact of laws and regulations upon the industry.

**3. Customers** _G_     c. the productivity enhancing potential of recent and expected technological innovations might influence the need.

**4. Macroeconomic Factors** _F_     d. the variety and diversity of suppliers might be an influencer, as can the power that suppliers have over their customers.

**5. Political and Regulatory Environment** _B_     e. individual industries have distinct ways in which value is created within that industry; this is a particularly important influencer if a proposed change involves entering a new industry.

**6. Suppliers** _D_     f. the constraints and opportunities that exist within the existing and expected macroeconomic environment (for example, trade, unemployment, or inflation) might influence the need.

**7. Technology** _C_     g. the size and nature of existing and potential customer segments can provide influences such as negotiating power and a degree of price sensitivity. Alternatively, the emergence of new alternative ways that customers can meet their needs may drive the enterprise to deliver greater value.

## 6.2 Define Future State

### 6.2.1 Purpose

To determine the set of necessary conditions to meet the business need.

### 6.2.2 Description

The future state description can include any context about the proposed future state. It describes the new, removed, and modified components of the enterprise. It can include changes to the boundaries of the organization itself, such as entering a new market or performing a merger or acquisition. Descriptions may include visual models and text to clearly show the scope boundaries and details. Relevant relationships between entities are identified and described. Business analysts work to ensure that the future state of the enterprise is well defined, that it is achievable with the resources available, and that key stakeholders have a shared consensus vision of the outcome.

Chapter 6 Strategy Analysis

**Figure 6.2.1: Define Future State Input/Task/Output Diagram**

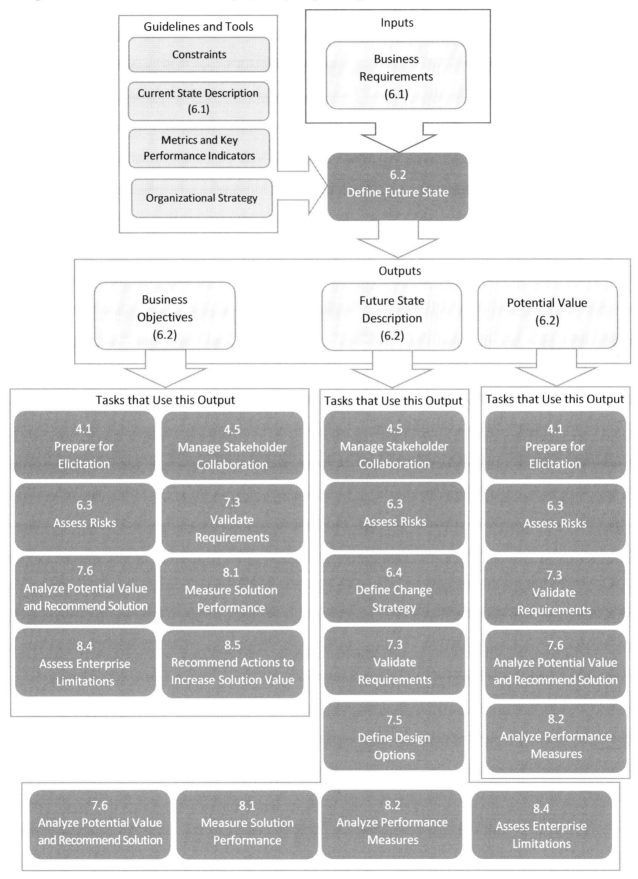

### 6.2.3 Inputs

- **Business Requirements (6.1)**: the problems, opportunities, or constraints that the future state will address.

### 6.2.4 Elements

#### 6.2.4.1 Business Goals and Objectives

A future state can be described in terms of business objectives or goals in order to guide the development of the change strategy and identify potential value. Business goals and objectives describe the ends that the organization is seeking to achieve. A common test for assessing objectives is to ensure that they are **SMART**.

#### 6.2.4.2 Scope of Solution Space

Decisions must be made about the range of solutions that will be considered to meet the business goals and objectives. The scope of the solution space defines which kinds of options will be considered when investigating possible solutions, including changes to the organizational structure or culture, capabilities and processes, technology and infrastructure, policies, products, or services, or even creating or changing relationships with organizations currently outside the scope of the extended enterprise.

#### 6.2.4.3 Constraints

Constraints describe aspects of the current state, aspects of the planned future state that may not be changed by the solution, or mandatory elements of the design.

#### 6.2.4.4 Organizational Structure and Culture

The formal and informal working relationships that exist within the enterprise may need to change to facilitate the desired future state.

#### 6.2.4.5 Capabilities and Processes

Identify new kinds of activities or changes in the way activities will be performed to realize the future state. New or changed capabilities and processes will be needed to deliver new products or services, to comply with new regulations, or to improve the performance of the enterprise.

#### 6.2.4.6 Technology and Infrastructure

If current technology and infrastructure are insufficient to meet the business need, the business analyst identifies the changes necessary for the desired future state. The existing technology may impose technical constraints on the design of the solution.

#### 6.2.4.7 Policies

If current polices are insufficient to meet the business need, the business analyst identifies the changes necessary for the desired future state. Policies are a common source of constraints on a solution.

#### 6.2.4.8 Business Architecture

The elements of any future state must effectively support one another and all contribute to meeting the business goals and objectives. In addition, they should be integrated into the overall desired future state of the enterprise as a whole, and support that future state.

## Chapter 6 Strategy Analysis

### 6.2.4.9 Internal Assets

The analysis of resources might indicate that existing resources need to be increased or require increased capabilities, or that new resources need to be developed. When analyzing resources, business analysts examine the resources needed to maintain the current state and implement the change strategy, and determine what resources can be used as part of a desired future state.

### 6.2.4.10 Identity Assumptions

Most strategies are predicated on a set of assumptions that will determine whether or not the strategy can succeed, particularly when operating in a highly uncertain environment.

### 6.2.4.11 Potential Value

Meeting the business objectives alone does not justify the transition to a future state; the potential value must be evaluated to see if it is sufficient to justify a change.

## 6.2.5 Guidelines and Tools

| Guideline or Tool | How Utilized in this Task |
| --- | --- |
| **Current State Description (6.1)** | provides the context within which the work needs to be completed. It is often used as a starting point for the future state. |
| **Metrics and KPIs** | the key performance indicators and metrics which will be used to determine whether the desired future state has been achieved. |
| **Organizational Strategy** | describes the path, method, or approach an enterprise or organization will take to achieve its desired future state. This can be implicitly or explicitly stated. |

## 6.2.6 Techniques

| Technique | How Utilized in this Task |
| --- | --- |
| **10.1 Acceptance and Evaluation Criteria** | used to identify what may make the future state acceptable and/or how options may be evaluated. |
| **10.3 Balanced Scorecard** | used to set targets for measuring the future state. |
| **10.4 Benchmarking and Market Analysis** | used to make decisions about future state business objectives. |
| **10.5 Brainstorming** | used to collaboratively come up with ideas for the future state. |
| **10.6 Business Capability Analysis** | used to prioritize capability gaps in relation to value and risk. |
| **10.7 Business Cases** | used to capture the desired outcomes of the change initiative. |
| **10.8 Business Model Canvas** | used to plan strategy for the enterprise by mapping out the needed infrastructure, target customer base, financial cost structure, and revenue streams required to fulfill the value proposition to customers in the desired future state. |

| Technique | How Utilized in this Task |
|---|---|
| **10.16 Decision Analysis** | used to compare the different future state options and understand which is the best choice. |
| **10.17 Decision Modeling** | used to model complex decisions regarding future state options. |
| **10.20 Financial Analysis** | used to estimate the potential financial returns to be delivered by a proposed future state. |
| **10.22 Functional Decomposition** | used to break down complex systems within the future state for better understanding. |
| **10.25 Interviews** | used to talk to stakeholders to understand their desired future state, which needs they want to address, and what desired business objectives they want to meet. |
| **10.27 Lessons Learned** | used to determine which opportunities for improvement will be addressed and how the current state can be improved upon. |
| **10.28 Metrics and KPIs** | used to determine when the organization has succeeded in achieving the business objectives. |
| **10.29 Mind Mapping** | used to develop ideas for the future state and understand relationships between them. |
| **10.32 Organizational Modeling** | used to describe the roles, responsibilities, and reporting structures that would exist within the future state organization. |
| **10.35 Process Modeling** | used to describe how work would occur in the future state. |
| **10.36 Prototyping** | used to model future state options and could also help determine potential value. |
| **10.41 Scope Modeling** | used to define the boundaries of the enterprise in the future state. |
| **10.45 Survey and Questionnaire** | used to understand stakeholders' desired future state, which needs they want to address, and what desired business objectives they want to meet. |
| **10.46 SWOT Analysis** | used to evaluate the strengths, weaknesses, opportunities, and threats that may be exploited or mitigated by the future state. |
| **10.49 Vendor Assessment** | used to assess potential value provided by vendor solution options. |
| **10.50 Workshops** | used to work with stakeholders to collaboratively describe the future state. |

### 6.2.7 Stakeholders

| Stakeholder | How Involved in this Task |
|---|---|
| **Customer** | might be targeted purchasers or consumers in a future state who might or might not be ready or able to consume a new state. |
| **Domain Subject Matter Expert** | provides insight into current state and potential future states. |

Chapter 6 Strategy Analysis

| Stakeholder | How Involved in this Task |
|---|---|
| End User | expected to use, or be a component of, a solution that implements the future state. |
| Implementation Subject Matter Expert | provides information regarding the feasibility of achieving the future state. |
| Operational Support | directly involved in supporting the operations of the enterprise and provides information on their ability to support the operation of a proposed future state. |
| Project Manager | might have input on what is a reasonable and manageable desired future state. |
| Regulator | ensures that laws, regulations, or rules are adhered to in the desired future state. Interpretations of relevant regulations must be included in the future state description in the form of business policies, business rules, procedures, or role responsibilities. |
| Sponsor | helps determine which business needs to address and sets the business objectives that a future state will achieve. Authorizes and ensures funding to support moving towards the future state. |
| Supplier | might help define the future state if they are supporting delivery of the change or deliver any part of the future state operation. |
| Tester | responsible for ensuring an envisioned future state can be sufficiently tested and can help set an appropriate level of quality to target. |

## 6.2.8 Outputs

- **Business Objectives (6.2)**: the desired direction that the business wishes to pursue in order to achieve the future state.
- **Future State Description (6.2)**: the future state description includes boundaries of the proposed new, removed, and modified components of the enterprise and the potential value expected from the future state. The description might include the desired future capabilities, policies, resources, dependencies, infrastructure, external influences, and relationships between each element.
- **Potential Value (6.2)**: the value that may be realized by implementing the proposed future state.

## 6.2.9 Define Future State Student Exercises

1. Match the SMART objective test word on the left with its definition on the right.

    Specific \_\_\_        a. testing the feasibility of the effort

    Measurable \_\_\_    b. aligning with the enterprise's vision, mission, and goals

    Achievable \_\_\_    c. describing something that has an observable outcome

    Relevant \_\_\_       d. defining a time frame that is consistent with the need

    Time-bounded \_\_\_  e. tracking and measuring the outcome

# Answers to Student Exercises

1. Match the SMART objective test word on the left with its definition on the right.

   Specific _c_     a. testing the feasibility of the effort
   Measurable _e_   b. aligning with the enterprise's vision, mission, and goals
   Achievable _a_   c. describing something that has an observable outcome
   Relevant _b_     d. defining a time frame that is consistent with the need
   Time-bounded _d_ e. tracking and measuring the outcome

## 6.3 Assess Risks

**Figure 6.3.1: Assess Risks Input/Task/Output Diagram**

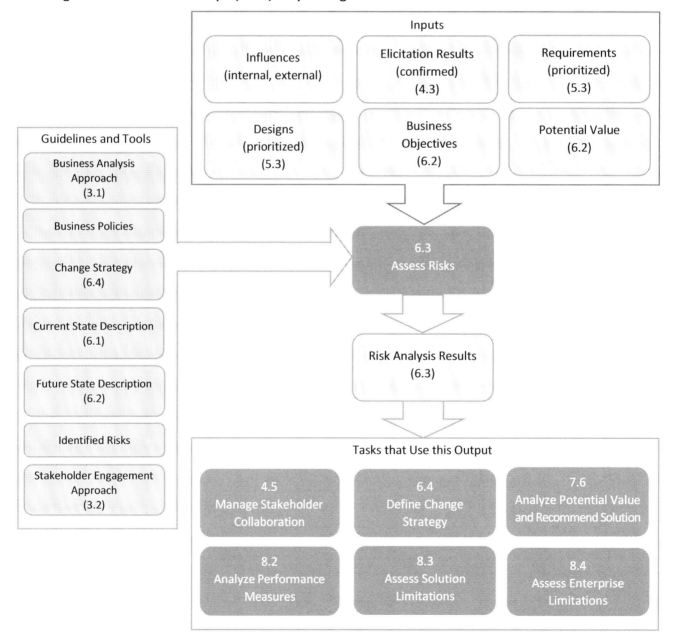

Chapter 6 Strategy Analysis

## 6.3.1 Purpose

To understand the undesirable consequences of internal and external forces on the enterprise during a transition to, or once in, the future state. An understanding of the potential impact of those forces can be used to make a recommendation about a course of action.

## 6.3.2 Description

Risks might be related to the current state, a desired future state, a change itself, a change strategy, or any tasks being performed by the enterprise. The risks are analyzed for the possible consequences if the risk occurs, impact of those consequences, likelihood of the risk, and potential time frame when the risk might occur.

## 6.3.3 Inputs

- **Business Objectives (6.2)**: describing the desired direction needed to achieve the future state can be used to identify and discuss potential risks.
- **Elicitation Results (confirmed) (4.3)**: an understanding of what the various stakeholders perceive as risks to the realization of the desired future state.
- **Influences**: factors inside of the enterprise (internal) and factors outside of the enterprise (external) which will impact the realization of the desired future state.
- **Potential Value (6.2)**: describing the value to be realized by implementing the proposed future state provides a benchmark against which risks can be assessed.
- **Requirements (prioritized) (5.3)**: depending on their priority, requirements will influence the risks to be defined and understood as part of solution realization.

## 6.3.4 Elements

### 6.3.4.1 Unknowns

When assessing a risk, there will be uncertainty in the likelihood of it occurring, and the impact if it does occur. Business analysts collaborate with stakeholders to assess risks based on current understanding. Even when it is not possible to know all that will occur as a result of a particular change strategy, it is still possible to estimate the impact of unknown or uncertain events or conditions occurring.

### 6.3.4.2 Constraints, Assumptions and Dependencies

Constraints, assumptions, and dependencies can be analyzed for risks and sometimes should be managed as risks themselves. If the constraint, assumption, or dependency is related to an aspect of a change, it can be restated as a risk by identifying the event or condition and consequences that could occur because of the constraint, assumption, or dependency.

### 6.3.4.3 Negative Impact to Value

Risks are expressed as conditions that increase the likelihood or severity of a negative impact to value. Business analysts clearly identify and express each risk and estimate its likelihood and impact to determine the level of risk.

#### 6.3.4.4 Risk Tolerance

How much uncertainty a stakeholder or an enterprise is willing to take on in exchange for potential value is referred to as risk tolerance. In general, there are three broad ways of describing attitude toward risk: 1) **Risk-aversion** (unwillingness), 2) **Neutrality** (some level of risk is acceptable), and 3) **Risk-seeking** (willingness to accept or even take on more risk in return for a higher potential value).

#### 6.3.4.5 Recommendation

Based on the analysis of risks, business analysts recommend a course of action. Business analysts work with stakeholders to understand the overall risk level and their tolerance for risk.

### 6.3.5 Guidelines and Tools

| Guideline or Tool | How Utilized in this Task |
|---|---|
| **Business Analysis Approach (3.1)** | guides how the business analyst analyzes risks. |
| **Business Policies** | define the limits within which decisions must be made. These may mandate or govern aspects of risk management. |
| **Change Strategy (6.4)** | provides the plan to transition from the current state to the future state and achieve the desired business outcomes. This approach must be assessed to understand risks associated with the change. |
| **Current State Description (6.1)** | provides the context within which the work needs to be completed. It can be used to determine risks associated with the current state. |
| **Future State Description (6.2)** | determines risks associated with the future state. |
| **Identified Risks** | can be used as a starting point for more thorough risk assessment. These can come from Risk Analysis Results, from elicitation activities, from previous business analysis experience, or based on expert opinion. |
| **Stakeholder Engagement Approach (3.2)** | understanding stakeholders and stakeholder groups helps identify and assess the potential impact of internal and external forces. |

### 6.3.6 Techniques

| Technique | How Utilized in this Task |
|---|---|
| **10.5 Brainstorming** | used to collaboratively identify potential risks for assessment. |
| **10.7 Business Cases** | used to capture risks associated with alternative change strategies. |
| **10.16 Decision Analysis** | used to assess problems. |
| **10.18 Document Analysis** | used to analyze existing documents for potential risks, constraints, assumptions, and dependencies. |

Chapter 6 Strategy Analysis

| Technique | How Utilized in this Task |
|---|---|
| 10.20 Financial Analysis | used to understand the potential effect of risks on the financial value of the solution. |
| 10.25 Interviews | used to understand what stakeholders think might be risks and the various factors of those risks. |
| 10.27 Lessons Learned | used as a foundation of past issues that might be risks. |
| 10.29 Mind Mapping | used to identify and categorize potential risks and understand their relationships. |
| 10.38 Risk Analysis and Management | used to identify and manage risks. |
| 10.40 Root Cause Analysis | used to identify and address the underlying problem creating a risk. |
| 10.45 Survey and Questionnaire | used to understand what stakeholders think might be risks and the various factors of those risks. |
| 10.50 Workshops | used to understand what stakeholders think might be risks and the various factors of those risks. |

## 6.3.7 Stakeholders

| Stakeholder | How Involved in this Task |
|---|---|
| Domain Subject Matter Expert | provides input to the risk assessment based on their knowledge of preparation required in their area of expertise. |
| Implementation Subject Matter Expert | provides input to the risk assessment based on their knowledge of preparation required in their area of expertise. |
| Operational Support | supports the operations of the enterprise and can identify likely risks and their impact. |
| Project Manager | helps to assess risk and is primarily responsible for managing and mitigating risk to the project. |
| Regulator | identifies any risks associated with adherence to laws, regulations, or rules. |
| Sponsor | needs to understand risks as part of authorizing and funding change. |
| Supplier | there might be risk associated with using a supplier. |
| Tester | identifies risks in the change strategy, from a validation or verification perspective. |

## 6.3.8 Outputs

- **Risk Analysis Results (6.3):** an understanding of the risks associated with achieving the future state, and the mitigation strategies which will be used to prevent those risks, reduce the impact of the risk, or reduce the likelihood of the risk occurring.

## 6.4 Define Change Strategy

### Figure 6.4.1: Define Change Strategy Input/Task/Output Diagram

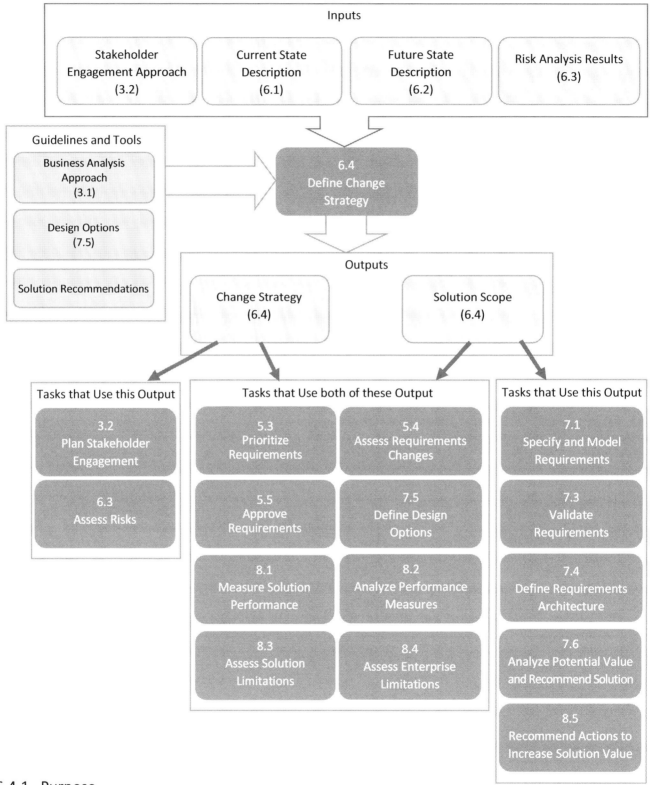

### 6.4.1 Purpose

To develop and assess alternative approaches to the change, and then select the recommended approach.

## 6.4.2 Description

Developing a change strategy is simpler when the current state and the future state are already defined because they provide some context for the change. The change strategy clearly describes the nature of the change in terms of:

- context of the change,
- identified alternative change strategies,
- justification for why a particular change strategy is the best approach,
- investment and resources required to work toward the future state,
- how the enterprise will realize value after the solution is delivered,
- key stakeholders in the change, and
- transition states along the way.

The appropriate representation of a change strategy depends on the perspective of the change team and their stakeholders. The change strategy might be presented as part of a business case, Statement of Work (SOW), an enterprise's strategic plan, or in other formats.

## 6.4.3 Inputs

- **Current State Description (6.1)**: provides context about the current state, and includes assessments of internal and external influences to the enterprise under consideration.
- **Future State Description (6.2)**: provides context about the desired future state.
- **Risk Analysis Results (6.3)**: describe identified risks and exposure of each risk.
- **Stakeholder Engagement Approach (3.2)**: understanding stakeholders' communication and collaboration needs can help identify change-related activities that need to be included as part of the change strategy.

## 6.4.4 Elements

### 6.4.4.1 Solution Scope

The solution is the outcome of a change that allows an enterprise to satisfy a need. The solution scope defines the boundaries of the solution, and is described in enough detail to enable stakeholders to understand which new capabilities the change will deliver. It also describes how the proposed solution enables the future state's goals. The solution scope can also include descriptions of out-of-scope solution components to provide clarity. The solution scope might evolve throughout an initiative as more information is discovered.

### 6.4.4.2 Gap Analysis

A gap analysis identifies the difference between current state and future state capabilities. To perform gap analysis, both current state and future state should be defined. Using the same techniques to describe both current and future states assists in gap analysis, as it simplifies the comparison.

### 6.4.4.3 Enterprise Readiness Assessment

Business analysts analyze the enterprise to assess its capacity to make the change and to sustain the change in the future state.

#### 6.4.4.4 Change Strategy

A change strategy is a high-level plan of key activities and events that will be used to transform the enterprise from the current state to the future state. During the course of the development of a change strategy, several options are identified, explored, and described in enough detail to determine which options are feasible.

#### 6.4.4.5 Transition States and Release Planning

In many cases, the future state will need to be achieved over time rather than through a single change, meaning that the enterprise will have to operate in one or more transition states. Release planning is concerned with determining which requirements to include in each release, phase, or iteration of the change. Business analysts help facilitate release planning discussions to help stakeholders reach decisions. There are many factors that guide these decisions, such as the overall budget, deadlines or time constraints, resource constraints, training schedules, and the ability of the business to absorb changes within a defined time frame. Business analysts assist in planning the timing of the implementation in order to cause minimal disruption to business activities, and to ensure all parties understand the impact to the organization.

### 6.4.5 Guidelines and Tools

| Guideline or Tool | How Utilized in this Task |
|---|---|
| **Business Analysis Approach (3.1)** | guides how the business analyst defines a change strategy. |
| **Design Options (7.5)** | describe various ways to satisfy the business needs. Each option will come with its own set of change challenges and the change strategy will be impacted by the option selected as well as the specific change approach that will be used. |
| **Solution Recommendations** | identifying the possible solutions which can be pursued in order to achieve the future state, which includes the recommendations of various subject matter experts (SMEs), helps the business analyst determine the types of changes to the organization. |

### 6.4.6 Techniques

| Technique | How Utilized in this Task |
|---|---|
| **10.3 Balanced Scorecard** | used to define the metrics that will be used to evaluate the effectiveness of the change strategy. |
| **10.4 Benchmarking and Market Analysis** | used to make decisions about which change strategy is appropriate. |
| **10.5 Brainstorming** | used to collaboratively come up with ideas for change strategies. |
| **10.6 Business Capability Analysis** | used to prioritize capability gaps in relation to value and risk. |

Chapter 6 Strategy Analysis

| Technique | How Utilized in this Task |
|---|---|
| 10.7 Business Cases | used to capture information about the recommended change strategy and other potential strategies that were assessed but not recommended. |
| 10.8 Business Model Canvas | used to define the changes needed in the current infrastructure, customer base, and financial structure of the organization in order to achieve the potential value. |
| 10.16 Decision Analysis | used to compare different change strategies and choose which is most appropriate. |
| 10.19 Estimation | used to determine timelines for activities within the change strategy. |
| 10.20 Financial Analysis | used to understand the potential value associated with a change strategy, and evaluate strategies against targets set for return on investments. |
| 10.21 Focus Groups | used to bring customers or end users together to solicit their input on the solution and change strategy. |
| 10.22 Functional Decomposition | used to break down the components of the solution into parts when developing a change strategy. |
| 10.25 Interviews | used to talk to stakeholders in order to fully describe the solution scope and change scope, and to understand their suggestions for a change strategy. |
| 10.27 Lessons Learned | used to understand what went wrong in past changes in order to improve this change strategy. |
| 10.29 Mind Mapping | used to develop and explore ideas for change strategies. |
| 10.32 Organizational Modeling | used to describe the roles, responsibilities, and reporting structures that are necessary during the change and are part of the solution scope. |
| 10.35 Process Modeling | used to describe how work would occur in the solution scope or during the change. |
| 10.41 Scope Modeling | used to define the boundaries on the solution scope and change scope descriptions. |
| 10.46 SWOT Analysis | used to make decisions about which change strategy is appropriate. |
| 10.49 Vendor Assessment | used to determine whether any vendors are part of the change strategy, either to implement the change or to be part of the solution. |
| 10.50 Workshops | used in work with stakeholders to collaboratively develop change strategies. |

### 6.4.7 Stakeholders

| Stakeholder | How Involved in this Task |
|---|---|
| Customer | might be purchasing or consuming the solution that results from the change. Customers can also be involved in a change as testers or focus group members, whose input is considered in the enterprise readiness assessment. |
| Domain Subject Matter Expert | have expertise in some aspect of the change. |
| End User | uses a solution, is a component of the solution, or is a user temporarily during the change. End users could be customers or people who work within the enterprise experiencing a change. Users might be involved in a change as testers or focus group members, whose input is considered in the enterprise readiness assessment. |
| Implementation Subject Matter Expert | have expertise in some aspect of the change. |
| Operational Support | directly involved in supporting the operations of the enterprise, and provide information on their ability to support the operation of a solution during and after a change. |
| Project Manager | responsible for managing change and planning the detailed activities to complete a change. In a project, the project manager is responsible for the project scope, which covers all the work to be performed by the project team. |
| Regulator | ensures adherence to laws, regulations, or rules during and at the completion of the change. The regulator might have unique input to the enterprise readiness assessment, as there might be laws and regulations that must be complied with prior to or as a result of a planned or completed change. |
| Sponsor | authorizes and ensures funding for solution delivery, and champions the change. |
| Supplier | might help implement the change or be part of the solution once the change is completed. |
| Tester | responsible for ensuring that the change will function within acceptable parameters, accomplish the desired result, and deliver solutions that meet an appropriate level of quality. The tester is often involved in validation of components of a solution for which the results will be included in an enterprise readiness assessment. |

### 6.4.8 Outputs

- **Change Strategy (6.4)**: the approach that the organization will follow to guide change.
- **Solution Scope (6.4)**: the solution scope that will be achieved through execution of the change strategy.

## 6.5 Strategy Analysis Pop-up Quiz

1. What are the tasks in the Strategy Analysis knowledge area?

    a. Define Current State, Define Future State, Assess Potential Value, and Build Business Case.

    b. Define Current State, Define Future State, Assess Risks, and Build Business Cases.

    c. Analyze Current State, Define Future State, Assess Risks, and Define Change Strategy.

    d. Analyze Current State, Define Future State, Assess Potential Value, and Define Change Strategy.

2. Which of the following describe the common test for assessing objectives?

    a. Strategic, Measurable, Achievable, Relevant, and Testable.

    b. Specific Measurable, Achievable, Realistic, and Time-bounded.

    c. Strategic, Maximum, Achievable, Realistic, and Testable.

    d. Specific, Measurable, Achievable, Relevant, and Time-bounded.

3. When should Strategic Analysis be performed?

    a. All the time.

    b. Any time it makes sense to.

    c. When a business need is identified.

    d. Prior to planning the business analysis approach.

## Answers to Pop-up Quiz

| Question | Answer | Description |
|----------|--------|-------------|
| 1 | C | BABOK sections 6.1, 6.2, 6.3 and 6.4 |
| 2 | D | BABOK section 6.2.4. |
| 3 | C | BABOK section 6.0. Strategy analysis should be performed as a business need is identified. |

# Requirements Analysis and Design Definition

## Overview

Requirements Analysis and Design Definition (RADD) is about structuring and organizing requirements and designs discovered through elicitation. It includes activities to specify, model, verify, and validate requirements so that the business analyst, through collaboration with stakeholders, can estimate potential value, derive viable solution options and recommend the best solution to meet the need. These activities are done incrementally and iteratively from exploring the business need through determining solutions.

The business analyst's role in modeling needs, requirements, designs, and solutions is instrumental in conducting thorough analysis and communicating with other stakeholders. The form, level of detail, and what is being modeled are all dependent on the context, audience, and purpose.

*The end goal of RADD is to consider many options for creating a solution to a business need, and determining and recommending the BEST solution.*

**Goal:** Analyze requirements and designs from elicitation activities, explore solution options, and recommend the solution that will most effectively meet the business need and delivers the greatest value.

Requirements Analysis and Design Definition is the largest knowledge area on the ECBA™, and all of the IIBA® core certification exams. It is given such great importance because many business analysts spend a great deal of their time performing the tasks defined in this knowledge area. You will notice expanded coverage of this knowledge area in this study guide at an appropriate level for the ECBA designation. What you should gleam from that statement is *this is one chapter to know its content thoroughly well.*

The following image illustrates the spectrum of value as business analysis activities progress from delivering potential value to actual value.

**Figure 7.0.1: Business Analysis Value Spectrum**

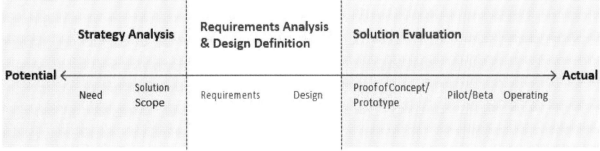

## What You Will Learn

When you are finished with this chapter, you will know:
- How to define Requirements Analysis and Design Definition.
- The six tasks in Requirements Analysis and Design Definition.
- A deeper understanding of the business analyst role in context of Requirements Analysis and Design Definition.

Important learnings in Requirements Analysis and Design Definition Knowledge Area:
1. Throughout the chapter, including task names, the BABOK often refers to requirements, but the meaning is both requirements and designs.
2. Portions of the BABOK refer only to "modeling" without mentioning the word "specifying" when the intention is to include both.

**Figure 7.0.2: Requirements Analysis and Design Definition Input/Task/Output Diagram**

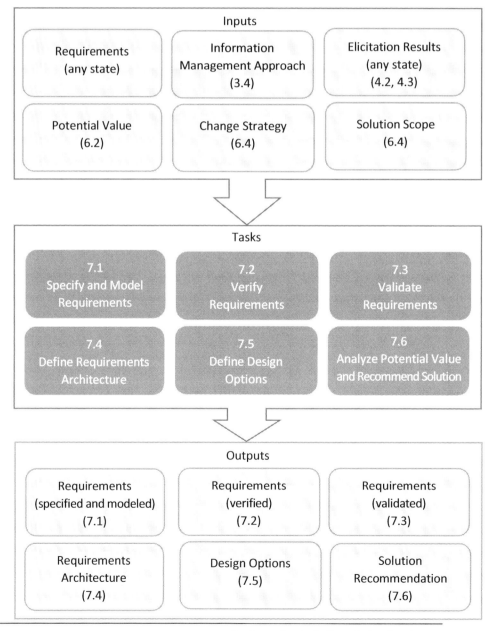

# Chapter 7 Requirements Analysis and Design Definition

## The BACCM™ in Requirements Analysis and Design Definition

The following model describes the usage and application of each of the core concepts within the context of Requirements Analysis and Design Definition.

**Figure 7.0.3: Core Concepts application In Requirements Analysis and Design Definition**

**Change**: transform elicitation results into requirements and designs in order to define the change

**Need**: analyze the needs in order to recommend a solution that meets the needs

**Solution**: define solution options and recommend the one that is most likely to address the need and has the most value

**Stakeholder**: tailor the requirements and designs so that they are usable by each stakeholder group

**Context**: model and describe the context in formats that are usable by all stakeholders

**Value**: analyze and quantify the potential value of the solution options

## Tasks in Requirements Analysis and Design Definition

There are six tasks in the Requirements Analysis and Design Definition Knowledge Area:

1. <u>S</u>pecify and Model Requirements
2. <u>V</u>erify Requirements
3. <u>V</u>alidate Requirements
4. Define Requirements <u>A</u>rchitecture
5. Define Solution <u>O</u>ptions
6. Analyze <u>P</u>otential Value and Recommend <u>S</u>olution

| Mnemonic |
|---|
| SVVA OPS |
| <u>S</u>pecify, <u>V</u>erify, <u>V</u>alidate <u>A</u>lways for great <u>O</u>perations (<u>OPS</u>) |

# Detailed ITTSO Table

The following table summarizes the Inputs, Tasks, Techniques, Stakeholders and Outputs (ITTSO) in the Requirements Analysis and Design Definition Knowledge Area.

Table 7.0.1: Inputs, Tasks, Techniques, Stakeholders and Outputs Summary

| ITTSO Summary for Requirements Analysis and Design Definition | | | | | |
|---|---|---|---|---|---|
| **Inputs** | **Tasks** | **M*** | **Techniques** | **Stakeholders** | **Outputs** |
| • Elicitation Results (any state) (4.2, 4.3) | 7.1 Specify and Model Requirements | S | 10.1 Acceptance and Evaluation Criteria<br>10.6 Business Capability Analysis<br>10.8 Business Model Canvas<br>10.9 Business Rules Analysis<br>10.11 Concept Modeling<br>10.12 Data Dictionary<br>10.13 Data Flow Diagram<br>10.15 Data Modeling<br>10.17 Decision Modeling<br>10.22 Functional Decomposition<br>10.23 Glossary<br>10.24 Interface Analysis<br>10.30 Non-Functional Requirements Analysis<br>10.32 Organizational Modeling<br>10.35 Process Modeling<br>10.36 Prototyping<br>10.39 Roles and Permissions Matrix<br>10.40 Root Cause Analysis<br>10.41 Scope Modeling<br>10.42 Sequence Diagrams<br>10.43 Stakeholder List, Map or Personas<br>10.44 State Modeling<br>10.47 Use Cases and Scenarios<br>10.48 User Stories | • Any stakeholder | • Requirements (specified and modele0d) (7.1) |

# Chapter 7 Requirements Analysis and Design Definition

| | | | | | |
|---|---|---|---|---|---|
| • Requirements (specified and modeled) (7.1) | 7.2 Verify Requirements | V | 10.1 Acceptance and Evaluation Criteria<br>10.26 Item Tracking<br>10.28 Metrics and KPIs<br>10.37 Reviews | • All stakeholders | • Requirements (verified) (7.2) |
| • Requirements (specified and modeled) (7.1) | 7.3 Validate Requirements | V | 10.1 Acceptance and Evaluation Criteria<br>10.18 Document Analysis<br>10.20 Financial Analysis<br>10.26 Item Tracking<br>10.28 Metrics and KPIs<br>10.37 Reviews<br>10.38 Risk Analysis and Management | • All stakeholders | • Requirements (validated) (7.3) |
| • Requirements (any state)<br>• Information Management Approach (3.4)<br>• Solution Scope (6.4) | 7.4 Define Requirements Architecture | A | 10.15 Data Modeling<br>10.22 Functional Decomposition<br>10.25 Interviews<br>10.32 Organizational Modeling<br>10.41 Scope Modeling<br>10.50 Workshops | • Domain SME<br>• Implementation SME<br>• Project Manager<br>• Sponsor<br>• Tester<br>• Any stakeholder | • Requirements Architecture (7.4) |
| • Requirements (validated, prioritized) (5.3, 7.3)<br>• Change Strategy (6.4)<br>• Requirements Architecture (7.4) | 7.5 Define Solution Options | O | 10.4 Benchmarking and Market Analysis<br>10.5 Brainstorming<br>10.18 Document Analysis<br>10.25 Interviews<br>10.27 Lessons Learned<br>10.29 Mind Mapping<br>10.40 Root Cause Analysis<br>10.45 Survey and Questionnaire<br>10.49 Vendor Assessment<br>10.50 Workshops | • Domain SME<br>• Implementation SME<br>• Operational Support<br>• Project Manager<br>• Supplier | • Design Options (7.5) |

| | | | | | |
|---|---|---|---|---|---|
| • Potential Value (6.2)<br>• Design Options (7.5) | 7.6 Analyze Potential Value and Recommend Solution | PS | 10.1 Acceptance and Evaluation Criteria<br>10.2 Backlog Management<br>10.5 Brainstorming<br>10.7 Business Cases<br>10.8 Business Model Canvas<br>10.16 Decision Analysis<br>10.19 Estimation<br>10.20 Financial Analysis<br>10.21 Focus Groups<br>10.25 Interviews<br>10.28 Metrics and KPIs<br>10.38 Risk Analysis and Management<br>10.45 Survey or Questionnaire<br>10.46 SWOT Analysis<br>10.50 Workshops | • Customer<br>• Domain SME<br>• End User<br>• Implementation SME<br>• Project Manager<br>• Regulator<br>• Sponsor | • Solution Recommendation (7.6) |

\* Mnemonic = SVVA OPS

# Chapter 7 Requirements Analysis and Design Definition

# Requirements Analysis and Design Definition Student Exercises

**Exercise 1:** Fill in the blanks to complete the Requirements Analysis and Design Definition task name, then enter the Mnemonic letter used in this chapter to help remember the tasks in this knowledge area.

| RADD Tasks | Mnemonic Letter |
|---|---|
| _____ Requirements | |
| _____ Requirements | |
| _____ Requirements | |
| Define _____ | |
| Define _____ _ | |
| Analyze _____ _ | |

**Bonus:** Enter below the phrase used in this chapter to help remember the tasks in RADD knowledge area.

_____

**Exercise 2:** For each stakeholder indicate which task they are involved in by putting an 'X' in the appropriate column under the stakeholder. Some stakeholders may not be involved in any tasks while some stakeholders may be involved in multiple tasks.

| Stakeholder / Task | All Stakeholders | Any Stakeholders | Customers | Domain SME | End User | Implementation SME | Operational Support | Project Manager | Regulator | Sponsor | Supplier | Tester |
|---|---|---|---|---|---|---|---|---|---|---|---|---|
| 7.1 Specify and Model Requirements | | | | | | | | | | | | |
| 7.2 Verify Requirements | | | | | | | | | | | | |
| 7.3 Validate Requirements | | | | | | | | | | | | |
| 7.4 Define Business Architecture | | | | | | | | | | | | |
| 7.5 Define Solution Options | | | | | | | | | | | | |
| 7.6 Analyze Potential Value and Recommend Solution | | | | | | | | | | | | |

## Answers to Student Exercises

**Exercise 1:** Fill in the blanks to complete the Requirements Analysis and Design Definition task name, then enter the Mnemonic letter used in this chapter to help remember the tasks in this knowledge area.

| RADD Tasks | Mnemonic Letter |
|---|---|
| _Specify and Model_ Requirements | S |
| _Verify_ Requirements | V |
| _Validate_ Requirements | V |
| Define _Business Architecture_ | A |
| Define _Solution Options_ | O |
| Analyze _Potential Value and Recommend Solution_ | PS |

**Bonus:** Enter below the phrase used in this chapter to help remember the tasks in RADD knowledge area.

___Specify, Verify and Validate Always for great Operations___

**Exercise 2:** For each stakeholder indicate which task they are involved in by putting an 'X' in the appropriate column under the stakeholder. Some stakeholders may not be involved in any tasks while some stakeholders may be involved in multiple tasks.

| Task \ Stakeholder | All Stakeholders | Any Stakeholders | Customers | Domain SME | End User | Implementation SME | Operational Support | Project Manager | Regulator | Sponsor | Supplier | Tester |
|---|---|---|---|---|---|---|---|---|---|---|---|---|
| 7.1 Specify and Model Requirements | | X | | | | | | | | | | |
| 7.2 Verify Requirements | X | | | | | | | | | | | |
| 7.3 Validate Requirements | X | | | | | | | | | | | |
| 7.4 Define Business Architecture | | X | | X | | X | | X | | X | | X |
| 7.5 Define Solution Options | | | | X | | X | X | X | | | X | |
| 7.6 Analyze Potential Value and Recommend Solution | | | X | X | X | X | | X | X | X | | |

## 7.1 Specify and Model Requirements

**Figure 7.1.1: Specify and Model Requirements Input/Task/Output Diagram**

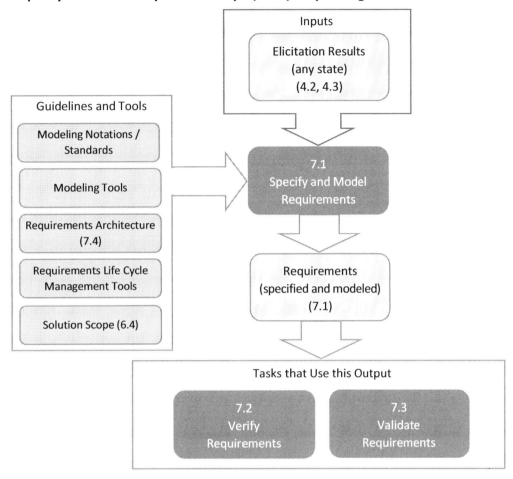

### 7.1.1 Purpose

To analyze, synthesize, and refine elicitation results into requirements and designs.

### 7.1.2 Description

Specify and Model Requirements describes what is involved in analyzing and synthesizing elicitation results and translating those into stakeholder, solution, and transition requirements and designs. The output can be textual documentation and/or diagrams and models of the requirements and designs. When these outputs (specifications and designs) refer to the need, the output in considered "requirements"; when they refer to the solution, they are considered "designs". In addition to the models used to represent the requirements, this task also includes capturing information about attributes or metadata about the requirements.

### 7.1.3 Inputs

- **Elicitation Results (any state) (4.2, 4.3)**: modeling can begin with any elicitation result and may lead to the need for more elicitation to clarify or expand upon requirements. Elicitation and modeling may occur sequentially, iteratively, or concurrently.

## 7.1.4 Elements

### 7.1.4.1 Model Requirements

Business analysts use models to convey information to a specific audience in order to support analysis, communication, and understanding. Models may also be used to confirm knowledge, identify information gaps that the business analyst may have, and identify duplicate information. These models may be in the form of a matrix or diagram:

- **Matrices**: a matrix is used when for modeling a requirement or set of requirements that have a complex but uniform structure, which can be broken down into elements that apply to every entry in the table. Matrices may be used for data dictionaries, requirements traceability, or for gap analysis. Matrices are also used for prioritizing requirements and recording other requirements attributes and metadata.
- **Diagrams**: a diagram is a visual, often pictorial, representation of a requirement or set of requirements. A diagram is especially useful to depict complexity in a way that would be difficult to do with words. Diagrams can also be used to define boundaries for business domains, to categorize and create hierarchies of items, and to show components of objects such as data and their relationships.

Business analysts can use a combination of models to convey the idea or concept they wish to communicate to the stakeholders within a given context. These models can be in any of the following categories:

- **People and Roles**: models represent organizations, groups of people, roles, and their relationships within an enterprise and to a solution. Techniques used to represent people and their roles include Organizational Modeling, Roles and Permissions Matrix and Stakeholder List, Map, or Personas.
- **Rationale**: models represent the 'why' of a change. Techniques used to represent the rationale include Decision Modeling, Scope Modeling, Business Model Canvas, Root Cause Analysis, and Business Rules Analysis.
- **Activity Flow**: models represent a sequence of actions, events, or a course that may be taken. Techniques used to represent activity flows include Process Modeling, Use Cases and Scenarios, and User Stories.
- **Capability**: models focus on features or functions of an enterprise or a solution. Techniques used to represent capabilities include Business Capability Analysis, Functional Decomposition, and Prototyping.
- **Data and Information**: models represent the characteristics and the exchange of information within an enterprise or a solution. Techniques used to represent data and information include Data Dictionary, Data Flow Diagrams, Data Modeling, Glossary, State Modeling, and Interface Analysis.

### 7.1.4.2 Analyze Requirements

Business analysis information is decomposed into components to further examine for anything that must change to meet the business need, anything that should stay the same to meet the business need, missing components, unnecessary components, and any constraints or assumptions that impact the components.

The level of decomposition required, and the level of detail to be specified, varies depending on the knowledge and understanding of the stakeholders, the potential for misunderstanding or miscommunication, organizational standards, and contractual or regulatory obligations, among other factors.

Analysis provides a basis for discussion to reach a conclusion about solution options.

#### 7.1.4.3 Represent Requirements and Attributes

Business analysts identify information for requirements and their attributes as part of the elicitation results. Requirements should be explicitly represented and should include enough detail such that they exhibit the characteristics of requirements and designs quality. Various attributes can be specified for each requirement or set of requirements. These attributes are selected when planning for information management (see 3.4 Plan Business Analysis Information Management task in Business Analysis Planning and Monitoring Knowledge Area).

As part of specifying requirements, they can also be categorized according to the schema described in task Requirements Classification Schema (p. 23). Categorizing requirements can help ensure the requirements are fully understood, a set of any type is complete, and that there is appropriate traceability between the types.

#### 7.1.4.4 Implement the Appropriate Level of Abstraction

The level of abstraction of a requirement varies based on the type of requirement and audience for the requirement. Not all stakeholders require or find value in the complete set of requirements and models. It may be appropriate to produce different viewpoints of requirements to represent the same need for different stakeholders. Business analysts take special care to maintain the meaning and intent of the requirements over all representations.

## 7.1.5 Guidelines and Tools

| Guideline or Tool | How Utilized in this Task |
| --- | --- |
| **Modeling Notations/Standards** | allow requirements and designs to be precisely specified, as is appropriate for the audience and the purpose of the models. Standard templates and syntax help to ensure that the right information is provided about the requirements. |
| **Modeling Tools** | software products that facilitate drawing and storing matrices and diagrams to represent requirements. This functionality may or may not be part of requirements life cycle management tools. |
| **Requirements Architecture (7.4)** | the requirements and interrelationships among them can be used to ensure models are complete and consistent. |
| **Requirements Life Cycle Management Tools** | software products that facilitate recording, organizing, storing, and sharing requirements and designs. |
| **Solution Scope (6.4)** | the boundaries of the solution provide the boundaries for the requirements and designs models. |

## 7.1.6 Techniques

| Technique | How Utilized in this Task |
|---|---|
| 10.1 Acceptance and Evaluation Criteria | used to represent the acceptance and evaluation criteria attributes of requirements. |
| 10.6 Business Capability Analysis | used to represent features or functions of an enterprise. |
| 10.8 Business Model Canvas | used to describe the rationale for requirements. |
| 10.9 Business Rules Analysis | used to analyze business rules so that they can be specified and modeled alongside requirements. |
| 10.11 Concept Modeling | used to define terms and relationships relevant to the change and the enterprise. |
| 10.12 Data Dictionary | used to record details about the data involved in the change. Details may include definitions, relationships with other data, origin, format, and usage. |
| 10.13 Data Flow Diagram | used to visualize data flow requirements. |
| 10.15 Data Modeling | used to model requirements to show how data will be used to meet stakeholder information needs. |
| 10.17 Decision Analysis | used to represent decisions in a model in order to show the elements of decision making required. |
| 10.22 Functional Decomposition | used to model requirements in order to identify constituent parts of an overall complex business function. |
| 10.23 Glossary | used to record the meaning of relevant business terms while analyzing requirements. |
| 10.24 Interface Analysis | used to model requirements in order to identify and validate inputs and outputs of the solution they are modeling. |
| 10.30 Non-Functional Requirements Analysis | used to define and analyze the quality of service attributes. |
| 10.32 Organizational Modeling | used to allow business analysts to model the roles, responsibilities, and communications within an organization. |
| 10.35 Process Modeling | used to show the steps or activities that are performed in the organization, or that must be performed to meet the desired change. |
| 10.36 Prototyping | used to assist the stakeholders in visualizing the appearance and capabilities of a planned solution. |
| 10.39 Roles and Permissions Matrix | used to specify and model requirements concerned with the separation of duties among users and external interfaces in utilizing a solution. |

Chapter 7 Requirements Analysis and Design Definition

| Technique | How Utilized in this Task |
|---|---|
| **10.40 Root Cause Analysis** | used to model the root causes of a problem as part of rationale. |
| **10.41 Scope Modeling** | used to visually show a scope boundary. |
| **10.42 Sequence Diagrams** | used to specify and model requirements to show how processes operate and interact with one another, and in what order. |
| **10.43 Stakeholder List, Map or Personas** | used to identify the stakeholders and their characteristics. |
| **10.44 State Modeling** | used to specify the different states of a part of the solution throughout a life cycle, in terms of the events that occur. |
| **10.47 Use Cases and Scenarios** | used to model the desired behavior of a solution, by showing user interactions with the solution, to achieve a specific goal or accomplish a particular task. |
| **10.48 User Stories** | used to specify requirements as a brief statement about what people do or need to do when using the solution. |

## 7.1.7 Stakeholders

| Stakeholder | How Involved in this Task |
|---|---|
| **Any Stakeholder** | business analysts may choose to perform this task themselves and then separately package and communicate the requirements to stakeholders for their review and approval, or they might choose to invite some or all stakeholders to participate in this task. |

## 7.1.8 Outputs

- **Requirements (specified and modeled) (7.1)**: any combination of requirements and/or designs in the form of text, matrices, and diagrams.

## 7.1.9 Specify and Model Requirements Student Exercises

1. Match the model category on the left with its description on the right.

    1. Activity Flow ___          a. Models relationships within an enterprise and to a solution
    2. Capability ___             b. models focus on features or functions of an enterprise or a solution
    3. Data and Information ___   c. models the 'why' of a change
    4. People and Roles ___       d. models a sequence of actions, events, or a course that may be taken
    5. Rationale ___              e. models represent the characteristics and the exchange of information within an enterprise or a solution

2. Match the business analysis technique on the left with how it is utilized to specify and model requirements on the right.

1. Acceptance and Evaluation Criteria ___
2. Business Capability Analysis ___
3. Business Model Canvas ___
4. Data Flow Diagram ___
5. Functional Decomposition ___
6. Interface Analysis ___
7. Process Modeling ___
8. Prototyping ___
9. Root Cause Analysis ___
10. Use Cases and Scenarios ___

a. used to specify requirements as a brief statement about what people do or need to do when using the solution.
b. used to model requirements in order to identify constituent parts of an overall complex business function.
c. used to assist the stakeholders in visualizing the appearance and capabilities of a planned solution.
d. used to represent features or functions of an enterprise.
e. used to visualize data flow requirements.
f. used to model the root causes of a problem as part of rationale.
g. used to represent the acceptance criteria attributes of requirements.
h. used to describe the rationale for requirements.
i. used to show the steps or activities that are performed in the organization, or that must be performed to meet the desired change.
j. used to model requirements in order to identify and validate inputs and outputs of the solution they are modeling.

## Answers to Student Exercises

1. Match the model category on the left with its description on the right.

    1. Activity Flow  _d_
    2. Capability  _b_
    3. Data and Information  _e_
    4. People and Roles  _a_
    5. Rationale  _c_

    a. Models relationships within an enterprise and to a solution
    b. models focus on features or functions of an enterprise or a solution
    c. models the 'why' of a change
    d. models a sequence of actions, events, or a course that may be taken
    e. models represent the characteristics and the exchange of information within an enterprise or a solution

2. Match the business analysis technique on the left with how it is utilized to specify and model requirements on the right.

| | |
|---|---|
| 1. Acceptance and Evaluation Criteria _g_ | a. used to specify requirements as a brief statement about what people do or need to do when using the solution. |
| 2. Business Capability Analysis _d_ | b. used to model requirements in order to identify constituent parts of an overall complex business function. |
| 3. Business Model Canvas _h_ | c. used to assist the stakeholders in visualizing the appearance and capabilities of a planned solution. |
| 4. Data Flow Diagram _e_ | d. used to represent features or functions of an enterprise. |
| 5. Functional Decomposition _b_ | e. used to visualize data flow requirements. |
| 6. Interface Analysis _j_ (jay) | f. used to model the root causes of a problem as part of rationale. |
| 7. Process Modeling _i_ (eye) | g. used to represent the acceptance criteria attributes of requirements. |
| 8. Prototyping _c_ | h. used to describe the rationale for requirements. |
| 9. Root Cause Analysis _f_ | i. used to show the steps or activities that are performed in the organization, or that must be performed to meet the desired change. |
| 10. Use Cases and Scenarios _a_ | j. used to model requirements in order to identify and validate inputs and outputs of the solution they are modeling. |

## 7.2 Verify Requirements

### 7.2.1 Purpose

To ensure that requirements and designs specifications and models meet quality standards and are usable for the purpose they serve.

### 7.2.2 Description

Verifying requirements ensures that the requirements and designs have been defined correctly and are usable for the change initiative and stakeholders so that further work toward the solution may continue. The most important characteristic of quality requirements and designs is fitness for use. They must meet the needs of stakeholders who will use them for a particular purpose. Quality is ultimately determined by stakeholders.

A high-quality specification is well written and easily understood by its intended audience. A high-quality model follows the formal or informal notation standards and effectively represents reality.

### 7.2.3 Inputs

- **Requirements (specified and modeled) (7.1)**: any requirement, design, or set of those may be verified to ensure that text is well structured and that matrices and modeling notation are used correctly.

You will notice that the input to the next task, 7.3 Validate Requirements, is also Requirements (specified and modeled) (7.1). This is showing that these two tasks are not sequential and one can be performed prior to the other, or they can be performed simultaneously.

**Figure 7.2.1: Verify Requirements Input/Task/Output Diagram**

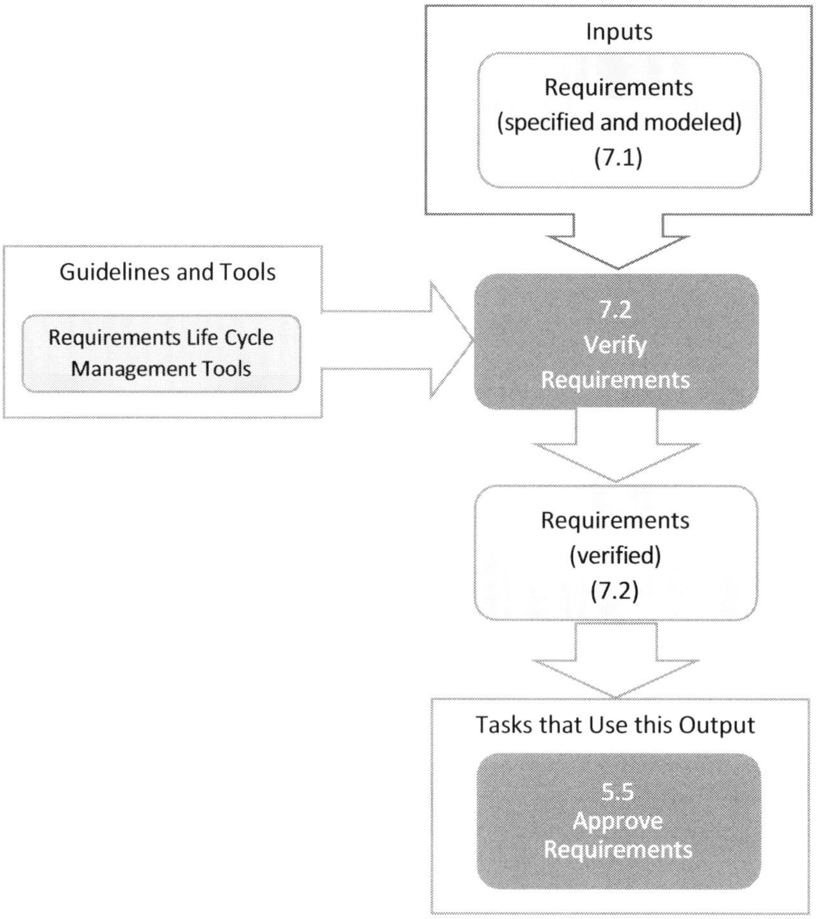

### 7.2.4 Elements

#### 7.2.4.1 Characteristics of Requirements and Designs Quality

While quality is ultimately determined by the needs of the stakeholders who will use the requirements or the designs, acceptable quality requirements exhibit many of the following characteristics:

- **Atomic**: self-contained and capable of being understood independently.
- **Complete**: enough to guide further work and at the appropriate level of detail for work to continue. The level of completeness required differs based on perspective, and point in the life cycle.
- **Consistent**: aligned with the needs of the stakeholders and not conflicting with other requirements.
- **Concise**: contains no extraneous and unnecessary content.
- **Feasible**: reasonable and possible within the agreed-upon risk, schedule, and budget, or considered feasible enough to investigate further through experiments or prototypes.
- **Unambiguous**: clearly stated in such a way to make it clear whether a solution does or does not meet the associated need.

- **Testable**: able to verify that the requirement or design has been fulfilled. Acceptable levels of verifying fulfillment depend on the level of abstraction of the requirement or design.
- **Prioritized**: ranked, grouped, or negotiated in terms of importance and value against all other requirements.
- **Understandable**: represented using common terminology of the audience.

### 7.2.4.2 Verification Activities

Verification activities are typically performed iteratively throughout the requirements analysis process. Verification activities include checking for compliance with organizational performance standards for business analysis, such as using the right tools and methods, checking for correct use of modeling notation, templates, or forms, checking for completeness within each model, comparing each model against other relevant models, checking for elements that are mentioned in one model but are missing in other models, and verifying that the elements are referenced consistently, ensuring the terminology used in expressing the requirement is understandable to stakeholders and consistent with the use of those terms within the organization, and adding examples where appropriate for clarification.

### 7.2.4.3 Checklists

Checklists may include a standard set of quality elements used to verify the requirements, or they may be specifically developed to capture issues of concern. The purpose of a checklist is to ensure that known important items are included in the final requirements deliverables, or that steps required for the verification process are followed.

## 7.2.5 Guidelines and Tools

| Guideline or Tool | How Utilized in this Task |
| --- | --- |
| **Requirements Life Cycle Management Tools** | some tools have functionality to check for issues related to many of the characteristics, such as atomic, unambiguous, and prioritized. |

## 7.2.6 Techniques

| Technique | How Utilized in this Task |
| --- | --- |
| **10.1 Acceptance and Evaluation Criteria** | used to ensure that requirements are stated clearly enough to devise a set of tests that can prove that the requirements have been met. |
| **10.26 Item Tracking** | used to ensure that any problems or issues identified during verification are managed and resolved. |
| **10.28 Metrics and KPIs** | used to identify how to evaluate the quality of the requirements. |
| **10.37 Reviews** | used to inspect requirements documentation to identify requirements that are not of acceptable quality. |

### 7.2.7 Stakeholders

| Stakeholder | How Involved in this Task |
|---|---|
| **All Stakeholders** | the business analyst, in conjunction with the domain and implementation subject matter experts, has the primary responsibility for determining that this task has been completed. Other stakeholders may discover problematic requirements during requirements communication. Therefore, all stakeholders could be involved in this task. |

### 7.2.8 Outputs

- **Requirements (verified) (7.2)**: a set of requirements or designs that is of sufficient quality to be used as a basis for further work.

**NOTES:**

*Use this space to write notes concerning this chapter that you want to remember and will help you pass the ECBA™ exam.*

Chapter 7 Requirements Analysis and Design Definition

## 7.2.9 Verify Requirements Student Exercises

1. Determine the requirement quality characteristics that the clues below describe, then put that characteristic in the crossword puzzle.

**ACROSS**

1. Ranked in terms of importance or value. _____
2. Requirement must be clearly stated in such a way to make it clear whether a solution does or does not meet the associated need. _____
3. Contains no extraneous and unnecessary content. _____
4. Reasonable and possible within the agreed-upon risk, schedule, and budget. _____

**DOWN**

1. Self-contained and capable of being understood independently of other requirements or designs._____
2. Aligned with the identified needs of the stakeholders and not conflicting with other requirements. _____
3. Represented using common terminology of the audience. _____
4. Stated well enough to guide further work._____
5. Able to verify that the requirement or design has been fulfilled. _____

## Answers to Student Exercises

1. Determine the requirement quality characteristics that the clues below describe, then put that characteristic in the crossword puzzle.

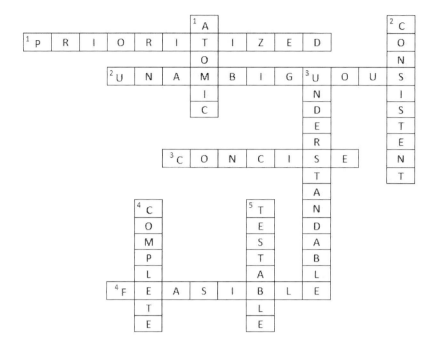

**ACROSS**

1. Ranked in terms of importance or value.  **Prioritized**
2. Requirement must be clearly stated in such a way to make it clear whether a solution does or does not meet the associated need.  **Unambiguous**
3. Contains no extraneous and unnecessary content.  **Concise**
4. Reasonable and possible within the agreed-upon risk, schedule, and budget.  **Feasible**

**DOWN**

1. Self-contained and capable of being understood independently of other requirements or designs. **Atomic**
2. Aligned with the identified needs of the stakeholders and not conflicting with other requirements.  **Consistent**
3. Represented using common terminology of the audience.  **Understandable**
4. Stated well enough to guide further work. **Complete**
5. Able to verify that the requirement or design has been fulfilled.  **Testable**

## 7.3 Validate Requirements

**Figure 7.3.1: Validate Requirements Input/Task/Output Diagram**

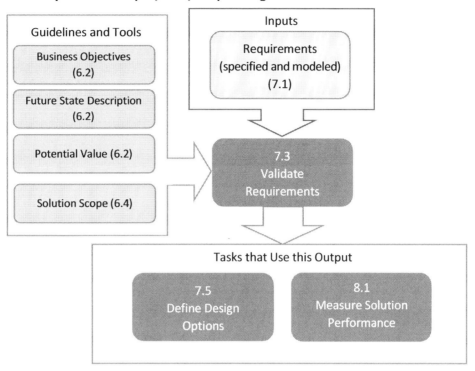

### 7.3.1 Purpose

To ensure that all requirements and designs align to the business requirements and support the delivery of needed value.

### 7.3.2 Description

Requirements validation is an ongoing process to ensure that stakeholder, solution, and transition requirements align to the business requirements and that the designs satisfy the requirements.

The overall goal of implementing the requirements is to achieve the stakeholders' desired future state. In many cases, stakeholders have different, conflicting needs and expectations that may be exposed through the validation process.

### 7.3.3 Inputs

- **Requirements (specified and modeled) (7.1)**: any types of requirements and designs can be validated. Validation activities may begin before requirements are completely verified. However, validation activities cannot be completed before requirements are completely verified.

You will notice that the input to the last task, 7.2 Verify Requirements, is also Requirements (specified and modeled) (7.1). This is showing that these two tasks are not sequential and one can be performed prior to the other, or they can be performed simultaneously.

### 7.3.4 Elements

#### 7.3.4.1 Identify Assumptions

It is often necessary to make assumptions about customer or stakeholder response, especially when there are no similar previous experiences on which to rely. Stakeholders may have assumed that certain benefits will result from the implementation of a requirement. These assumptions are identified and defined so that associated risks can be managed, and work can progress to confirm or disprove the assumptions.

#### 7.3.4.2 Define Measurable Evaluation Criteria

While the expected benefits are defined as part of the future state, the specific measurement criteria and evaluation process may not have been included.

Business analysts define the evaluation criteria that will be used to evaluate how successful the change has been after the solution is implemented. Baseline metrics might be established based on the current state. Target metrics can be developed to reflect the achievement of the business objectives or some other measurement of success.

#### 7.3.4.3 Evaluate Alignment and Solution Scope

A requirement can be of benefit to a stakeholder and still not be a desirable part of a solution. A requirement that does not deliver benefit to a stakeholder is a strong candidate for elimination. When requirements do not align, either the future state must be re-evaluated and the solution scope changed, or the requirement removed from the solution scope.

If a design cannot be validated to support a requirement, there might be a missing or misunderstood requirement, or the design must change.

### 7.3.5 Guidelines and Tools

| Guideline or Tool | How Utilized in this Task |
| --- | --- |
| **Business Objectives (6.2)** | ensure the requirements deliver the desired business benefits. |
| **Future State Description (6.2)** | helps to ensure the requirements that are part of the solution scope do help achieve the desired future state. |
| **Potential Value (6.2)** | can be used as a benchmark against which the value delivered by requirements can be assessed. |
| **Solution Scope (6.4)** | ensures the requirements that provide benefit are within the scope of the desired solution. |

### 7.3.6 Techniques

| Technique | How Utilized in this Task |
| --- | --- |
| **10.1 Acceptance and Evaluation Criteria** | used to define the quality metrics that must be met to achieve acceptance by a stakeholder. |
| **10.18 Document Analysis** | used to identify previously documented business needs in order to validate requirements. |

| Technique | How Utilized in this Task |
|---|---|
| **10.20 Financial Analysis** | used to define the financial benefits associated with requirements. |
| **10.26 Item Tracking** | used to ensure that any problems or issues identified during validation are managed and resolved. |
| **10.28 Metrics and KPIs** | used to select appropriate performance measures for a solution, solution component, or requirement. |
| **10.37 Reviews** | used to confirm whether or not the stakeholder agrees that their needs are met. |
| **10.38 Risk Analysis and Management** | used to identify possible scenarios that would alter the benefit delivered by a requirement. |

### 7.3.7 Stakeholders

| Stakeholder | How Involved in this Task |
|---|---|
| **All Stakeholders** | the business analyst, in conjunction with the customer, end users, and sponsors, has the primary responsibility for determining whether or not requirements are validated. Other stakeholders may discover problematic requirements during requirements communication. Therefore, virtually all project stakeholders are involved in this task. |

### 7.3.8 Outputs

- **Requirements (validated) (7.3)**: validated requirements and designs are those that can be demonstrated to deliver benefit to stakeholders and align with the business goals and objectives of the change. If a requirement or design cannot be validated, it either does not benefit the organization, does not fall within the solution scope, or both.

## 7.4 Define Requirements Architecture

### 7.4.1 Purpose

To ensure that the requirements collectively support one another to fully achieve the objectives.

### 7.4.2 Description

Requirements architecture is the structure of all of the requirements of a change. A requirements architecture fits the individual models and specifications together to ensure that all of the requirements form a single whole that supports the overall business objectives and produces a useful outcome for stakeholders.

Business analysts use a requirements architecture to:
- understand which models are appropriate for the domain, solution scope, and audience,
- organize requirements into structures relevant to different stakeholders,
- illustrate how requirements and models interact with and relate to each other, and show how the parts fit together into a meaningful whole,
- ensure the requirements work together to achieve the overall objectives, and
- make trade-off decisions about requirements while considering the overall objectives.

Requirements architecture is not intended to demonstrate traceability, but rather to show how elements work in harmony with one another to support the business requirements, and to structure them in various ways to align the viewpoints of different stakeholders.

**Figure 7.4.1: Define Requirements Architecture Input/Task/Output Diagram**

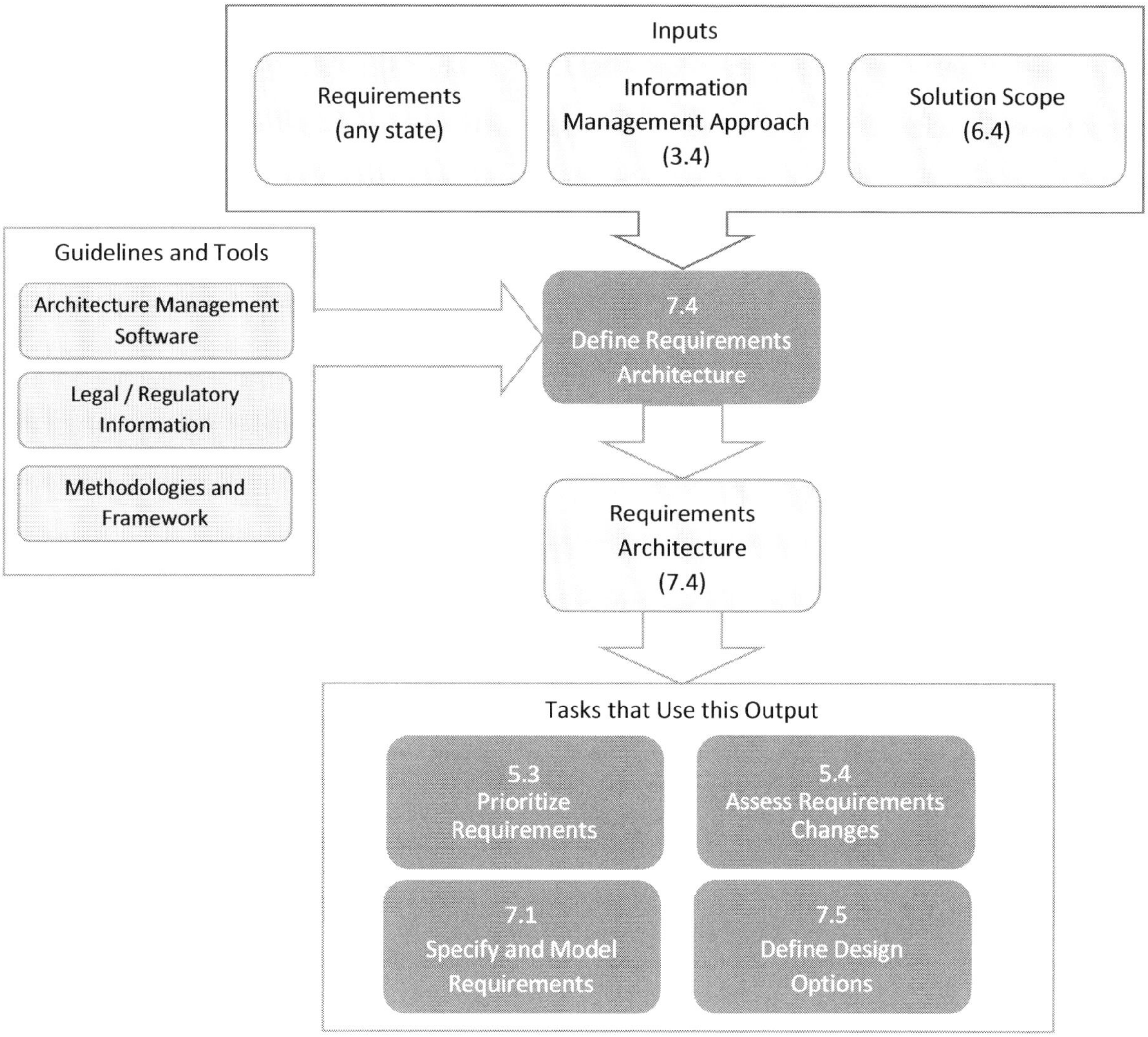

### 7.4.3 Inputs

- **Information Management Approach (3.4)**: defines how the business analysis information (including requirements and models) will be stored and accessed.
- **Requirements (any state)**: every requirement should be stated once, and only once, and incorporated into the requirements architecture so that the entire set may be evaluated for completeness.
- **Solution Scope (6.4)**: must be considered to ensure the requirements architecture is aligned with the boundaries of the desired solution.

## 7.4.4 Elements

### 7.4.4.1 Requirements Viewpoints and Views

A viewpoint is a set of conventions that define how requirements will be represented, how these representations will be organized, and how they will be related. Viewpoints provide templates for addressing the concerns of particular stakeholder groups.

No single viewpoint alone can form an entire architecture. Trying to put too much information into any one viewpoint will make it too complex and degrade its purpose. Examples of viewpoints include business process models, data models and information, user interactions, including use cases and/or user experience, audit and security, and business models.

The actual requirements and designs for a particular solution from a chosen viewpoint are referred to as a view. A collection of views makes up the requirements architecture for a specific solution. Business analysts align, coordinate, and structure requirements into meaningful views for the various stakeholders. This set of coordinated, complementary views provides a basis for assessing the completeness and coherence of the requirements.

### 7.4.4.2 Template Architecture

An architectural framework is a collection of viewpoints that is standard across an industry, sector, or organization. Business analysts can treat frameworks as predefined templates to start from in defining their architecture.

### 7.4.4.3 Completeness

An architecture helps ensure that a set of requirements is complete. The entire set of requirements should be able to be understood by the audience in way that it can be determined that the set is cohesive and tells a full story. No requirements should be missing from the set, inconsistent with others, or contradictory to one another. The requirements architecture should take into account any dependencies between requirements that could keep the objectives from being achieved.

### 7.4.4.4 Relate and Verify Requirements Relationships

Requirements may be related to each other in several ways when defining the requirements architecture. Business analysts examine and analyze the requirements to define the relationships between them. Business analysts examine each relationship to ensure that the relationships satisfy the following quality criteria:

- **Defined**: there is a relationship and the type of the relationship is described.
- **Necessary**: the relationship is necessary for understanding the requirements holistically (big picture).
- **Correct**: the elements do have the relationship described.
- **Unambiguous**: there are no relationships that link elements in two different and conflicting ways.
- **Consistent**: relationships are described in the same way, using the same set of standard descriptions as defined in the viewpoints.

#### 7.4.4.5 Business Analysis Information Architecture

The structure of the business analysis information is also an information architecture. This type of architecture is defined as part of the task 3.4 Plan Business Analysis Information Management in the Business Analysis Planning and Monitoring Knowledge Area.

The information architecture is a component of the requirements architecture because it describes how all of the business analysis information for a change relates. It defines relationships for types of information such as requirements, designs, types of models, and elicitation results.

### 7.4.5 Guidelines and Tools

| Guideline or Tool | How Utilized in this Task |
|---|---|
| **Architecture Management Software** | modeling software can help to manage the volume, complexity, and versions of the relationships within the requirements architecture. |
| **Legal/Regulatory Information** | describes legislative rules or regulations that must be followed. They may impact the requirements architecture or its outputs. Additionally, contractual or standards-based constraints may also need to be considered. |
| **Methodologies and Frameworks** | a predetermined set of models, and relationships between the models, to be used to represent different viewpoints. |

### 7.4.6 Techniques

| Technique | How Utilized in this Task |
|---|---|
| **10.15 Data Modeling** | used to describe the requirements structure as it relates to data. |
| **10.22 Functional Decomposition** | used to break down an organizational unit, product scope, or other elements into its component parts. |
| **10.25 Interviews** | used to define the requirements structure collaboratively. |
| **10.32 Organizational Modeling** | used to understand the various organizational units, stakeholders, and their relationships which might help define relevant viewpoints. |
| **10.41 Scope Modeling** | used to identify the elements and boundaries of the requirements architecture. |
| **10.50 Workshops** | used to define the requirements structure collaboratively. |

### 7.4.7 Stakeholders

| Stakeholder | How Involved in this Task |
|---|---|
| **Any Stakeholder** | may assist in defining and confirming the requirements architecture and use the requirements architecture to assess the completeness of the requirements. |

## Chapter 7 Requirements Analysis and Design Definition

| Stakeholder | How Involved in this Task |
|---|---|
| **Domain Subject Matter Expert** | may assist in defining and confirming the requirements architecture. |
| **Implementation Subject Matter Expert** | may assist in defining and confirming the requirements architecture. |
| **Project Manager** | may assist in defining and confirming the requirements architecture. |
| **Sponsor** | may assist in defining and confirming the requirements architecture. |
| **Tester** | may assist in defining and confirming the requirements architecture. |

### 7.4.8 Outputs

- **Requirements Architecture (7.4)**: the requirements and the interrelationships among them, as well as any contextual information that is recorded.

## 7.5 Define Solution Options

**Figure 7.5.1: Define Solution Options Input/Task/Output Diagram**

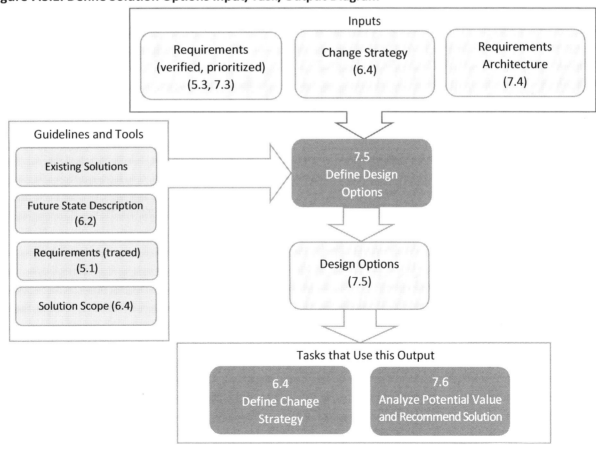

## 7.5.1 Purpose

To define the solution approach, identify opportunities to improve the business, allocate requirements across solution components, and represent design options that achieve the desired future state.

## 7.5.2 Description

This task is about defining as many options for the solution to meet a business need as possible. Design options exist at a lower level than the change strategy and are considered tactical rather than strategic. As a solution is developed, tactical trade-offs may need to be made among design alternatives. Business analysts must assess the effect these trade-offs will have on the delivery of value to stakeholders. As initiatives progress and requirements evolve, design options evolve as well.

## 7.5.3 Inputs

- **Change Strategy (6.4)**: describes the approach that will be followed to transition to the future state. This may have some impact on design decisions in terms of what is feasible or possible.
- **Requirements (validated (5.3), prioritized (7.3))**: only validated requirements are considered in design options. Knowing the requirement priorities aids in the suggestion of reasonable design options. Requirements with the highest priorities might deserve more weight in choosing solution components to best meet them as compared to lower priority requirements.
- **Requirements Architecture (7.4)**: the full set of requirements and their relationships is important for defining design options that can address the holistic set of requirements.

## 7.5.4 Elements

### 7.5.4.1 Define Solution Approaches

The solution approach describes whether solution components will be created or purchased, or some combination of both. Business analysts assess the merits of the solution approaches for each design option. Solution approaches include:

- **Create**: solution components are assembled, constructed, or developed by experts as a direct response to a set of requirements. The requirements and the design options have enough detail to make a decision about which solution to construct. This option includes modifying an existing solution.
- **Purchase**: solution components are selected from a set of offerings that fulfill the requirements. The requirements and design options have enough detail to make a recommendation about which solution to purchase. These offerings are usually products or services owned and maintained by third parties.
- **Combination of both**: not all design options will fall strictly into one of the categories above. Design options may include a combination of both creation and purchase of components.

### 7.5.4.2 Identify Improvement Opportunities

When proposing design options, a number of opportunities to improve the operation of the business may occur and are compared, including:

- **Increase Efficiencies**: automate or simplify the work people perform by re-engineering or sharing processes, changing responsibilities, or outsourcing. Automation may also increase consistency of behavior, reducing the likelihood of different stakeholders performing the same function in distinctly different fashions.

- **Improve Access to Information**: provide greater amounts of information to staff who interface directly or indirectly with customers, thereby reducing the need for specialists.
- **Identify Additional Capabilities**: highlight capabilities that have the potential to provide future value and can be supported by the solution. These capabilities may not necessarily be of immediate value to the organization (for example, a software application with features the organization anticipates using in the future).

#### 7.5.4.3 Requirements Allocation

Requirements allocation is the process of assigning requirements to solution components and releases to best achieve the objectives.

#### 7.5.4.4 Describe Design Options

Design options are investigated and developed while considering the desired future state, and in order to ensure the design option is valid. Solution performance measures are defined for each design option.

A design option usually consists of many design components, each described by a design element. Design elements may describe business policies, business rules, business processes, people who operate and maintain the solution (including their job functions and responsibilities), operational business decisions to be made, software applications and application components used in the solution, and organizational structures (including interactions between the organization, its customers, and its suppliers).

### 7.5.5 Guidelines and Tools

| Guideline or Tool | How Utilized in this Task |
|---|---|
| **Existing Solutions** | existing products or services, often third party, that are considered as a component of a design option. |
| **Future State Description (6.2)** | identifies the desired state of the enterprise that the design options will be part of, and helps to ensure design options are viable. |
| **Requirements (traced) (5.1)** | define the design options that best fulfill known requirements. |
| **Solution Scope (6.4)** | defines the boundaries when selecting viable design options. |

### 7.5.6 Techniques

| Technique | How Utilized in this Task |
|---|---|
| **10.5 Benchmarking and Market Analysis** | used to identify and analyze existing solutions and market trends. |
| **10.5 Brainstorming** | used to help identify improvement opportunities and design options. |
| **10.18 Document Analysis** | used to provide information needed to describe design options and design elements. |
| **10.25 Interviews** | used to help identify improvement opportunities and design options. |

| Technique | How Utilized in this Task |
|---|---|
| **10.27 Lessons Learned** | used to help identify improvement opportunities. |
| **10.29 Mind Mapping** | used to identify and explore possible design options. |
| **10.40 Root Cause Analysis** | used to understand the underlying cause of the problems being addressed in the change to propose solutions to address them. |
| **10.45 Survey and Questionnaire** | used to help identify improvement opportunities and design options. |
| **10.49 Vendor Assessment** | used to couple the assessment of a third-party solution with an assessment of the vendor to ensure that the solution is viable and all parties will be able to develop and maintain a healthy working relationship. |
| **10.50 Workshops** | used to help identify improvement opportunities and design options. |

### 7.5.7 Stakeholders

| Stakeholder | How Involved in this Task |
|---|---|
| **Domain Subject Matter Expert** | provides the expertise within the business to provide input and feedback when evaluating solution alternatives, particularly for the potential benefits of a solution. |
| **Implementation Subject Matter Expert** | use their expertise in terms of the design options being considered to provide needed input about the constraints of a solution and its costs. |
| **Operational Support** | can help evaluate the difficulty and costs of integrating proposed solutions with existing processes and systems. |
| **Project Manager** | plans and manages the solution definition process, including the solution scope and any risks associated with the proposed solutions. |
| **Supplier** | provides information on the functionality associated with a particular design option. |

### 7.5.8 Outputs

- **Design Options (7.5)**: describe various ways to satisfy one or more needs in a context. They may include solution approach, potential improvement opportunities provided by the option, and the components that define the option.

## 7.6 Analyze Potential Value and Recommend Solution

### 7.6.1 Purpose

To estimate the potential value for each design option and to establish which one is most appropriate to meet the enterprise's requirements.

# Chapter 7 Requirements Analysis and Design Definition

**Figure 7.6.1: Analyze Potential Value and Recommend Solution Input/Task/Output Diagram**

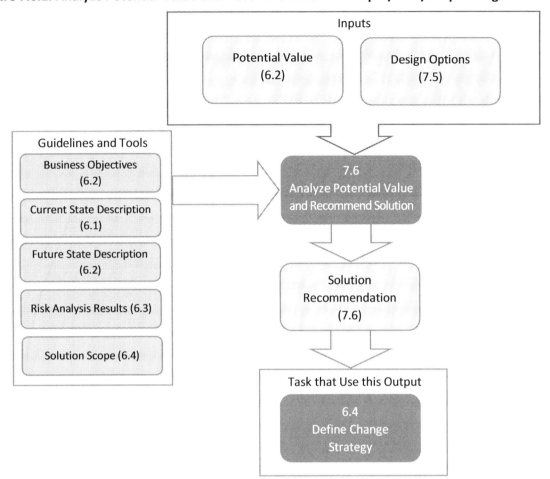

## 7.6.2 Description

Analyze Potential Value and Recommend Solution describes how to estimate and model the potential value delivered by a set of requirements, designs, or design options. Potential value is analyzed many times over the course of a change. The analysis of potential value includes consideration that there is uncertainty in the estimates. Value can be described in terms of finance, reputation, or even impact on the marketplace. Any change may include a mix of increases and decreases in value.

Design options are evaluated by comparing the potential value of each option to the other options. Sometimes determining the best option is clear, other times there may not be a clear best option to recommend. In this case, the best option may be to begin work on multiple competing solution options; perhaps to build proof of concepts for each, then measure the performance of each to help determine which will deliver the best value to the organization or its stakeholders. It is also possible that the best recommendation is to do nothing.

## 7.6.3 Inputs

- **Design Options (7.5)**: need to be evaluated and compared to one another to recommend one option for the solution.
- **Potential Value (6.2)**: can be used as a benchmark against which the value delivered by a design can be evaluated.

### 7.6.4 Elements

#### 7.6.4.1 Expected Benefit

Expected benefits describe the positive value that a solution is intended to deliver to stakeholders. Value can be more than monetary, including benefits, reduced risk, compliance with business policies and regulations, an improved user experience, or any other positive outcome. Benefits are determined based on the analysis of the benefit that stakeholders desire and the benefit that is possible to attain. Benefits are often realized over a period of time.

#### 7.6.4.2 Expected Costs

Expected costs include any potential negative value associated with a solution, including the cost to acquire the solution, any negative effects it may have on stakeholders, and the cost to maintain it over time. Expected costs for a design option consider the cumulative costs of the design components.

Business analysts also consider opportunity cost when estimating the expected cost of a change. Opportunity costs are alternative results that might have been achieved if the resources, time, and funds devoted to one design option had been allocated to another design option. The opportunity cost of any design option is equal to the value of the best alternative not selected.

#### 7.6.4.3 Determined Value

The potential value of a solution to a stakeholder is based on the benefits delivered by that solution and the associated costs. Value can be positive (if the benefits exceed the costs) or negative (if the costs exceed the benefits).

Business analysts consider potential value from the points of view of stakeholders. Value to the enterprise is almost always more heavily weighted than value for any individual stakeholder groups. There might be increases in value for one set of stakeholders and decreases in value for another set, but an overall positive increase in value for the enterprise as a whole justifies proceeding with the change.

Potential value is uncertain value. There are always events or conditions that could increase or decrease the actual value if they occur.

#### 7.6.4.4 Assess Design Options and Recommend Solution

Each design option is assessed based on the potential value it is expected to deliver. There are several factors to take into consideration:

- **Available Resources**: there may be limitations regarding the number of requirements that can be implemented based on the allocated resources. In some instances, a business case can be developed to justify additional investment.
- **Constraints on the Solution**: regulatory requirements or business decisions may require that certain requirements be handled manually or automatically, or that certain requirements be prioritized above all others.
- **Dependencies between Requirements**: some capabilities may in and of themselves provide limited value to the organization, but need to be delivered in order to support other high-value requirements.

## 7.6.5 Guidelines and Tools

| Guideline or Tool | How Utilized in this Task |
|---|---|
| **Business Objectives (6.2)** | used to calculate the expected benefit. |
| **Current State Description (6.1)** | provides the context within which the work needs to be completed. It can be used to identify and help quantify the value to be delivered from a potential solution. |
| **Future State Description (6.2)** | describes the desired future state that the solution will be part of in order to ensure the design options are appropriate. |
| **Risk Analysis Results (6.3)** | the potential value of design options includes an assessment of the level of risk associated with the design options or initiative. |
| **Solution Scope (6.4)** | defines the scope of the solution that is being delivered so that a relevant evaluation can be made that is within the scope boundaries. |

## 7.6.6 Techniques

| Technique | How Utilized in this Task |
|---|---|
| **10.1 Acceptance and Evaluation Criteria** | used to express requirements in the form of acceptance criteria to make them most useful when assessing proposed solutions and determining whether a solution meets the defined business needs. |
| **10.2 Backlog Management** | used to sequence the potential value. |
| **10.5 Brainstorming** | used to identify potential benefits of the requirements in a collaborative manner. |
| **10.7 Business Cases** | used to assess recommendations against business goals and objectives. |
| **10.8 Business Model Canvas** | used as a tool to help understand strategy and initiatives. |
| **10.16 Decision Analysis** | used to support the assessment and ranking of design options. |
| **10.19 Estimation** | used to forecast the costs and efforts of meeting the requirements as a step towards estimating their value. |
| **10.20 Financial Analysis** | used to evaluate the financial return of different options and choose the best possible return on investment. |
| **10.21 Focus Groups** | used to get stakeholder input on which design options best meet the requirements, and to evaluate a targeted, small group of stakeholders' value expectations. |
| **10.25 Interviews** | used to get stakeholder input on which design options best meet the requirements, and to evaluate individual stakeholders' value expectations. |
| **10.28 Metrics and KPIs** | used to create and evaluate the measurements used in defining value. |
| **10.38 Risk Analysis and Management** | used to identify and manage the risks that could affect the potential value of the requirements. |

| Technique | How Utilized in this Task |
|---|---|
| **10.45 Survey and Questionnaire** | used to get stakeholder input on which design options best meet the requirements, and to identify stakeholders' value expectations. |
| **10.46 SWOT Analysis** | used to identify areas of strength and weakness that will impact the value of the solutions. |
| **10.50 Workshops** | used to get stakeholder input on which design options best meet the requirements, and to evaluate stakeholders' value expectations. |

## 7.6.7 Stakeholders

| Stakeholder | How Involved in this Task |
|---|---|
| **Customer** | represents the market segments affected by the requirements and solutions, and will be involved in analyzing the benefit of those requirements and costs of the design options. |
| **Domain Subject Matter Expert** | may be called upon for their domain knowledge to assist in analyzing potential value and benefits, particularly for those requirements where they are harder to identify. |
| **End User** | provides an insight into the potential value of the change. |
| **Implementation Subject Matter Expert** | may be called upon for their expertise in implementing the design options in order to identify potential costs and risks. |
| **Project Manager** | manages the selection process so that when effecting the change they are aware of potential impacts on those supporting the change, including the risks associated with the change. |
| **Regulator** | may be involved in risk evaluation concerning outside regulatory bodies or place constraints on the potential benefits. |
| **Sponsor** | approves the expenditure of resources to purchase or develop a solution and approve the final recommendation. The sponsor will want to be kept informed of any changes in potential value or risk, as well as the resulting opportunity cost, as he/she may prefer another course of action. |

## 7.6.8 Outputs

- **Solution Recommendation (7.6)**: identifies the suggested, most appropriate solution based on an evaluation of all defined design options. The recommended solution should maximize the value provided to the enterprise.

Chapter 7 Requirements Analysis and Design Definition

## 7.7 Requirements Analysis and Design Definition Pop-up Quiz

1. What is the purpose for a business analyst to perform Requirements Analysis and Design Definition tasks?

    a. To structure and organize requirements discovered during elicitation activities, identify solution options that meet the business needs, and estimate the potential value of each option.

    b. To specify and model requirements and designs.

    c. To collaborate with stakeholders to ensure they understand the requirements and accept them.

    d. To collaborate with stakeholders to ensure they have a shared understanding of the elicitation results discovered during elicitation activities.

2. What is the input to the Specify and Model Requirements task?

    a. Existing business analysis information

    b. Solution Scope and Business Analysis Approach

    c. Elicitation Results (any state)

    d. Elicitation Results (confirmed)

3. The business analyst is working to ensure that all requirements align to the business requirements and support the delivery of needed value. Which task is the business analyst performing?

    a. Verify Requirements

    b. Validate Requirements

    c. Assess Potential Value and Recommend Solution

    d. Approve Requirements

4. Which of the following lists the quality characteristics of requirements?

    a. Time-bounded, Specific, Measurable, Relevant, and Achievable.

    b. Specific, Atomic, Complete, Measurable, Realistic, Testable, and Concise.

    c. Written in complete sentence.

    d. Complete, Concise, Testable, Atomic, Feasible, Consistent, Understandable, Unambiguous, and Prioritized.

5. What are the tasks in the Requirements Analysis and Design Definition knowledge area?

   a. Specify Requirements, Validate Requirements, Specify Solution Options, and Assess Potential Value and Recommend Solution.

   b. Specify and Model Requirements, Verify Requirements, Validate Requirements, Define Requirements Architecture, Define Solution Options, and Assess Potential Value and Recommend Solution.

   c. Specify and Model Requirements, Verify Requirements, Approve Requirements, Define Requirements Architecture, Define Solution Options, and Assess Potential Value and Recommend Solution.

   d. Specify Requirements, Verify Requirements, Validate Requirements, Specify Solution Options, Approve Requirements, and Assess Potential Value.

6. Requirements may be specified and modeled in a variety of formats; which of the following lists the ways that business analysts represent requirements and designs?

   a. Logical, physical, formal, and informal.

   b. Text, and graphical.

   c. Text, matrices, and diagrams.

   d. Throw-away, evolutionary, and functional.

7. Which of the following is NOT a correct statement of how business analysts use requirements architecture?

   a. Business analysts use requirements architecture to ensure every requirement links back to an objective and shows how an objective was met.

   b. Business analysts use requirements architecture to ensure requirements work together to achieve the overall objective.

   c. Business analysts use requirements architecture to make tradeoff decisions about requirements while considering the overall objectives.

   d. Business analysts use requirements architecture to understand which models are appropriate for the domain, solution scope, and audience.

Chapter 7 Requirements Analysis and Design Definition

8. Which of the following is NOT an element of the Analyze Potential Value and Recommend Solution task?

    a. Expected Costs

    b. Expected Outcome

    c. Determine Value

    d. Expected Benefits

9. Which of the following is NOT an input to the Define Design Options task?

    a. Requirements

    b. Change Strategy

    c. Requirements Architecture

    d. Solution Scope

10. Which techniques are used to verify requirements?

    a. Acceptance and evaluation criteria, workshops, reviews, and metrics and key performance indicators.

    b. Acceptance and evaluation criteria, item tracking, workshops, and metrics and key performance indicators.

    c. Acceptance and evaluation criteria, item tracking, reviews, and metrics and key performance indicators.

    d. Acceptance and evaluation criteria, workshops, reviews, and roles and permissions matrix.

## Answers to Pop-up Quiz

| Question | Answer | Description |
|---|---|---|
| 1 | A | BABOK section 7.0. The Requirements Analysis and Design Definition knowledge area describes the tasks that business analysts perform to structure and organize requirements discovered during elicitation activities, specify and model requirements and designs, validate and verify information, identify solution options that meet business needs, and estimate the potential value that could be realized for each solution option. |
| 2 | C | BABOK section 7.1.3 and figure 7.1.1. |
| 3 | B | BABOK section 7.3.1. The purpose of Validate Requirements is to ensure that all requirements and designs align to the business requirements and support the delivery of needed value. |
| 4 | D | BABOK section 7.2.4.1. |
| 5 | B | BABOK sections 7.1, 7.2, 7.3, 7.4, 7.5, and 7.6 |
| 6 | C | BABOK sections 7.1.4.1 and 7.1.8. any combination of requirements and/or designs in the form of text, matrices, and diagrams. |
| 7 | A | BABOK section 7.4.2. |
| 8 | B | BABOK section 7.6.4. |
| 9 | D | BABOK section 7.5.3 and figure 7.5.1. |
| 10 | C | BABOK section 7.2.6. |

# Solution Evaluation

## Overview

Solution Evaluation is about evaluating the performance of an implemented solution, or solution component, to verify if it is delivering the expected value to the organization or its stakeholders. This includes making recommendations to improve the value the organization is receiving from the solution. Value is achieved over time, and can increase as time passes. This may require multiple assessments of solution value at different intervals of time and a comparison of those assessments to evaluate the increase of performance over time.

**Goal:** To determine ways to increase solution value.

The following image illustrates the spectrum of value as business analysis activities progress from delivering potential value to actual value.

Figure 8.0.1: Business Analysis Value Spectrum

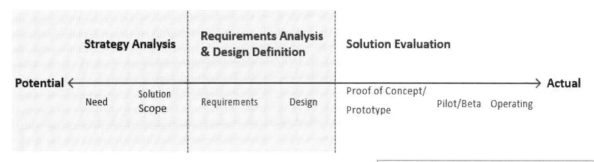

## What You Will Learn

When you are finished with this chapter, you will know:
- How to define Solution Evaluation
- The five tasks in Solution Evaluation
- A deeper understanding the business analyst role in evaluating solution performance and recommending improvements to gain greater value from those solutions

> *You have now seen the above diagram four times (chapters 1, 6, 7 and 8. A great indication that you should know the three knowledge areas that manage requirements before, during and after a change.*

Important learnings in Solution Evaluation Knowledge Area:
1. There are similar tasks for evaluating value in other knowledge areas, the uniqueness of evaluation in Solution Evaluation knowledge area is that it is evaluation of an existing solution.
2. Solution Evaluation can be done on a recently implemented solution or a solution that has been in operation for years.
3. Focus of evaluation may be one a solution component instead of an entire solution.
4. Solution Evaluation is 1% of the ECBA™ exam; meaning there will be one question on the exam from this knowledge area. You will note a very light coverage of this topic so you can spend your time in knowledge areas with higher coverage on the exam.

**Figure 8.0.2: Solution Evaluation Input/Task/Output Diagram**

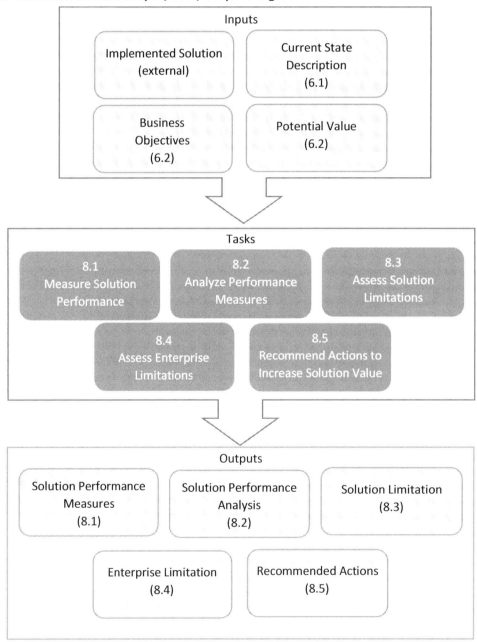

# Chapter 8 Solution Evaluation

## The BACCM™ in Solution Evaluation

The following model describes the usage and application of each of the core concepts within the context of Solution Evaluation.

**Figure 8.0.3: Core Concepts application In Solution Evaluation**

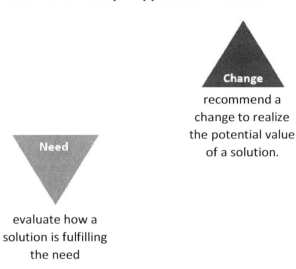

evaluate how a solution is fulfilling the need

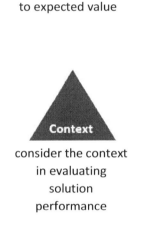

assess the performance of the solution, in relation to expected value

elicit information from the stakeholders on solution performance and value delivery

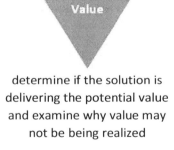

consider the context in evaluating solution performance

determine if the solution is delivering the potential value and examine why value may not be being realized

## Tasks in Solution Evaluation

There are five tasks in the Solution Evaluation Knowledge Area:

1. <u>M</u>easure Solution Performance
2. <u>A</u>nalyze Solution Performance
3. Assess <u>S</u>olution Limitations
4. Assess <u>E</u>nterprise Limitations
5. <u>R</u>ecommend Actions to Increase Solution Value

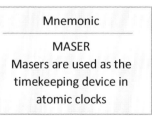

| Mnemonic |
| --- |
| MASER |
| Masers are used as the timekeeping device in atomic clocks |

# Detailed ITTSO Table

The following table summarizes the Inputs, Tasks, Techniques, Stakeholders and Outputs (ITTSO) in the Solution Evaluation Knowledge Area.

Table 8.0.1: Inputs, Tasks, Techniques, Stakeholders and Outputs Summary

| ITTSO Summary for Solution Evaluation | | | | | |
|---|---|---|---|---|---|
| Inputs | Tasks | M* | Techniques | Stakeholders | Outputs |
| • Implemented Solution (external)<br>• Business Objectives (6.2) | 8.1 Measure Solution Performance | M | 10.1 Acceptance and Evaluation Criteria<br>10.4 Benchmarking and Market Analysis<br>10.7 Business Cases<br>10.14 Data Mining<br>10.16 Decision Analysis<br>10.21 Focus Groups<br>10.28 Metrics and KPIs<br>10.30 Non-Functional Requirements Analysis<br>10.31 Observation<br>10.36 Prototyping<br>10.45 Survey and Questionnaire<br>10.47 Use Cases and Scenarios<br>10.49 Vendor Assessment | • Customer<br>• Domain SME<br>• End User<br>• Project Manager<br>• Regulator<br>• Sponsor | • Solution Performance Measures (8.1) |
| • Potential Value (6.2)<br>• Solution Performance Measures (8.1) | 8.2 Analyze Solution Performance | A | 10.1 Acceptance and Evaluation Criteria<br>10.4 Benchmarking and Market Analysis<br>10.14 Data Mining<br>10.25 Interviews<br>10.28 Metrics and KPIs<br>10.31 Observation<br>10.38 Risk Analysis and Management<br>10.40 Root Cause Analysis<br>10.45 Survey and Questionnaire | • Domain SME<br>• Project Manager<br>• Sponsor | • Solution Performance Analysis (8.2) |

# Chapter 8 Solution Evaluation

| | | | | | |
|---|---|---|---|---|---|
| • Implemented Solution (external)<br>• Solution Performance Analysis (8.2) | 8.3 Assess Solution Limitations | S | 10.1 Acceptance and Evaluation Criteria<br>10.4 Benchmarking and Market Analysis<br>10.9 Business Rules Analysis<br>10.14 Data Mining<br>10.16 Decision Analysis<br>10.25 Interviews<br>10.26 Item Tracking<br>10.27 Lessons Learned<br>10.38 Risk Analysis and Management<br>10.40 Root Cause Analysis<br>10.45 Survey and Questionnaire | • Customer<br>• Domain SME<br>• End User<br>• Regulator<br>• Sponsor<br>• Tester | • Solution Limitation (8.3) |
| • Implemented Solution (external)<br>• Current State Description (6.1)<br>• Solution Performance Analysis (8.2) | 8.4 Assess Enterprise Limitations | E | 10.4 Benchmarking and Market Analysis<br>10.5 Brainstorming<br>10.15 Data Mining<br>10.16 Decision Analysis<br>10.18 Document Analysis<br>10.25 Interviews<br>10.26 Item Tracking<br>10.27 Lessons Learned<br>10.31 Observation<br>10.32 Organizational Modeling<br>10.34 Process Analysis<br>10.35 Process Modeling<br>10.38 Risk Analysis and Management<br>10.39 Roles and Permissions Matrix<br>10.40 Root Cause Analysis<br>10.45 Survey and Questionnaire<br>10.46 SWOT Analysis<br>10.50 Workshops | • Customer<br>• Domain SME<br>• End User<br>• Regulator<br>• Sponsor | • Enterprise Limitation (8.4) |

| | | | | | |
|---|---|---|---|---|---|
| • Solution Limitation (8.3)<br>• Enterprise Limitation (8.4) | 8.5 Recommend Actions to Increase Solution Value | R | 10.14 Data Mining<br>10.16 Decision Analysis<br>10.20 Financial Analysis<br>10.21 Focus Groups<br>10.32 Organizational Modeling<br>10.33 Prioritization<br>10.34 Process Analysis<br>10.38 Risk Analysis and Management<br>10.45 Survey and Questionnaire | • Customer<br>• Domain SME<br>• End User<br>• Regulator<br>• Sponsor | • Recommended Actions (8.5) |

\* Mnemonic = MASER

# Chapter 8 Solution Evaluation

## Solution Evaluation Student Exercises

**Exercise 1:** Fill in the blanks to complete the Solution Evaluation task name, then enter the Mnemonic letter used in this chapter to help remember the tasks in this knowledge area.

| SE Tasks | Mnemonic Letter |
|---|---|
| _____ Solution Performance |  |
| _____ Solution Performance |  |
| Assess _____ |  |
| Assess _____ |  |
| _____ Actions to Increase Solution Value |  |

**Bonus:** Enter below the phrase used in this chapter to help remember the tasks in Solution Evaluation knowledge area.

_____

**Exercise 2:** For each stakeholder indicate which task they are involved in by putting an 'X' in the appropriate column under the stakeholder. Some stakeholders may not be involved in any tasks while some stakeholders may be involved in multiple tasks.

| Stakeholder / Task | All Stakeholders | Any Stakeholders | Customers | Domain SME | End User | Implementation SME | Operational Support | Project Manager | Regulator | Sponsor | Supplier | Tester |
|---|---|---|---|---|---|---|---|---|---|---|---|---|
| 8.1 Measure Solution Performance |  |  |  |  |  |  |  |  |  |  |  |  |
| 8.2 Analyze Solution Performance |  |  |  |  |  |  |  |  |  |  |  |  |
| 8.3 Assess Solution Limitations |  |  |  |  |  |  |  |  |  |  |  |  |
| 8.4 Assess Enterprise Limitations |  |  |  |  |  |  |  |  |  |  |  |  |
| 8.5 Recommend Actions to Increase Value |  |  |  |  |  |  |  |  |  |  |  |  |

# Answers to Student Exercises

**Exercise 1:** Fill in the blanks to complete the Solution Evaluation task name, then enter the Mnemonic letter used in this chapter to help remember the tasks in this knowledge area.

| SE Tasks | Mnemonic Letter |
|---|---|
| _Measure_ Solution Performance | M |
| _Analyze_ Solution Performance | A |
| Assess _Solution Limitations_ | S |
| Assess _Enterprise Limitations_ | E |
| _Recommend_ Actions to Increase Solution Value | R |

**Bonus:** Enter below the phrase used in this chapter to help remember the tasks in Solution Evaluation knowledge area.

_Masers are used as the timekeeping device in atomic clocks_

**Exercise 2:** For each stakeholder indicate which task they are involved in by putting an 'X' in the appropriate column under the stakeholder. Some stakeholders may not be involved in any tasks while some stakeholders may be involved in multiple tasks.

| Stakeholder / Task | All Stakeholders | Any Stakeholders | Customers | Domain SME | End User | Implementation SME | Operational Support | Project Manager | Regulator | Sponsor | Supplier | Tester |
|---|---|---|---|---|---|---|---|---|---|---|---|---|
| 8.1 Measure Solution Performance | | | X | X | X | | | X | X | X | | |
| 8.2 Analyze Solution Performance | | | | X | | | | X | | X | | |
| 8.3 Assess Solution Limitations | | | X | X | X | | | | X | X | | X |
| 8.4 Assess Enterprise Limitations | | | X | X | X | | | | X | X | | |
| 8.5 Recommend Actions to Increase Value | | | X | X | X | | | | X | X | | |

Chapter 8 Solution Evaluation

## 8.1 Measure Solution Performance

Figure 8.1.1: Measure Solution Performance Input/Task/Output Diagram

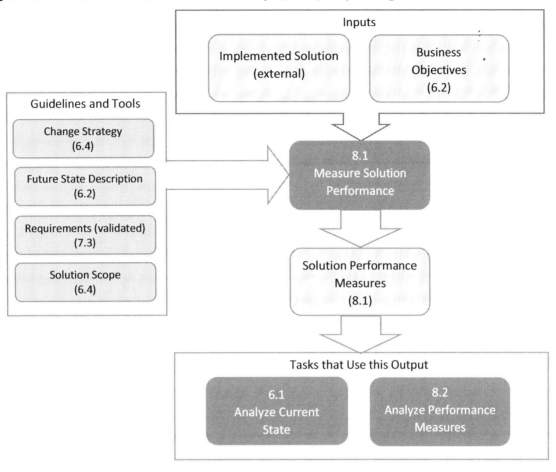

### 8.1.1 Purpose

To define performance measures and use the data collected to evaluate the effectiveness of a solution in relation to the value it brings.

### 8.1.2 Description

This task covers the activities of measuring the performance of a newly implemented, or existing, solution. The next task covers assessing actual performance against expected (potential) value, but first you must know how a solution is performing for the organization. The measures used depend on the solution itself, the context, and how the organization defines value.

### 8.1.3 Inputs

- **Business Objectives (6.2)**: the measurable results that the enterprise wants to achieve. Provides a benchmark against which solution performance can be assessed.
- **Implemented Solution (external)**: a solution (or component of a solution) that exists in some form. It may be an operating solution, a prototype, or a pilot or beta solution.

### 8.1.4 Elements

#### 8.1.4.1 Define Performance Measures

Business goals, objectives, and business processes are common sources of measures. Solution performance measures may be quantitative, qualitative, or both, depending on the value being measured.

#### 8.1.4.2 Validate Performance Measures

Specific performance measures should align with any higher-level measures that exist within the context affecting the solution. Decisions about which measures are used to evaluate solution performance often reside with the sponsor, but may be made by any stakeholder with decision-making authority.

#### 8.1.4.3 Collect Performance Measures

When defining performance measures, business analysts may employ basic statistical sampling concepts. Things to consider include volume and sample size, frequency and timing, and currency.

### 8.1.5 Guidelines and Tools

| Guideline or Tool | How Utilized in this Task |
| --- | --- |
| Change Strategy (6.4) | the change strategy used or in use to implement the potential value. |
| Future State Description (6.2) | boundaries of the proposed new, removed, or modified components of the enterprise, and the potential value expected from the future state. |
| Requirements (validated) (7.3) | a set of requirements that have been analyzed and appraised to determine their value. |
| Solution Scope (6.4) | the solution boundaries to measure and evaluate. |

### 8.1.6 Techniques

| Technique | How Utilized in this Task |
| --- | --- |
| 10.1 Acceptance and Evaluation Criteria | used to define acceptable solution performance. |
| 10.4 Benchmarking and Market Analysis | used to define measures and their acceptable levels. |
| 10.7 Business Cases | used to define business objectives and performance measures for a proposed solution. |
| 10.14 Data Mining | used to collect and analyze large amounts of data regarding solution performance. |
| 10.16 Decision Analysis | used to assist stakeholders in deciding on suitable ways to measure solution performance and acceptable levels of performance. |

| Technique | How Utilized in this Task |
|---|---|
| 10.21 Focus Groups | used to provide subjective assessments, insights, and impressions of a solution's performance. |
| 10.28 Metrics and KPIs | used to measure solution performance. |
| 10.30 Non-Functional Requirements Analysis | used to define expected characteristics of a solution. |
| 10.31 Observation | used either to provide feedback on perceptions of solution performance or to reconcile contradictory results. |
| 10.36 Prototyping | used to simulate a new solution so that performance measures can be determined and collected. |
| 10.45 Survey and Questionnaire | used to gather opinions and attitudes about solution performance. Surveys and questionnaires can be effective when large or disparate groups need to be polled. |
| 10.47 Use Cases and Scenarios | used to define the expected outcomes of a solution. |
| 10.39 Vendor Assessment | used to assess which of the vendor's performance measures should be included in the solution's performance assessment. |

## 8.1.7 Stakeholders

| Stakeholder | How Involved in this Task |
|---|---|
| Customer | may be consulted to provide feedback on solution performance. |
| Domain Subject Matter Expert | a person familiar with the domain who can be consulted to provide potential measurements. |
| End User | contributes to the actual value realized by the solution in terms of solution performance. They may be consulted to provide reviews and feedback on areas such as workload and job satisfaction. |
| Project Manager | responsible for managing the schedule and tasks to perform the solution measurement. For solutions already in operation, this role may not be required. |
| Regulator | an external or internal group that may dictate or prescribe constraints and guidelines that must be incorporated into solution performance measures. |
| Sponsor | responsible for approving the measures used to determine solution performance. May also provide performance expectations. |

### 8.1.8 Outputs

- **Solution Performance Measures (8.1)**: measures that provide information on how well the solution is performing or potentially could perform.

## 8.2 Analyze Solution Performance

**Figure 8.2.1: Analyze Solution Performance Input/Task/Output Diagram**

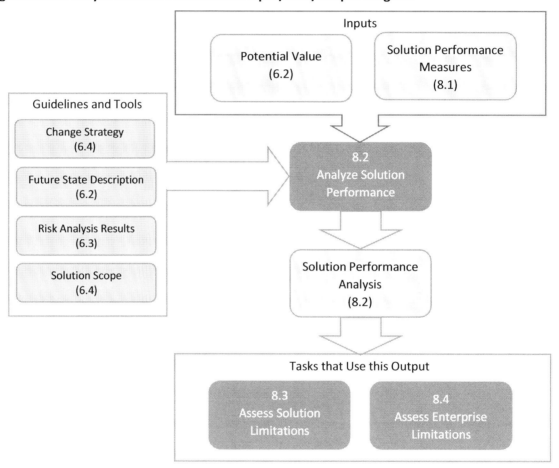

### 8.2.1 Purpose

To provide insights into the performance of a solution in relation to the value it brings.

### 8.2.2 Description

In the last task you identified what your performance measures are going to be for a particular solution in a given context. Now you assess those performance measures against potential value that was defined when developing the solution to determine if it is delivering the expected value.

## 8.2.3 Inputs

- **Potential Value (6.2)**: describes the value that may be realized by implementing the proposed future state. It can be used as a benchmark against which solution performance can be evaluated.
- **Solution Performance Measures (8.1)**: measures and provides information on how well the solution is performing or potentially could perform.

## 8.2.4 Elements

### 8.2.4.1 Solution Performance versus Desired Value

A solution might be high performing, such as an efficient online transaction processing system, but contributes lower value than expected (or compared to what it had contributed in the past). On the other hand, a low performing but potentially valuable solution, such as a core process that is inefficient, can be enhanced to increase its performance level. If the measures are not sufficient to help stakeholders determine solution value, business analysts either collect more measurements or treat the lack of measures as a solution risk.

### 8.2.4.2 Risks

Performance measures may uncover new risks to solution performance and to the enterprise. These risks are identified and managed like any other risks.

### 8.2.4.3 Trends

Consider the time period when the data was collected to guard against anomalies and skewed trends.

### 8.2.4.4 Accuracy

The accuracy of performance measures is essential to the validity of their analysis. To be considered accurate and reliable, the results of performance measures should be reproducible and repeatable.

### 8.2.4.5 Performance Variances

The difference between expected and actual performance represents a variance. Root cause analysis may be necessary to determine the underlying causes of significant variances within a solution. Recommendations of how to improve performance and reduce any variances are made in the task 8.5 Recommend Actions to Increase Solution Value.

## 8.2.5 Guidelines and Tools

| Guideline or Tool | How Utilized in this Task |
| --- | --- |
| **Change Strategy (6.4)** | the change strategy that was used or is in use to implement the potential value. |
| **Future State Description (6.2)** | boundaries of the proposed new, modified, or removed components of the enterprise and the potential value expected from the future state. |
| **Risk Analysis Results (6.3)** | the overall level of risk and the planned approach to modifying the individual risks. |
| **Solution Scope (6.4)** | the solution boundaries to measure and evaluate. |

## 8.2.6 Techniques

| Technique | How Utilized in this Task |
|---|---|
| 10.1 Acceptance and Evaluation Criteria | used to define acceptable solution performance through acceptance criteria. The degree of variance from these criteria will guide the analysis of that performance. |
| 10.4 Benchmarking and Market Analysis | used to observe the results of other organizations employing similar solutions when assessing risks, trends, and variances. |
| 10.14 Data Mining | used to collect data regarding performance, trends, common issues, and variances from expected performance levels and understand patterns and meaning in that data. |
| 10.25 Interviews | used to determine expected value of a solution and its perceived performance from an individual or small group's perspective. |
| 10.28 Metrics and KPIs | used to analyze solution performance, especially when judging how well a solution contributes to achieving goals. |
| 10.31 Observation | used to observe a solution in action if the data collected does not provide definitive conclusions. |
| 10.38 Risk Analysis and Management | used to identify, analyze, develop plans to modify the risks, and to manage the risks on an ongoing basis. |
| 10.40 Root Cause Analysis | used to determine the underlying cause of performance variance. |
| 10.45 Survey and Questionnaire | used to determine expected value of a solution and its perceived performance. |

## 8.2.7 Stakeholders

| Stakeholder | How Involved in this Task |
|---|---|
| Domain Subject Matter Expert | can identify risks and provide insights into data for analyzing solution performance. |
| Project Manager | within a project, responsible for overall risk management and may participate in risk analysis for new or changed solutions. |
| Sponsor | can identify risks, provide insights into data and the potential value of a solution. They will make decisions about the significance of expected versus actual solution performance. |

## 8.2.8 Outputs

- **Solution Performance Analysis (8.2)**: results of the analysis of measurements collected and recommendations to solve performance gaps and leverage opportunities to improve value.

Chapter 8 Solution Evaluation

## 8.3 Assess Solution Limitations

**Figure 8.3.1: Assess Solution Limitations Input/Task/Output Diagram**

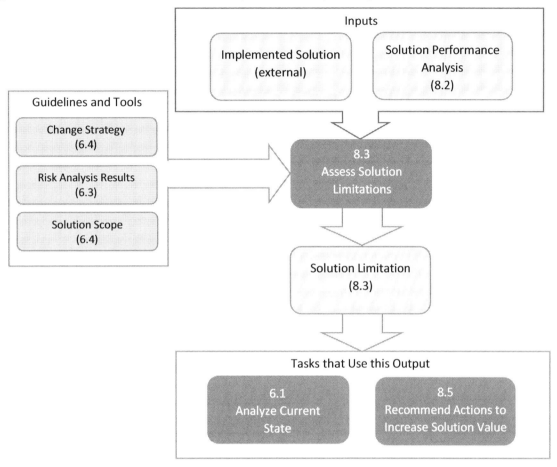

### 8.3.1 Purpose

To determine the factors internal to the solution that restrict the full realization of value.

### 8.3.2 Description

Assessing solution limitations identifies the root causes for under-performing and ineffective solutions. If the solution has not met its potential value, business analysts determine which factors, both internal and external to the solution, are limiting value. This task focuses on the assessment of those factors internal to the solution. This assessment may be performed at any point during the solution life cycle.

### 8.3.3 Inputs

- **Implemented Solution (external):** a solution that exists. The solution may or may not be in operational use; it may be a prototype. The solution must be in use in some form in order to be evaluated.
- **Solution Performance Analysis (8.2):** results of the analysis of measurements collected and recommendations to solve for performance gaps and leverage opportunities to improve value.

### 8.3.4 Elements

#### 8.3.4.1 Identify Internal Solution Component Dependencies

Solutions often have internal dependencies that limit the performance of the entire solution to the performance of the least effective component. Assessment of the overall performance of the solution or its components is performed in the last two tasks.

#### 8.3.4.2 Investigate Solution Problems

When it is determined that the solution is consistently or repeatedly producing ineffective outputs, problem analysis is performed in order to identify the source of the problem.

#### 8.3.4.3 Impact Assessment

Business analysts review identified problems in order to assess the effect they may have on the operation of the organization or the ability of the solution to deliver its potential value. This requires determining the severity of the problem, the probability of the re-occurrence of the problem, the impact on the business operations, and the capacity of the business to absorb the impact. Business analysts identify which problems must be resolved, which can be mitigated through other activities or approaches, and which can be accepted.


### 8.3.5 Guidelines and Tools

| Guideline or Tool | How Utilized in this Task |
|---|---|
| **Change Strategy (6.4)** | the change strategy used or in use to implement the potential value. |
| **Risks Analysis Results (6.3)** | the overall level of risk and the planned approach to modifying the individual risks. |
| **Solution Scope (6.4)** | the solution boundaries to measure and evaluate. |


### 8.3.6 Techniques

| Technique | How Utilized in this Task |
|---|---|
| **10.1 Acceptance and Evaluation Criteria** | used both to indicate the level at which acceptance criteria are met or anticipated to be met by the solution and to identify any criteria that are not met by the solution. |
| **10.4 Benchmarking and Market Analysis** | used to assess if other organizations are experiencing the same solution challenges and, if possible, determine how they are addressing it. |
| **10.9 Business Rules Analysis** | used to illustrate the current business rules and the changes required to achieve the potential value of the change. |
| **10.14 Data Mining** | used to identify factors constraining performance of the solution. |
| **10.16 Decision Analysis** | used to illustrate the current business decisions and the changes required to achieve the potential value of the change. |
| **10.25 Interviews** | used to help perform problem analysis. |

Chapter 8 Solution Evaluation

| Technique | How Utilized in this Task |
|---|---|
| 10.26 Item Tracking | used to record and manage stakeholder issues related to why the solution is not meeting the potential value. |
| 10.27 Lessons Learned | used to determine what can be learned from the inception, definition, and construction of the solution to have potentially impacted its ability to deliver value. |
| 10.38 Risk Analysis and Management | used to identify, analyze, and manage risks, as they relate to the solution and its potential limitations, that may impede the realization of potential value. |
| 10.40 Root Cause Analysis | used to identify and understand the combination of factors and their underlying causes that led to the solution being unable to deliver its potential value. |
| 10.45 Survey and Questionnaire | used to help perform problem analysis. |

## 8.3.7 Stakeholders

| Stakeholder | How Involved in this Task |
|---|---|
| Customer | is ultimately affected by a solution, and therefore has an important perspective on its value. A customer may be consulted to provide reviews and feedback. |
| Domain Subject Matter Expert | provides input into how the solution should perform and identifies potential limitations to value realization. |
| End User | uses the solution, or is a component of the solution, and therefore contributes to the actual value realized by the solution in terms of solution performance. An end user may be consulted to provide reviews and feedback on areas such as workload and job satisfaction. |
| Regulator | a person whose organization needs to be consulted about the planned and potential value of a solution, as that organization may constrain the solution, the degree to which actual value is realized, or when actual value is realized. |
| Sponsor | responsible for approving the potential value of the solution, for providing resources to develop, implement and support the solution, and for directing enterprise resources to use the solution. The sponsor is also responsible for approving a change to potential value. |
| Tester | responsible for identifying solution problems during construction and implementation; not often used in assessing an existing solution outside of a change. |

## 8.3.8 Outputs

- **Solution Limitation (8.3)**: a description of the current limitations of the solution including constraints and defects.

## 8.4 Assess Enterprise Limitations

### Figure 8.4.1: Assess Enterprise Limitations Input/Task/Output Diagram

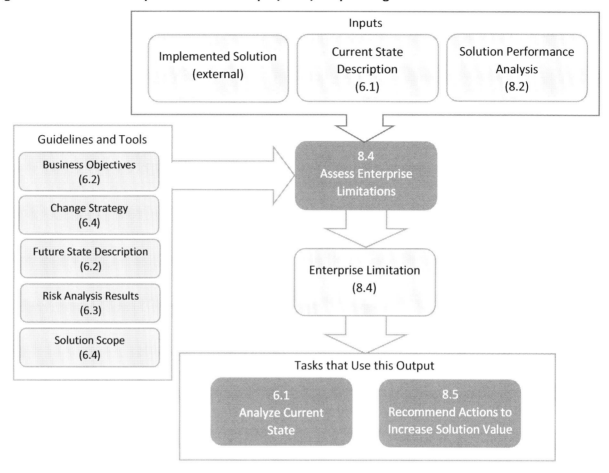

### 8.4.1 Purpose

To determine how factors external to the solution are restricting value realization.

### 8.4.2 Description

Enterprise limitations may include factors such as culture, operations, technical components, stakeholder interests, or reporting structures. Assessing enterprise limitations identifies root causes and describes how enterprise factors limit value realization. This assessment may be performed at any point during the solution life cycle.

### 8.4.3 Inputs

- **Current State Description (6.1)**: the current internal environment of the solution including the environmental, cultural, and internal factors influencing the solution limitations.
- **Implemented (or Constructed) Solution (external)**: a solution that exists. The solution may or may not be in operational use; it may be a prototype. The solution must be in use in some form in order to be evaluated.
- **Solution Performance Analysis (8.2)**: results of the analysis of measurements collected and recommendations to solve performance gaps and leverage opportunities to improve value.

### 8.4.4 Elements

#### 8.4.4.1 Enterprise Culture Assessment

Enterprise culture is defined as the deeply rooted beliefs, values, and norms shared by the members of an enterprise. Business analysts perform cultural assessments to identify whether or not stakeholders understand the reasons why a solution exists, ascertain whether or not the stakeholders view the solution as something beneficial and are supportive of the change, and determine if and what cultural changes are required to better realize value from a solution.

The enterprise culture assessment evaluates the extent to which the culture can accept a solution. If cultural adjustments are needed to support the solution, the assessment is used to judge the enterprise's ability and willingness to adapt to these cultural changes.

Business analysts also evaluate internal and external stakeholders to gauge understanding and acceptance of the solution, assess perception of value and benefit from the solution, and determine what communication activities are needed to ensure awareness and understanding of the solution.

#### 8.4.4.2 Stakeholder Impact Analysis

A stakeholder impact analysis provides insight into how the solution affects a particular stakeholder group. Business analysts consider functions, locations and concerns of the stakeholders.

#### 8.4.4.3 Enterprise Structure Changes

The use of a solution and the ability to adopt a change can be enabled or blocked by formal and informal relationships among stakeholders. The reporting structure may be too complex or too simple to allow a solution to perform effectively.

Assessing if the organizational hierarchy supports the solution is a key activity. On occasion, informal relationships within an organization, whether alliances, friendships, or matrix-reporting, impact the ability of a solution to deliver potential value. Business analysts consider these informal relationships in addition to the formal structure.

#### 8.4.4.4 Operational Assessment

The operational assessment is performed to determine if an enterprise is able to adapt to or effectively use a solution. This identifies which processes and tools within the enterprise are adequately equipped to benefit from the solution, and if sufficient and appropriate assets are in place to support it.

Consider policies and procedures, capabilities and processes that enable other capabilities, skill and training needs, human resources practices, risk tolerance and management approaches, and tools and technology that support a solution.

### 8.4.5 Guidelines and Tools

| Guideline or Tool | How Utilized in this Task |
|---|---|
| **Business Objectives (6.2)** | are considered when measuring and determining solution performance. |
| **Change Strategy (6.4)** | the change strategy used or in use to implement the potential value. |
| **Future State Descriptions (6.2)** | boundaries of the proposed new, removed, or modified components of the enterprise, as well as the potential value expected from the future state. |

| Guideline or Tool | How Utilized in this Task |
|---|---|
| **Risk Analysis Results (6.3)** | the overall level of risk and the planned approach to modifying the individual risks. |
| **Solution Scope (6.4)** | the solution boundaries to measure and evaluate. |

### 8.4.6 Techniques

| Technique | How Utilized in this Task |
|---|---|
| **10.4 Benchmarking and Market Analysis** | used to identify existing solutions and enterprise interactions. |
| **10.5 Brainstorming** | used to identify organizational gaps or stakeholder concerns. |
| **10.14 Data Mining** | used to identify factors constraining performance of the solution. |
| **10.16 Decision Analysis** | used to assist in making an optimal decision under conditions of uncertainty and may be used in the assessment to make decisions about functional, technical, or procedural gaps. |
| **10.18 Document Analysis** | used to gain an understanding of the culture, operations, and structure of the organization. |
| **10.25 Interviews** | used to identify organizational gaps or stakeholder concerns. |
| **10.26 Item Tracking** | used to ensure that issues are not neglected or lost and that issues identified by assessment are resolved. |
| **10.27 Lessons Learned** | Used to analyze previous initiatives and the enterprise interactions with the solutions. |
| **10.31 Observation** | used to witness the enterprise and solution interactions to identify impacts. |
| **10.32 Organizational Modeling** | used to ensure the identification of any required changes to the organizational structure that may have to be addressed. |
| **10.34 Process Analysis** | used to identify possible opportunities to improve performance. |
| **10.35 Process Modeling** | used to illustrate the current business processes and/or changes that must be made in order to achieve the potential value of the solution. |
| **10.38 Risk Analysis and Management** | used to consider risk in the areas of technology (if the selected technological resources provide required functionality), finance (if costs could exceed levels that make the change salvageable), and business (if the organization will be able to make the changes necessary to attain potential value from the solution). |
| **10.39 Roles and Permissions Matrix** | used to determine roles and associated permissions for stakeholders, as well as stability of end users. |
| **10.40 Root Cause Analysis** | used to determine if the underlying cause may be related to enterprise limitations. |

| Technique | How Utilized in this Task |
|---|---|
| 10.45 Survey and Questionnaire | used to identify organizational gaps or stakeholder concerns. |
| 10.46 SWOT Analysis | used to demonstrate how a change will help the organization maximize strengths and minimize weaknesses, and to assess strategies developed to respond to identified issues. |
| 10.50 Workshops | used to identify organizational gaps or stakeholder concerns. |

### 8.4.7 Stakeholders

| Stakeholder | How Involved in this Task |
|---|---|
| Customer | people directly purchasing or consuming the solution who may interact with the organization in the use of the solution. |
| Domain Subject Matter Expert | provides input into how the organization interacts with the solution and identifies potential limitations. |
| End User | people who use a solution or who are a component of the solution. Users could be customers or people who work within the organization. |
| Regulator | one or many governmental or professional entities that ensure adherence to laws, regulations, or rules; may have unique input to the organizational assessment, as relevant regulations must be included in the requirements. There may be laws and regulations that must be complied with prior to (or as a result of) a planned or implemented change. |
| Sponsor | authorizes and ensures funding for a solution delivery, and champions action to resolve problems identified in the organizational assessment. |

### 8.4.8 Outputs

- **Enterprise Limitation (8.4)**: a description of the current limitations of the enterprise including how the solution performance is impacting the enterprise.

## 8.5 Recommend Actions to Increase Solution Value

### 8.5.1 Purpose

To understand the factors that create differences between potential value and actual value, and to recommend a course of action to align them.

**Figure 8.5.1: Recommend Actions to Increase Solution Value Input/Task/Output Diagram**

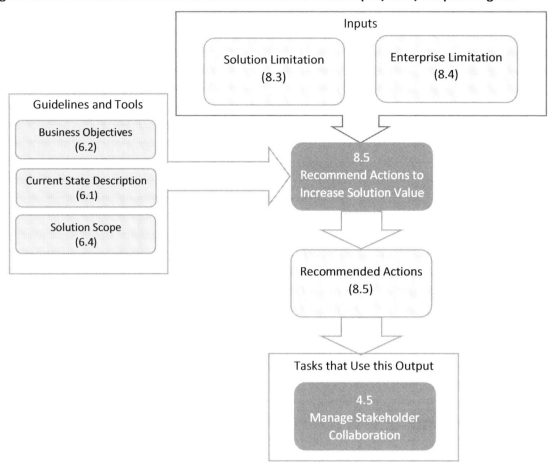

### 8.5.2 Description

Recommendations generally identify how a solution should be replaced, retired, or enhanced. They may include recommendations to adjust the organization to allow for maximum solution performance and value realization.

### 8.5.3 Inputs

- **Enterprise Limitation (8.4)**: a description of the current limitations of the enterprise including how the solution performance is impacting the enterprise.
- **Solution Limitation (8.3)**: a description of the current limitations of the solution including constraints and defects.

### 8.5.4 Elements

#### 8.5.4.1 Adjust Solution Performance Measures

In some cases, the performance of the solution is considered acceptable but may not support the fulfillment of business goals and objectives. An analysis effort to identify and define more appropriate measures may be required.

Chapter 8 Solution Evaluation

### 8.5.4.2 Recommendations

Depending on the reason for lower than expected performance, it may be reasonable to take no action, adjust factors that are external to the solution, or reset expectations for the solution.

Some common examples of recommendations include do nothing, organizational change, reduce complexity of interfaces, eliminate redundancy, avoid waste, identify additional capabilities, retire the solution (based on ongoing cost vs. initial investment, opportunity cost, necessity, or sunk cost).

## 8.5.5 Guidelines and Tools

| Guideline or Tool | How Utilized in this Task |
|---|---|
| **Business Objectives (6.2)** | are considered in evaluating, measuring, and determining solution performance. |
| **Current State Description (6.1)** | provides the context within which the work needs to be completed. It can be used to assess alternatives and better understand the potential increased value that could be delivered. It can also help highlight unintended consequences of alternatives that may otherwise remain undetected. |
| **Solution Scope (6.4)** | the solution boundaries to measure and evaluate. |

## 8.5.6 Techniques

| Technique | How Utilized in this Task |
|---|---|
| **10.14 Data Mining** | used to generate predictive estimates of solution performance. |
| **10.16 Decision Analysis** | used to determine the impact of acting on any of the potential value or performance issues. |
| **10.20 Financial Analysis** | used to assess the potential costs and benefits of a change. |
| **10.21 Focus Groups** | used to determine if solution performance measures need to be adjusted and used to identify potential opportunities to improve performance. |
| **10.32 Organizational Modeling** | used to demonstrate potential change within the organization's structure. |
| **10.33 Prioritization** | used to identify relative value of different actions to improve solution performance. |
| **10.34 Process Analysis** | used to identify opportunities within related processes. |
| **10.38 Risk Analysis and Management** | used to evaluate different outcomes under specific conditions. |
| **10.45 Survey and Questionnaire** | used to gather feedback from a wide variety of stakeholders to determine if value has been met or exceeded, if the metrics are still valid or relevant in the current context, and what actions might be taken to improve the solution. |

### 8.5.7 Stakeholders

| Stakeholder | How Involved in this Task |
|---|---|
| **Customer** | people directly purchasing or consuming the solution and who may interact with the organization in the use of the solution. |
| **Domain Subject Matter Expert** | provides input into how to change the solution and/or the organization in order to increase value. |
| **End User** | people who use a solution or who are a component of the solution. Users could be customers or people who work within the organization. |
| **Regulator** | one or many governmental or professional entities that ensure adherence to laws, regulations, or rules. Relevant regulations must be included in requirements. |
| **Sponsor** | authorizes and ensures funding for implementation of any recommended actions. |

### 8.5.8 Outputs

- **Recommended Actions (8.5)**: recommendation of what should be done to improve the value of the solution within the enterprise.

**NOTES:**

*Use this space to write notes concerning this chapter that you want to remember and will help you pass the ECBA™ exam.*

## 8.6 Solution Evaluation Pop-up Quiz

1. The business analyst is recommending a change to either the solution or the enterprise in order to realize the potential value of the solution. Which of the business analysis core concept is the business analyst applying in Solution Evaluation?

    a. Need

    b. Change

    c. Solution

    d. Context

2. Which of the following is NOT a reason a business analyst would perform an organizational cultural assessment when Assessing Enterprise Limitations?

    a. to ascertain whether the organization is ready for the change.

    b. to ascertain whether or not the stakeholders view the solution as something beneficial and are supportive of the change.

    c. to identify whether or not stakeholders understand the reasons why a solution exists.

    d. to determine if and what cultural changes are required to better realize value from a solution.

## Answers to Pop-up Quiz

| Question | Answer | Description |
|---|---|---|
| 1 | B | BABOK table 8.0.1. Change: recommend a change to either a solution or the enterprise in order to realize the potential value of a solution. |
| 2 | A | BABOK section 8.4.4.1. |

# Underlying Competencies

## Overview

The Underlying Competencies chapter provides a description of the behaviors, characteristics, knowledge, and personal qualities that business analysis practitioners should have to provide effective business analysis service to their stakeholders. These competencies grow over time as the business analysis practitioner gains experience in practicing business analysis.

These competencies are grouped into six categories:
- Analytical Thinking and Problem Solving
- Behavioral Characteristics
- Business Knowledge
- Communication Skills
- Interaction Skills
- Tools and Technology

This chapter touches lightly on the competencies described in the *BABOK® Guide*. There won't be many questions, if any, on the ECBA™ exam on underlying competencies. So, we will just lightly touch on these competencies. It will help you understand how business analysis practitioners perform the tasks described in the knowledge areas in the last six chapters, using the techniques described in the next chapter by understanding the personal characteristics the business analysis practitioner must possess. This light understanding of the underlying competencies will be enough to answer the questions on the ECBA exam; but as in other areas of this study guide, it is recommended you study these competencies by studying them in the BABOK and this study guide together.

Each underlying competency is defined with a purpose, definition, and effectiveness measures.

## What You Will Learn

When you are finished with this chapter, you will know:
- Basic understanding of competencies for business analysts.
- A high-level definition of these competencies and their effective measures.

## 9.1 Analytical Thinking and Problem Solving

Analytical thinking and problem-solving skills are required for business analysts to analyze problems and opportunities effectively, identify which changes may deliver the most value, and work with stakeholders to understand the impact of those changes. Core competencies for analytical thinking and problem-solving include:

- Creative Thinking,
- Decision Making,
- Learning,
- Problem Solving,
- Systems Thinking,
- Conceptual Thinking, and
- Visual Thinking.

**Figure 9.1.1: Analytical Thinking and Problem Solving Competency Diagram**

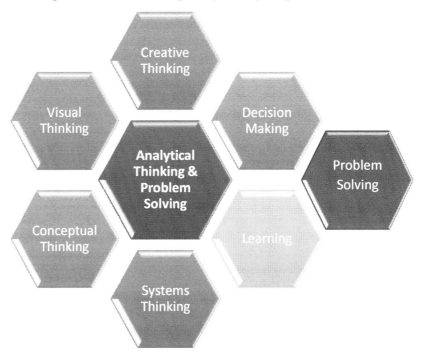

## 9.1.1 Creative Thinking

| | |
|---|---|
| Purpose | To generate new ideas, approaches, and alternatives to problem solving and opportunities. |
| Description | Creative thinking involves generating new ideas and concepts as well as finding new or different associations between existing ideas and concepts. It questions conventional approaches and encourages new ideas and innovations that are appropriate to the situation. Creative thinking may involve combining, changing, and reapplying existing concepts or ideas. Business analysts can be effective in promoting creative thinking in others by identifying and proposing alternatives, and by asking questions and challenging assumptions. |
| Effective Measures | <ul><li>generating and productively considering new ideas,</li><li>exploring concepts and ideas that are new,</li><li>exploring changes to existing concepts and ideas,</li><li>generating creativity for self and others, and</li><li>applying new ideas to resolve existing problems.</li></ul> |

## 9.1.2 Decision Making

| | |
|---|---|
| Purpose | To understand the criteria involved in making a decision, and in assisting others to make better decisions. |
| Description | Used when a decision must be made which is the most advantageous for the stakeholders and the enterprise. Determining this involves gathering the information that is relevant to the decision, analyzing the relevant information, making comparisons and trade-offs options, and identifying the most desirable option. Business analysts document decisions (and the rationale supporting them) to use them as a reference in the event a similar decision is required in the future or if they are required to explain why a decision was made. |
| Effective Measures | <ul><li>the appropriate stakeholders are represented,</li><li>stakeholders understand the decision-making process and the rationale behind the decision,</li><li>the pros and cons of all available options are clearly communicated,</li><li>the decision reduces or eliminates uncertainty, and any remaining uncertainty is accepted,</li><li>the decision made addresses the need or the opportunity and is in the best interest of all stakeholders,</li><li>stakeholders understand all the conditions, environment, and measures in which the decision will be made, and</li><li>a decision is made.</li></ul> |

### 9.1.3 Learning

| | |
|---|---|
| Purpose | To quickly absorb new and different types of information and also modify and adapt existing knowledge. |
| Description | Learning is the process of gaining knowledge or skills. Learning is done in stages from initial acquisition through comprehension to applying the knowledge. Business analysts must be able to synthesize information to identify opportunities to create new solutions and evaluate those solutions to ensure that they are effective.<br><br>Learning techniques to consider include:<br>• **Visual**: learning through the presentation of pictures, photographs, diagrams, models, and videos.<br>• **Auditory**: learning through verbal and written language and text.<br>• **Kinesthetic**: learning by doing.<br><br>Most people experience faster understanding and longer retention of information when more than one learning technique is used. |
| Effective Measures | • understanding that learning is a process for all stakeholders,<br>• learning the concepts presented and then demonstrating an understanding of them,<br>• demonstrating the ability to apply concepts to new areas or relationships,<br>• rapidly absorbing new facts, ideas, concepts, and opinions, and<br>• effectively presenting new facts, ideas, concepts, and opinions to others. |

### 9.1.4 Problem Solving

| | |
|---|---|
| Purpose | To ensure that the real, underlying root cause of a problem is understood by all stakeholders and that solution options address that root cause. |
| Description | Ensure that the nature of the problem and any underlying issues are clearly understood. Ensure that stakeholder points of view are articulated and addressed to understand any conflicts between the goals and objectives of different groups of stakeholders. Ensure that assumptions are identified and validated. Ensure that the objectives that will be met once the problem is solved are clearly specified, and alternative solutions are considered and possibly developed. |
| Effective Measures | • inspire confidence in the problem-solving process,<br>• select solutions that meet the defined objectives and address the root cause of the problem,<br>• evaluate new solution options using the problem-solving framework, and<br>• avoid making decisions based on unvalidated assumptions, preconceived notions, or other biases that may cause a sub-optimal solution to be selected. |

# Chapter 9 Underlying Competencies

## 9.1.5 Systems Thinking

| | |
|---|---|
| Purpose | To understand the enterprise from a holistic view as a system with relationships and interactions between people, processes, and technology. |
| Description | A system is more than the sum of its parts. It is made up of properties, behaviors, and characteristics that emerge from the interaction of its components. You must understand these interactions, not just the output. A system includes people, their interactions, external forces, and other relevant factors. |
| Effective Measures | Ability to communicate:<br>• how a change to a component affects the system as a whole,<br>• how a change to a system affects the environment it is in, and<br>• how systems adapt to internal and/or external pressures and changes. |

## 9.1.6 Conceptual Thinking

| | |
|---|---|
| Purpose | To understand large amounts of disparate information and how it fits into a larger picture; what details are important, and to connect seemingly abstract information. |
| Description | Conceptual thinking abstract thinking, creativity, intuition, past experiences, and knowledge to generate alternatives, understand where details fit into the larger context, and connect information and patterns that may not be obviously related. It is about understanding the linkage between contexts, solutions, needs, changes, stakeholders, and value abstractly and in the big picture. |
| Effective Measures | Ability to:<br>• connect disparate information and better understand the relationship,<br>• confidently understanding concepts being communicated,<br>• formulate abstract concepts using information and uncertainty, and<br>• draw on past experiences to understand the situation. |

### 9.1.7 Visual Thinking

| | |
|---|---|
| Purpose | To engage stakeholders and help them understand by translating complex concepts and models into understandable visual representations. |
| Description | Help stakeholders to quickly understand complex concepts by communicating them in graphical representations. |
| Effective Measures | • Communicate complex information through visual models,<br>• Convey comparisons, patterns, and ideas through visual models,<br>• Provide quick learning via visual models that can lead to increased productivity,<br>• Engage stakeholders at a deeper level, and<br>• Help stakeholders understand critical information. |

## 9.2 Behavioral Characteristics

Behavioral characteristics increases business analysis practitioner's effectiveness and impacts the outcome of their work effort. Always acting in an ethical manner, completing tasks on time and to expectations, efficiently delivering quality results, and demonstrating adaptability to changing needs gains the trust and respect of stakeholders. These characteristics include:

- Ethics
- Personal Accountability
- Trustworthiness
- Organization and Time Management
- Adaptability

**Figure 9.2.1: Behavioral Characteristics Competencies Diagram**

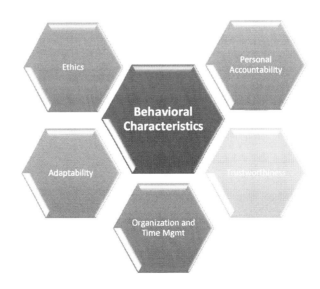

## 9.2.1 Ethics

| | |
|---|---|
| Purpose | To earn the trust and respect of the stakeholders by identifying when a proposed solution or requirement may present ethical difficulties. |
| Description | To identify when ethical dilemmas occur and recommend resolutions to these dilemmas. Focus on fairness, consideration, and moral behavior. Makes consideration of the impact that a proposed solution can have on all stakeholder groups and working to ensure that those groups are treated as fairly as possible, and understands the reasons for decisions. |
| Effective Measures | <ul><li>prompt identification and resolution of ethical dilemmas,</li><li>feedback from stakeholders confirming they feel decisions and actions are transparent and fair,</li><li>decisions made with consideration of the interests of all stakeholders,</li><li>reasoning for decisions that is clearly articulated and understood,</li><li>full and prompt disclosure of potential conflicts of interest, and</li><li>honesty regarding one's abilities, the performance of one's work, and accepting responsibility for failures or errors.</li></ul> |

## 9.2.2 Personal Accountability

| | |
|---|---|
| Purpose | Establishes credibility with stakeholders by ensuring business analysis tasks are completed on time and to expectations. |
| Description | Effectively planning business analysis work to achieve targets and goals, ensuring that value is delivered and aligned to business needs. Follow through on business analysis tasks to produce complete, accurate and relevant solutions. Ensure that decision makers have information needed to assess impact and make informed decisions. |
| Effective Measures | <ul><li>work effort is planned and easily articulated to others,</li><li>work is completed as planned or re-planned with sufficient reasoning and lead time,</li><li>status of both planned and unplanned work is known,</li><li>stakeholders feel that work is organized,</li><li>risks and issues are identified and appropriately acted on,</li><li>completely traceable requirements are delivered on time, and stakeholder needs are met.</li></ul> |

### 9.2.3 Trustworthiness

| | |
|---|---|
| Purpose | Earn the trust of the stakeholders so they will participate in business analysis activities to work to the common goal and have confidence in your recommendations and suggestions. |
| Description | Earning the trust of stakeholders is crucial to the business analysts' ability to collaborate with them to achieve their common goal. Several factors can contribute to earning trust:<br><br>• intentionally and consistently completing tasks and deliverables on time, within budget, and achieving expected results so that colleagues and stakeholders consider the business analyst's behavior dependable and diligent,<br><br>• presenting a consistent attitude of confidence, so that colleagues and stakeholders consider the business analyst's demeanor as strong,<br><br>• acting in an honest and straightforward manner, addressing conflict and concerns immediately so that colleagues and stakeholders consider the business analyst's morals as being honest and transparent, and<br><br>• maintaining a consistent schedule over a long period of time so that colleagues and stakeholders consider the business analyst's availability predictable and reliable. |
| Effective Measures | • stakeholders involve the business analyst in discussions and decision making,<br>• stakeholders bring issues and concerns to the business analyst,<br>• stakeholders are willing to discuss difficult or controversial topics with the business analyst,<br>• stakeholders do not blame the business analyst when problems occur,<br>• stakeholders respect the business analyst's ideas and referrals, and<br>• stakeholders respond to the business analyst's referrals with positive feedback. |

## 9.2.4 Organization and Time Management

| | |
|---|---|
| Purpose | Organization and Time Management skills will help you perform your tasks effectively and use time efficiently. |
| Description | Show ability to prioritize tasks, perform them efficiently, and manage time effectively to complete your work in a timely manner. Organize and store information and knowledge so it can be accessed and used on an ongoing basis. Be able to determine relevant and important information. Be able to set goals, use checklists to stay organized, manage interruptions, and show the ability to meet deadlines. |
| Effective Measures | <ul><li>the ability to produce deliverables in a timely manner,</li><li>stakeholders feel that the business analyst focuses on the correct tasks at the right time,</li><li>schedule of work effort and deadlines is managed and communicated to stakeholders,</li><li>stakeholders feel their time in meetings and in reading communications is well spent,</li><li>complete preparation for meetings, interviews, and requirements workshops,</li><li>relevant business analysis information is captured, organized, and documented,</li><li>adherence to the project schedule and the meeting of deadlines,</li><li>provides accurate, thorough, and concise information in a logical manner which is understood by stakeholders, and</li><li>maintains up-to-date information on the status of each work item and all outstanding work.</li></ul> |

### 9.2.5 Adaptability

| | |
|---|---|
| Purpose | Show the ability to adapt your behavior style and approach to effectively work in a rapidly changing environment with a variety of stakeholders. |
| Description | Show the ability to change techniques, style, methods, and approach to work effectively for a particular situation. Adjust your style to a manner that stakeholders prefer. This will increase your effectiveness in working with stakeholders, and therefore, the quality of the service you provide them. Have the curiosity to learn what others need and the courage to try different approaches to work to adjust to the given situation and context. Show the ability to adjust to changing goals, objectives, needs, stakeholders, risks, and priorities throughout the life cycle of an initiative. |
| Effective Measures | <ul><li>demonstrating the courage to act differently from others,</li><li>adapting to changing conditions and environments,</li><li>valuing and considering other points of view and approaches,</li><li>demonstrating a positive attitude in the face of ambiguity and change,</li><li>demonstrating a willingness to learn new methods, procedures, or techniques in order to accomplish goals and objectives,</li><li>changing behavior to perform effectively under changing or unclear conditions,</li><li>acquiring and applying new information and skills to address new challenges,</li><li>acceptance of having changes made to tasks, roles and project assignments as organizational realities change,</li><li>altering interpersonal style to highly diverse individuals and groups in a range of situations, and</li><li>evaluating what worked, what did not, and what could be done differently next time.</li></ul> |

## 9.3 Business Knowledge

Business knowledge is required for the business analyst to perform effectively within their business, industry, organization, solution, and methodology. Business knowledge enables the business analyst to better understand the overarching concepts that govern the structure, benefits, and value of the situation as it relates to a change or a need.

Business Knowledge underlying competencies include:
- Business Acumen
- Industry Knowledge
- Organization Knowledge
- Solution Knowledge
- Methodology Knowledge

**Figure 9.3.1: Business Knowledge Competencies Diagram**

### 9.3.1 Business Acumen

| | |
|---|---|
| Purpose | Requires understanding of fundamental business principles and best practices to ensure they are considered as solutions are reviewed. |
| Description | Use your experience and knowledge obtained from previous working relationships to show the ability to understand the business domain. Translate experience from similar practices but from a different perspective to help your current work effort. You may never have helped a Sales & Marketing department as a business analyst before, but you have seen advertisements and shopped online and in stores. Use that knowledge to understand the business concepts from a different perspective. |
| Effective Measures | <ul><li>demonstrating the ability to recognize potential limitations and opportunities,</li><li>demonstrating the ability to recognize when changes to a situation may require a change in the direction of an initiative or effort,</li><li>understanding the risks involved, ability to make decisions on managing risks,</li><li>demonstrating the ability to recognize an opportunity to decrease expenses and increase profits, and</li><li>understanding the options available to address emerging changes in the situation.</li></ul> |

### 9.3.2 Industry Knowledge

| | |
|---|---|
| Purpose | Show ability to understand current practices and activities within an industry, and across industries. |
| Description | Show understanding of:<br><br>    current trends    customer segments    suppliers<br>    market forces    Products    services<br>    market drivers    Practices    definitions<br>    key processes    Regulations    other factors<br><br>Also show understanding of how a company is positioned within an industry, and its impacts and dependencies to market and human resources. |
| Effective Measures | <ul><li>being aware of activities within both the enterprise and the broader industry,</li><li>having knowledge of major competitors and partners,</li><li>the ability to identify key trends shaping the industry,</li><li>being familiar with the largest customer segments,</li><li>having knowledge of common products and product types,</li><li>being knowledgeable of sources of information about the industry, including relevant trade organizations or journals,</li><li>understanding of industry specific terms, standards, processes and methodologies, and</li><li>understanding of the industry regulatory environment.</li></ul> |

# Chapter 9 Underlying Competencies

## 9.3.3 Organizational Knowledge

| | |
|---|---|
| Purpose | Show understanding of management structure and business architecture of an enterprise. |
| Description | Show understanding of how the enterprise makes profits, accomplishes goals, communication channels, relationships between business units, key stakeholders, and internal politics that influence decision making. |
| Effective Measures | • the ability to act according to informal and formal communications and authority channels,<br>• understanding of terminology or jargon used in the organization,<br>• understanding of the products or services offered by the organization,<br>• the ability to identify subject matter experts (SMEs) in the organization, and<br>• the ability to navigate organizational relationships and politics. |

## 9.3.4 Solution Knowledge

| | |
|---|---|
| Purpose | Show understanding of existing departments, environments, or technology to identify the most effective means of implementing change. |
| Description | Leverage previous experience to shorten the time frame of discovery of alternative options for a solution, including commercially available products and suppliers, enhancing the existing solution, or replace and rebuild internally. |
| Effective Measures | • reduced time or cost to implement a required change,<br>• shortened time on requirements analysis and/or solution design,<br>• understanding when a larger change is, or is not, justified based on business benefit, and<br>• understanding how additional capabilities that are present, but not currently used, can be deployed to provide value. |

### 9.3.5 Methodology Knowledge

| Purpose | Show an understanding of methodologies in use by the organization including context, dependencies, opportunities, and constraints. |
|---|---|
| Description | Methodologies determine the timing, approach, user roles, acceptable risk, and other aspects of how a change is approached and managed. Knowledge of variety of methodologies will allow you to adapt to what is in use in the organization. |
| Effective Measures | <ul><li>the ability to adapt to changes in methodologies,</li><li>the willingness to use or learn a new methodology,</li><li>the successful integration of business analysis tasks and techniques to support the current methodology,</li><li>familiarity with the terms, tools, and techniques prescribed by a methodology, and</li><li>the ability to play multiple roles within activities prescribed by a</li><li>methodology.</li></ul> |

## 9.4 Communication Skills

Effective communication skills help to deepen understanding and builds trust with stakeholders. Understanding the nuances of verbal, non-verbal, written communication, and listening skills, allows the business analyst to effectively collaborate with stakeholders. Words, gestures, and phrases may have different meanings to different people. This understanding may be influenced by native language, culture, motivations, priorities, and thinking style. The ability to adjust your communication style to fit a give set of stakeholders in a given context is an essential skill for business analysts.

Communication skills core competencies include:

- Verbal Communication
- Non-Verbal Communication
- Written Communication
- Listening

**Figure 9.4.1: Communication Skills Competencies Diagram**

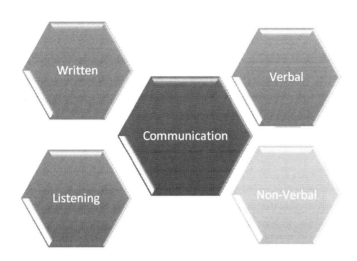

| 9.4.1 Verbal Communication | |
|---|---|
| Purpose | Effectively convey ideas, concepts, facts, and opinions through verbal communication. |
| Description | Use choice of words and tone of voice to effectively verbalize ideas and be easily understood by your stakeholders. |
| Effective Measures | <ul><li>restating concepts to ensure all stakeholders clearly understand the same information,</li><li>assisting conversations to reach productive conclusions,</li><li>delivering effective presentations by designing and positioning content and objectives appropriately, and</li><li>communicating an issue's important points in a calm and rational manner,</li><li>and presenting solution options.</li></ul> |

### 9.4.2 Non-Verbal Communication

| | |
|---|---|
| Purpose | Effectively send and receive messages through body movement, posture, facial expressions, gestures, and eye contact. |
| Description | Non-verbal communication conveys more meaning that words alone, spoken or written. Effective use of non-verbal communication can show a confident, trustworthy, capable business analyst...or not. |
| Effective Measures | <ul><li>being aware of body language in others, but not assuming a complete understanding through non-verbal communication,</li><li>intentional awareness of personal non-verbal communication,</li><li>improving trust and communication as a result of non-verbal communication, and</li><li>effectively addressing and resolving situations when a stakeholder's nonverbal communication does not agree with their verbal message.</li></ul> |

### 9.4.3 Written Communication

| | |
|---|---|
| Purpose | Effectively convey ideas, concepts, facts, and opinions through the written word. |
| Description | Utilize text, symbols, models, and sketches to convey and share information. Show the ability to tailor the message to the audience. A broad vocabulary, strong grasp of spelling, grammar, style, and technical jargon will help you effectively communicate with your stakeholders. |
| Effective Measures | <ul><li>adjusting the style of writing for the needs of the audience,</li><li>proper use of grammar and style,</li><li>choosing words the audience will understand the intended meaning of, and</li><li>ability of the reader to paraphrase and describe the content of the written communication.</li></ul> |

### 9.4.4 Listening

| | |
|---|---|
| Purpose | Show understanding of information that has been verbally communicated to you. |
| Description | Show ability to not only hear the words but understand their meaning. You may have to convey this message to other stakeholders, understanding the message is the first step of being able to communicate it to others. |
| Effective Measures | <ul><li>giving the speaker undivided attention,</li><li>acknowledging the speaker with verbal or non-verbal encouragement,</li><li>providing feedback to the person or the group that is speaking to ensure there is an understanding, and</li><li>using active listening skills by deferring judgment and responding appropriately.</li></ul> |

## 9.5 Interaction Skills

Interaction skills is the ability to relate, cooperate, and communicate with different kinds of people including executives, sponsors, colleagues, team members, developers, vendors, learning and development professionals, end users, customers, and subject matter experts (SMEs).

Interaction Skills core competencies include:
- Facilitation
- Leadership and Influencing
- Teamwork
- Negotiation and Conflict Resolution
- Teaching

**Figure 9.5.1: Interaction Skills Competencies Diagram**

### 9.5.1 Facilitation

| | |
|---|---|
| Purpose | Business analysts often facilitate conversations between stakeholders to support work and decisions. |
| Description | Facilitation is a skill for moderating discussions to assist participants to articulate their point of view while understanding the viewpoints of other participants. |
| Effective Measures | <ul><li>making it clear to the participants that the facilitator is a third party to the process and not a decision maker nor the owner of the topic,</li><li>encouraging participation from all attendees,</li><li>remaining neutral and not taking sides, but at the same time being impartial and intervening when required in order to make suggestions and offer insights,</li><li>establishing ground rules such as being open to suggestions, building on what is there, not dismissing ideas, and allowing others to speak and express themselves,</li><li>ensuring that participants in a discussion correctly understand each other's positions,</li><li>using meeting management skills and tools to keep discussions focused and organized,</li><li>preventing discussions from being sidetracked onto irrelevant topics, and</li><li>understanding and considering all parties' interests, motivations, and objectives.</li></ul> |

### 9.5.2 Leadership and Influencing

| | |
|---|---|
| Purpose | Ability to guide stakeholders through the discovery of requirements, pertinent information, and solution options. |
| Description | Show ability to motivate stakeholders to enable them to collaborate to achieve shared goals and objectives. Understanding the individual motives, needs, and capabilities of each stakeholder helps in meeting the shared objectives of the organization. |
| Effective Measures | <ul><li>reduced resistance to necessary changes,</li><li>articulation of a clear and inspiring vision of a desired future state,</li><li>success in inspiring others to turn vision into action,</li><li>influence on stakeholders to understand mutual interests,</li><li>effective use of collaboration techniques to influence others,</li><li>influence on stakeholders to consider broader objectives over personal motivations, and</li><li>re-framing issues so alternate perspectives can be understood and accommodated to influence stakeholders towards shared goals.</li></ul> |

Chapter 9 Underlying Competencies

### 9.5.3 Teamwork

| | |
|---|---|
| Purpose | Have the ability to work productively with team members, stakeholders, and any other vested partners toward a shared goal. |
| Description | Working as part of a team involves creating business relationships with those with whom you work. Understanding team dynamics and how they play a role as the team progresses through their work is crucial to your role on the team. Being able to handle team conflict can strengthen your role on the team. |
| Effective Measures | <ul><li>fostering a collaborative working environment,</li><li>effectively resolving conflict,</li><li>developing trust among team members,</li><li>support among the team for shared high standards of achievement, and</li><li>promoting a shared sense of ownership of the team goals.</li></ul> |

### 9.5.4 Negotiation and Conflict Resolution

| | |
|---|---|
| Purpose | Show ability to mediate negotiations between stakeholders and resolve differences of opinions while preserving the working relationships. |
| Description | This involves mediating discussions between participants in order to help them recognize that there are differing views on the topic, resolve differences, and reach conclusions that have the agreement of all participants. Successful negotiation and conflict resolution includes identifying the underlying interests of the parties, distinguishing those interests from their stated positions, and helping the parties identify solutions that satisfy those underlying interests |
| Effective Measures | <ul><li>a planned approach to ensure that the negotiation takes into account the tone of voice, the conveyed attitude, the methods used, and the concern for the other side's feelings and needs,</li><li>the ability to recognize that the needs of the parties are not always in opposition and that it is often possible to satisfy both parties without either side losing,</li><li>an objective approach to ensure the problem is separated from the person so that the real issues are debated without damaging working relationships, and</li><li>the ability to recognize that effective negotiation and conflict resolution are not always achieved in a single autonomous meeting, and that sometimes several meetings are required in order to achieve the stated goals.</li></ul> |

### 9.5.5 Teaching

| | |
|---|---|
| Purpose | Effectively communicate ideas, concepts, information and issues in a way that makes it easy for stakeholders to understand. |
| Description | Teaching is the process of leading others to gain knowledge. It is helping other learn contexts. It requires visual, verbal, written, and kinesthetic teaching skills. |
| Effective Measures | <ul><li>utilizing different methods to communicate information to be learned by</li><li>stakeholders,</li><li>discovering new information through high levels of stakeholder engagement,</li><li>validating that audiences have a clear understanding of the key messages that are intended to be learned, and</li><li>verifying that the stakeholders can demonstrate the new knowledge, facts, concepts, and ideas.</li></ul> |

## 9.6 Tools and Technology

Business analysts use a variety of software applications to support communication and collaboration, create and maintain requirements artifacts, model concepts, track issues, and increase overall productivity.

Requirements management technologies support requirements workflow, approvals, baselining, and change control. These technologies can also support the traceability between requirements and assist in determining the impact of changes to requirements.

Interacting with the stakeholders and team members may require the use of communication and collaboration tools, as well as presentation software in order to showcase ideas and generate discussion among stakeholders and team members.

Business Analysis Tools and Technology core competencies include:
- Office Productivity Tools and Technology
- Business Analysis Tools and Technology
- Communication Tools and Technology

### Figure 9.6.1: Tools and Technology Competencies Diagram

| 9.6.1 Office Productivity Tools and Technology | |
|---|---|
| Purpose | To document and track information and artifacts. |
| Description | They provide the ability to organize, dissect, manipulate, understand, and communicate information. Utilizing these tools requires becoming familiar with available resources, and understanding one software program may provide insights into comparable abilities or operations in similar programs. |
| Effective Measures | • increased efficiencies and streamlining of processes by exploring features and functions of tools,<br>• awareness of available tools, their operation, and abilities,<br>• the ability to determine the tool that will best meet stakeholder needs, and<br>• the ability to clearly communicate the major features of available tools. |

### 9.6.2 Business Analysis Tools and Technology

| | |
|---|---|
| Purpose | To model, document, and manage outputs of business analysis activities and deliverables to stakeholders. |
| Description | Some business analysis tools and technologies focus solely on a single business analysis activity and some integrate multiple business analysis functions into a single tool. Tools specifically designed for business analysis may include such functionality as modeling, requirements management, issue tracking, prototyping and simulation, computer aided software engineering (CASE), and survey engines. |
| Effective Measures | <ul><li>the ability to apply an understanding of one tool and other similar tools,</li><li>being able to identify major tools currently available and describe their strengths, weaknesses, and how they may be used in any given situation,</li><li>understanding of and the ability to use the major features of the tool,</li><li>ability to select a tool or tools that support organizational processes,</li><li>the ability to use the tools to complete requirements-related activities more rapidly than otherwise possible, and</li><li>the ability to track changes to the requirements and their impact on the solution implementation, stakeholders, and value.</li></ul> |

### 9.6.3 Communication Tools and Technology

| | |
|---|---|
| Purpose | To perform business analysis activities, manage teams, and collaborate with stakeholders. |
| Description | Communication tools are used to plan and complete tasks related to conversational interactions and collaborative interactions. Communication tools allow business analysts to work with virtual and co-located teams. Understanding the options available with these tools can enable more efficient and accurate communication and more effective decision making. |
| Effective Measures | <ul><li>the selection of appropriate and effective tools for the audience and purpose,</li><li>effectively choosing when to use communication technology and when not to,</li><li>the ability to identify tools to meet communication needs, and understanding of and the ability to use features of the tool.</li></ul> |

# 10 Techniques

Techniques are methods business analysts use to perform business analysis tasks. The *BABOK® Guide* contains the techniques most commonly used by business analysts in performing their duties.

This chapter provides a summary of the 50 techniques in the *BABOK® Guide*. As a summary it does not provide the detail that is in the BABOK, but gives a level of detail that allows someone new to the concept a basic understanding of the technique. As suggested in chapter 1 of this guide, we suggest that you study each technique by utilizing both the BABOK and this study guide at the same time.

## Techniques Usage by Knowledge Area

**KNOWLEDGE AREA KEY:**

**BAPM**: Business Analysis Planning and Monitoring  **SA**: Strategy Analysis

**EC**: Elicitation and Collaboration  **RADD**: Requirements Analysis and Design Definition

**RLCM**: Requirements Life Cycle Management  **SE**: Solution Evaluation

| # | Technique Name | BAPM | EC | RCLM | SA | RADD | SE |
|---|---|---|---|---|---|---|---|
| 10.1 | Acceptance and Evaluation Criteria | | | X | X | X | X |
| 10.2 | Backlog Management | | | X | | X | |
| 10.3 | Balanced Scorecard | | | | X | | |
| 10.4 | Benchmarking and Market Analysis | | X | | X | X | X |
| 10.5 | Brainstorming | X | X | | X | X | X |
| 10.6 | Business Capability Analysis | | | | X | X | |
| 10.7 | Business Cases | X | | X | X | X | X |
| 10.8 | Business Model Canvas | | | | X | X | |
| 10.9 | Business Rules Analysis | X | X | X | | X | X |
| 10.10 | Collaborative Games | | X | | | | |
| 10.11 | Concept Modeling | | X | | X | X | |
| 10.12 | Data Dictionary | | | | | X | |
| 10.13 | Data Flow Diagrams | | | X | | X | |
| 10.14 | Data Mining | | X | | X | | X |

| # | Technique Name | BAPM | EC | RCLM | SA | RADD | SE |
|---|---|---|---|---|---|---|---|
| 10.15 | Data Modeling | | X | X | | X | |
| 10.16 | Decision Analysis | | | X | X | X | X |
| 10.17 | Decision Modeling | | | | X | X | |
| 10.18 | Document Analysis | X | X | X | X | X | X |
| 10.18 | Estimation | X | X | X | X | X | |
| 10.20 | Financial Analysis | X | | X | X | X | X |
| 10.21 | Focus Groups | | X | | X | X | X |
| 10.22 | Functional Decomposition | X | | X | X | X | |
| 10.23 | Glossary | | | | | X | |
| 10.24 | Interface Analysis | | X | X | | X | |
| 10.25 | Interviews | X | X | X | X | X | X |
| 10.26 | Item Tracking | X | | X | X | X | X |
| 10.27 | Lessons Learned | X | X | | X | X | X |
| 10.28 | Metrics and Key Performance Indicators (KPIs) | X | | | X | X | X |
| 10.29 | Mind Mapping | X | X | | X | X | |
| 10.30 | Non-Functional Requirements Analysis | | | | | X | X |
| 10.31 | Observation | X | X | | X | | X |
| 10.32 | Organizational Modeling | X | | | X | X | X |
| 10.33 | Prioritization | | | X | | | X |
| 10.34 | Process Analysis | X | X | | X | | X |
| 10.35 | Process Modeling | X | X | X | X | X | X |
| 10.36 | Prototyping | | X | | X | X | X |
| 10.37 | Reviews | X | X | X | | X | |
| 10.38 | Risk Analysis and Management | X | X | X | X | X | X |
| 10.39 | Roles and Permissions Matrix | | | | | X | X |
| 10.40 | Root Cause Analysis | X | | | X | X | X |
| 10.41 | Scope Modeling | X | | X | X | X | |
| 10.42 | Sequence Diagrams | | | | | X | |
| 10.43 | Stakeholder List, Map or Personas | X | X | | | X | |
| 10.44 | State Modeling | | | | | X | |
| 10.45 | Survey or Questionnaire | X | X | | X | X | X |
| 10.46 | SWOT Analysis | | | | X | X | X |
| 10.47 | Use Cases and Scenarios | | | X | | X | X |
| 10.48 | User Stories | | | X | | X | |
| 10.49 | Vendor Assessment | | | | X | X | X |
| 10.50 | Workshops | X | X | X | X | X | X |

# Techniques

## 10.1 Acceptance and Evaluation Criteria

| | |
|---|---|
| Purpose | Used to assess and compare solutions, alternative designs, and requirements. They provide objective and consistent of all solutions and designs across the project and enterprise. |
| Description | **Acceptance Criteria:** used to define the minimum set of conditions for a solution to consider it acceptable by stakeholders and worth implementing. *(assess one solution)* <br><br> **Evaluation Criteria:** used to assess a set of requirements in order to choose between alternative solution options or designs. *(deciding between multiple solutions)* |
| Details | Acceptance criteria are written textual statements of value attributes that a solution must have to satisfy the stakeholders needs. These are attached to requirements or user stories. They must be written in such a way that a test case can be written to verify that the solution meets that criteria *(testable)*. Evaluation criteria provide a way to determine if a solution component provides value to stakeholders. |
| Strengths | - Agile methodologies may require that all requirements be expressed in the form of testable acceptance criteria.<br>- Acceptance criteria are necessary when the requirements express contractual obligations.<br>- Acceptance criteria provide the ability to assess requirements based on agreed-upon criteria.<br>- Evaluation criteria provide the ability to assess diverse needs based on agreed-upon criteria, such as features, common indicators, local or global benchmarks, and agreed ratios.<br>- Evaluation criteria assist in the delivery of expected return on investment (ROI) or otherwise specified potential value.<br>- Evaluation criteria helps in defining priorities. |
| Limitations | - Acceptance criteria may express contractual obligations and as such maybe difficult to change for legal or political reasons.<br>- Achieving agreement on evaluation criteria for different needs among diverse stakeholders can be challenging. |
| Knowledge Areas | RLCM, SA, RADD, SE |

## 10.2 Backlog Management

| | |
|---|---|
| Purpose | A planning approach to record, track, and prioritize remaining work items for an initiative. |
| Description | A backlog occurs when the remaining work exceeds the delivery team's capacity to complete them. The backlog is an ordered and prioritized list of items for the team to complete. The backlog rarely stays stagnant. Items are added to the backlog and the team removes items from the backlog that they have completed through the time of the initiative. Items at the top of the backlog have the greatest value to stakeholders, and therefore, the highest priority. These are the items that the team should work on next to deliver. |
| Details | **Backlog items:** the individual items on the backlog, sometimes called product backlog items (PBIs). These are typically user stories, but can be other types of items such as use cases, defects, change requests, etc.<br><br>**Priority:** items on the backlog must be prioritized so that the delivery team knows which items the stakeholders consider the most valuable; so that they can plan their work to deliver the items. Backlog items are prioritized relative to other items on the backlog. Stakeholders priorities change over time, so backlog item priorities may change over time.<br><br>**Estimation:** each item needs to be estimated as to how much effort the delivery team must put in to deliver the solution for the backlog item. Each backlog item must be described in enough detail so that a fairly accurate estimation can be determined. When an item is first added to the backlog, it may not have enough detail to estimate. The item is elaborated over time until enough detail is known that the team can give a relative estimation of the item.<br><br>**Manage the backlog:** things change over time; stakeholders' priorities, business environment changes, organizational changes, and other changes may affect priorities and the value of backlog items. Items may need removed because they are no longer valuable to the stakeholders. |
| Strengths | - An effective approach to responding to changing stakeholder needs and priorities because the next work items selected from the backlog are always aligned with current stakeholder priorities.<br>- Only items near the top of the backlog are elaborated and estimated in detail; items near the bottom of the backlog reflect lower priorities and receive less attention and effort.<br>- Can be an effective communication vehicle because stakeholders can understand what items are about to be worked on, what items are scheduled farther out, and which ones may not be worked on for some time. |
| Limitations | - Large backlogs may become cumbersome and difficult to manage.<br>- It takes experience to be able to break down the work to be done into enough detail for accurate estimation.<br>- A lack of detail in the items in the backlog can result in lost information over time. |
| Knowledge Areas | RCLM, RADD |

# Chapter 10 Techniques

## 10.3 Balanced Scorecard

| | |
|---|---|
| Purpose | To manage performance in any business model, organizational structure, or business process. |
| Description | A strategic planning and management tool used to measure organizational performance beyond the traditional financial measures. It is outcome focused and provides a balanced view of an enterprise by implementing the strategic plan as an active framework of objectives and performance measures. |
| Details | The balanced scorecard is composed of four dimensions: Learning and Growth, Business Process, Customer, and Financial. The balanced scorecard includes tangible objectives, specific measures, and targeted outcomes derived from an organization's vision and strategy. |
| Strengths | <ul><li>Facilitates holistic and balanced planning and thinking.</li><li>Short-, medium-, and long-term goals can be harmonized into programs with incremental success measures.</li><li>Strategic, tactical, and operational teams are more easily aligned in their work.</li><li>Encourages forward thinking and competitiveness.</li></ul> |
| Limitations | <ul><li>A lack of a clear strategy makes aligning the dimensions difficult.</li><li>Can be seen as the single tool for strategic planning rather than just one tool to be used in a suite of strategic planning tools.</li><li>Can be misinterpreted as a replacement for strategic planning, execution, and measurement.</li></ul> |
| Knowledge Areas | SA |

## 10.4 Benchmarking and Market Analysis

| | |
|---|---|
| Purpose | Analytical technique to improve organizational operations, increase customer satisfaction, and increase value to stakeholders. |
| Description | Benchmark studies are conducted to compare organizational practices against the best-in-class practices. The objective of benchmarking is to evaluate enterprise performance and ensure that the enterprise is operating efficiently. Benchmarking may also be performed against standards for compliance purposes. The results from the benchmark study may initiate change within an organization.<br><br>Market analysis involves researching customers in order to determine the products and services that they need or want, the factors that influence their decisions to purchase, and the competitors that exist in the market. The objective of market analysis is to acquire this information in order to support the various decision-making processes within an organization. Market analysis can also help determine when to exit a market. It may be used to determine if partnering, merging, or divesting are viable alternatives for an enterprise. |
| Details | Benchmarking includes identifying the areas to be studied, identifying enterprises that are leaders in the sector (including competitors), conducting a survey of selected enterprises to understand their practices, using a Request for Information (RFI) to gather information about capabilities, arranging visits to best-in-class organizations, determining gaps between current and best practices, and developing a project proposal to implement best practices.<br><br>Market Analysis requires that business analysts identify customers and understand their preferences, identify opportunities that may increase value to stakeholders, identify competitors and investigate their operations, look for trends in the market, anticipate growth rate, and estimate potential profitability, define appropriate business strategies, gather market data, use existing resources such as company records, research studies, and books and apply that information to the questions at hand, and review data to determine trends and draw conclusions. |
| Strengths | <ul><li>Benchmarking provides organizations with information about new and different methods, ideas, and tools to improve organizational performance.</li><li>An organization may use benchmarking to identify best practices by its competitors in order to meet or exceed its competition.</li><li>Benchmarking identifies why similar companies are successful and what processes they used to become successful.</li><li>Market analysis can target specific groups and can be tailored to answer specific questions.</li><li>Market analysis may expose weaknesses within a certain company or industry.</li><li>Market analysis may identify differences in product offerings and services that are available from a competitor.</li></ul> |

## 10.4 Benchmarking and Market Analysis

| | |
|---|---|
| Limitations | - Benchmarking is time-consuming; organizations may not have the expertise to conduct the analysis and interpret useful information.<br>- Benchmarking cannot produce innovative solutions or solutions that will produce a sustainable competitive advantage because it involves assessing solutions that have been shown to work elsewhere with the goal of reproducing them.<br>- Market analysis can be time-consuming and expensive, and the results may not be immediately available.<br>- Without market segmentation, market analysis may not produce the expected results or may provide incorrect data about a competitor's products or services. |
| Knowledge Areas | EC, SA, RADD, SE |

## 10.5 Brainstorming

| | |
|---|---|
| Purpose | To foster creative thinking about a problem. The aim of brainstorming is to produce numerous new ideas, and to derive from them themes for further analysis. |
| Description | Brainstorming is a technique intended to produce a broad or diverse set of options.<br><br>It helps answer specific questions such as (but not limited to):<br>• What options are available to resolve the issue at hand?<br>• What factors are constraining the group from moving ahead with an approach or option?<br>• What could be causing a delay in activity 'A'?<br>• What can the group do to solve problem 'B'?<br><br>This is a facilitation technique to focus a group of stakeholders on one specific problem or topic with the goal of cultivating as many ideas on that problem or topic as possible in a short amount of time. You should encourage stakeholders to create ideas without judgement on them, that will come later. When facilitated properly, brainstorming can be fun, engaging, and productive. |
| Details | **1. Preparation**: Define Area of Interest → Determine Time Limit → Identify Participants → Establish Evaluation Criteria<br><br>**2. Session**: Share Ideas → Record Ideas → Build on each others ideas → Elicit as many ideas as possible<br><br>**3. Wrap-up**: Discuss and Evaluate → Create List → Rate Ideas → Distribute Final List<br><br>© 2017 International Institute of Business Analysis |
| Strengths | • Ability to elicit many ideas in a short time period.<br>• Non-judgmental environment enables creative thinking.<br>• Can be useful during a workshop to reduce tension between participants. |
| Limitations | • Participation is dependent on individual creativity and willingness to participate.<br>• Organizational and interpersonal politics may limit overall participation.<br>• Group participants must agree to avoid debating the ideas raised during brainstorming. |
| Knowledge Areas | BAPM, EC, SA, RADD, SE |

## 10.6 Business Capability Analysis

| | |
|---|---|
| Purpose | Provide a framework for scoping and planning by generating a shared understanding of outcomes, identifying alignment with strategy, and providing a scope and prioritization filter. |
| Description | Describes current capabilities of the enterprise, or part of the enterprise. Used to identify capability gaps to obtaining a business goal or objective. This is done by comparing what activities are needed to achieve that goal or object to current activities of the enterprise. The missing activities, what the enterprise doesn't currently do that they need to, is the capability gap. |
| Details | Capabilities are the abilities of an enterprise to perform or transform something that helps achieve the business goal or objective. Capabilities are used to increase or protect revenue, reduce or prevent cost, improve service, achieve compliance, or position the company for the future. Performance of capabilities, and enabling a capability change, comes with risk; in either business risk, technology risk, organizational risk or market risk. Business Capability Analysis is used for strategic planning for the enterprise. |
| Strengths | <ul><li>Provides a shared articulation of outcomes, strategy, and performance, which help create very focused and aligned initiatives.</li><li>Helps align business initiatives across multiple aspects of the organization.</li><li>Useful when assessing the ability of an organization to offer new products and services.</li></ul> |
| Limitations | <ul><li>Requires an organization to agree to collaborate on this model.</li><li>When created unilaterally or in a vacuum it fails to deliver on the goals of alignment and shared understanding.</li><li>Requires a broad, cross-functional collaboration in defining the capability model and the value framework.</li></ul> |
| Knowledge Areas | SA, RADD |

### Figure 10.6.1: Business Capability Gap Map Example

| ORGANIZATIONAL ANALYSIS | Business Value | | | Customer Value | | | Performance Gap | | | Risk | | |
|---|---|---|---|---|---|---|---|---|---|---|---|---|
| | High | Med | Low | High | Med | Low | High | Med | Low | High | Med | Low |
| Capability Analysis | ■ | | | | | ░ | ■ | | | | ▓ | |
| Root Cause Analysis | | | ░ | ■ | | | | | | | | ░ |
| Process Analysis | | ▓ | | ■ | | | | | ░ | | ▓ | |
| Stakeholder Analysis | ■ | | | ■ | | | | ▓ | | ■ | | |
| Roadmap Construction | | ▓ | | | ▓ | | | ▓ | | | ▓ | |

| PROJECT ANALYSIS | Business Value | | | Customer Value | | | Performance Gap | | | Risk | | |
|---|---|---|---|---|---|---|---|---|---|---|---|---|
| | High | Med | Low | High | Med | Low | High | Med | Low | High | Med | Low |
| Requirements Elicitation | ■ | | | | ▓ | | ■ | | | | | ░ |
| Requirements Management | | ▓ | | ■ | | | | | ░ | ■ | | |
| Requirements Communication | ■ | | | | | ░ | | ▓ | | | | ░ |
| User Acceptance Testing | | ▓ | | | ▓ | | | ▓ | | ■ | | |
| Usability Testing | | | ░ | | ▓ | | | | ░ | | ▓ | |

| PROFESSIONAL DEVELOPMENT | Business Value | | | Customer Value | | | Performance Gap | | | Risk | | |
|---|---|---|---|---|---|---|---|---|---|---|---|---|
| | High | Med | Low | High | Med | Low | High | Med | Low | High | Med | Low |
| Organizational Consulting | | ▓ | | ■ | | | | | | | | |
| Project Analysis Consulting | | | ░ | | | ░ | ■ | | | | | ░ |
| Training | ■ | | | ■ | | | ■ | | | | ▓ | |
| Mentoring | | | ░ | | | | | | ░ | | | |
| Resources Maintenance | | ▓ | | | ▓ | | | ▓ | | ■ | | |

| MANAGEMENT | Business Value | | | Customer Value | | | Performance Gap | | | Risk | | |
|---|---|---|---|---|---|---|---|---|---|---|---|---|
| | High | Med | Low | High | Med | Low | High | Med | Low | High | Med | Low |
| Performance Management | ■ | | | | ▓ | | | | | ■ | | |
| Resource Allocations | | | ░ | | ▓ | | ■ | | | | ▓ | |
| Employee Dev Planning | | | ░ | | ▓ | | | | ░ | ■ | | |

© 2015 International Institute of Business Analysis

## 10.7 Business Cases

| | |
|---|---|
| Purpose | Provide a justification for a course of action based on the benefits to be realized by using the proposed solution, as compared to the cost, effort, and other considerations to acquire and live with that solution. |
| Description | A business case captures the rationale for undertaking a change. Typically, a formal textual document with sufficient detail to inform and request approval without providing specific details about the method and/or approach to the implementation of the change. It is used to define the need, define desired outcome, assess alternative solutions, and recommend a solution. |
| Details | The **need** is the driver for the business case. It is the relevant business goal or objective that must be met. Objectives are linked to a strategy or the strategies of the enterprise. The need assessment identifies the problem or the potential opportunity.<br><br>The **desired outcomes** describe the state which should result if the need is fulfilled. They should include measurable outcomes that can be utilized to determine the success of the business case or the solution.<br><br>The business case identifies and assesses various **alternative solutions**. Alternatives may include (but are not limited to) different technologies, processes, or business models. Alternatives may also include different ways of acquiring these and different timing options. The 'do-nothing' alternative should be assessed and considered for the recommended solution. Each alternative should be assessed in terms of scope, feasibility, assumptions, risks and constraints, financial analysis and value assessment.<br><br>The **recommended solution** describes the most desirable way to solve the problem or leverage the opportunity. The solution is described in sufficient detail for decision makers to understand the solution and determine if the recommendation will be implemented. |
| Strengths | • Provides an amalgamation of the complex facts, issues, and analysis required to make decisions regarding change.<br>• Provides a detailed financial analysis of cost and benefits.<br>• Provides guidance for ongoing decision making throughout the initiative. |
| Limitations | • May be subject to the biases of authors.<br>• Frequently not updated once funding for the initiative is secured.<br>• Contains assumptions regarding costs and benefits that may prove invalid upon further investigation. |
| Knowledge Areas | BAPM, RLCM, SA, RADD, SE |

## 10.8 Business Model Canvas

| | |
|---|---|
| Purpose | Describes how an enterprise creates, delivers, and captures value for and from its customers. |
| Description | A business model canvas is comprised of nine building blocks that describe how an organization intends to deliver value:<br><br>- Key Partnerships
- Key Activities
- Key Resources
- Value Proposition
- Customer Relationships
- Channels
- Customer Segments
- Cost Structures
- Revenue Stream<br><br>These building blocks are arranged on a business canvas that shows the relationship between the organization's operations, finance, customers, and offerings. The business model canvas also serves as a blueprint for implementing a strategy. A business model canvas can be used as a diagnostic and planning tool regarding strategy and initiatives. |
| Details | **Key partnerships** frequently involve some degree of sharing of proprietary information, including technologies. The benefits in engaging in key partnerships include optimization and economy, reduction of risk and uncertainty, acquisition of particular resources and activities, and lack of internal capabilities.<br><br>**Key activities** are those that are critical to the creation, delivery, and maintenance of value, as well as other activities that support the operation of the enterprise. Key activities can be classified as:<br><br>- **Value-add**: characteristics, features, and business activities for which the customer is willing to pay.
- **Non-value-add**: aspects and activities for which the customer is not willing to pay.
- **Business non-value-add**: characteristics that must be included in the offering, activities performed to meet regulatory and other needs, or costs associated with doing business, for which the customer is not willing to pay.<br><br>**Key Resources** are the assets needed to execute a business model. Resources can be classified as physical, financial, intellectual, or human.<br><br>A **value proposition** represents what a customer is willing to exchange for having their needs met. The proposition may consist of a single product or service, or may be comprised of a set of goods and services that are bundled together to address the needs of a customer or customer segment to help them solve their problem.<br><br>**Customer relationships** are classified as customer acquisition and customer retention. The methods used in establishing and maintaining customer relationships vary depending on the level of interaction desired and the method of communication. |

## 10.8 Business Model Canvas

|  |  |
|---|---|
|  | **Channels** are the different ways an enterprise interacts with and delivers value to its customers. |
|  | **Customer segments** group customers with common needs and attributes so that the enterprise can more effectively and efficiently address the needs of each segment. |
|  | **Cost structure** is made up of the cost to produce product or service, and conduct the activities within an enterprise. |
|  | A **revenue stream** is a way or method by which revenue comes into an enterprise from each customer segment in exchange for the realization of a value proposition. |
| Strengths | - It is a widely used and effective framework that can be used to understand and optimize business models.<br>- It is simple to use and easy to understand. |
| Limitations | - Does not account for alternative measures of value such as social and environmental impacts.<br>- The primary focus on value propositions does not provide a holistic insight for business strategy.<br>- Does not include the strategic purpose of the enterprise within the canvas. |
| Knowledge Areas | SA, RADD |

## 10.9 Business Rules Analysis

| | |
|---|---|
| Purpose | To identify, express, validate, refine, and organize the rules that shape day-to-day business behavior and guide operational business decision making. |
| Description | Business policies and rules guide the day-to-day operation of the business and its processes, and shape operational business decisions. A business policy is a directive concerned with broadly controlling, influencing, or regulating the actions of an enterprise and the people in it. A business rule is a specific, testable directive that serves as a criterion for guiding behavior, shaping judgments, or making decisions.<br><br>Analysis of business rules involves capturing business rules from sources, expressing them clearly, validating them with stakeholders, refining them to best align with business goals, and organizing them so they can be effectively managed and reused. |
| Details | Business rules require consistent use of business terms, a glossary of definitions for the underlying business concepts, and an understanding of the structural connections among the concepts.<br><br>Definitional rules shape concepts, or produce knowledge or information. They indicate something that is necessarily true (or untrue) about some concept, thereby supplementing its definition.<br><br>Behavioral rules are people rules—even if the behavior is automated. Behavioral rules serve to shape (govern) day-to-day business activity. They do so by placing some obligation or prohibition on conduct, action, practice, or procedure. |
| Strengths | • When enforced and managed by a single enterprise-wide engine, changes to business rules can be implemented quickly.<br>• A centralized repository creates the ability to reuse business rules across an organization.<br>• Business rules provide structure to govern business behaviors.<br>• Clearly defining and managing business rules allows organizations to make changes to policy without altering processes or systems. |
| Limitations | • Organizations may produce lengthy lists of ambiguous business rules.<br>• Business rules can contradict one another or produce unanticipated results when combined unless validated against one another.<br>• If available vocabulary is insufficiently rich, not business-friendly, or poorly defined and organized, resulting business rules will be inaccurate or contradictory. |
| Knowledge Areas | BAPM, EC, RCLM, RADD, SE |

## 10.10 Collaborative Games

| | |
|---|---|
| Purpose | Get participants in an elicitation activity to collaborate in building a joint understanding of a problem or a solution. |
| Description | Elicitation technique inspired by game play. Each game includes rules to keep participants focused on a specific objective. The games are used to help the participants share their knowledge and experience on a given topic, identify hidden assumptions, and explore that knowledge in ways that may not occur during the course of normal interactions. Collaborative games often benefit from the involvement of a neutral facilitator who helps the participants understand the rules of the game and enforces those rules. |
| Details | Each collaborative game has a defined purpose. The facilitator helps the participants in the game understand the purpose and work toward the successful realization of that purpose. Games typically have at least three steps:<br>1. an opening step, in which the participants get involved, learn the rules of the game, and start generating ideas,<br>2. the exploration step, in which participants engage with one another and look for connections between their ideas, test those ideas, and experiment with new ideas, and<br>3. a closing step, in which the ideas are assessed and participants work out which ideas are likely to be the most useful and productive.<br>At the end of a collaborative game, the facilitator and participants work through the results and determine any decisions or actions that need to be taken as a result of what the participants have learned. |
| Strengths | • May reveal hidden assumptions or differences of opinion.<br>• Encourages creative thinking by stimulating alternative mental processes.<br>• Challenges participants who are normally quiet or reserved to take a more active role in team activities.<br>• Some collaborative games can be useful in exposing business needs that aren't being met. |
| Limitations | • The playful nature of the games may be perceived as silly and make participants with reserved personalities or cultural norms uncomfortable.<br>• Games can be time-consuming and may be perceived as unproductive, especially if the objectives or outcomes are unclear.<br>• Group participation can lead to a false sense of confidence in the conclusions reached. |
| Knowledge Areas | EC |

## 10.11 Concept Modeling

| | |
|---|---|
| Purpose | To organize the business vocabulary needed to consistently and thoroughly communicate the knowledge of a domain. |
| Description | A concept model starts with a glossary, which typically focuses on the core noun concepts of a domain. Concept models put a premium on high-quality, design- independent definitions that are free of data or implementation biases. Concept models also emphasize rich vocabulary. Concept models can be effective where:<br><br>• the enterprise seeks to organize, retain, build-on, manage, and communicate core knowledge,<br>• the initiative needs to capture large numbers of business rules,<br>• there is resistance from stakeholders about the perceived technical nature of data models, class diagrams, or data element nomenclature and definition,<br>• innovative solutions are sought when re-engineering business processes or other aspects of business capability, and<br>• the enterprise faces regulatory or compliance challenges. |
| Details | **Noun concepts** of the domain are simply 'givens' for the space.<br>**Verb concepts** provide basic structural connections between noun concepts.<br>Since concept models must support rich meaning (semantics), other types of standard **connections** are used besides verb concepts. These include but are not limited to categorizations, classifications, partitive connections, and roles. |
| Strengths | • Provide a business-friendly way to communicate with stakeholders about precise meanings and subtle distinctions.<br>• Is independent of data design biases and the often limited business vocabulary coverage of data models.<br>• Proves highly useful for white-collar, knowledge-rich, decision-laden business processes.<br>• Helps ensure that large numbers of business rules and complex decision tables are free of ambiguity and fit together cohesively. |
| Limitations | • May set expectations too high about how much integration based on business semantics can be achieved on relatively short notice.<br>• Requires a specialized skill set based on the ability to think abstractly and non- procedurally about know-how and knowledge.<br>• The knowledge-and-rule focus may be foreign to stakeholders.<br>• Requires tooling to actively support real-time use of standard business terminology in writing business rules, requirements, and other forms of business communication. |
| Knowledge Areas | EC, SA, RADD |

# Chapter 10 Techniques

## 10.12 Data Dictionary

| | |
|---|---|
| Purpose | To standardize a definition of a data element and enable a common interpretation of data elements. |
| Description | A data dictionary is used to document standard definitions of data elements, their meanings, and allowable values. A data dictionary contains definitions of each data element and indicates how those elements combine into composite data elements. |
| Details | Data dictionaries describe data element characteristics including the description of the data element in the form of a definition that will be used by stakeholders. For each data element it defines name, alias, values/meanings, and descriptions. |
| Strengths | • Provides all stakeholders with a shared understanding of the format and content of relevant information.<br>• A single repository of corporate metadata promotes the use of data throughout the organization in a consistent manner. |
| Limitations | • Requires regular maintenance, otherwise the metadata could become obsolete or incorrect.<br>• All maintenance is required to be completed in a consistent manner in order to ensure that stakeholders can quickly and easily retrieve the information they need. This requires time and effort on the part of the stewards responsible for the accuracy and completeness of the data dictionary.<br>• Unless care is taken to consider the metadata required by multiple scenarios, it may have limited value across the enterprise. |
| Knowledge Areas | RADD |

## 10.13 Data Flow Diagrams

| | |
|---|---|
| Purpose | Pictorial diagram to show how data flows through activities within a system, how it is stored, and between the system and external entities. |
| Description | Data flow diagrams portray the transformation of data. They are useful for depicting a transaction-based system and illustrating the boundaries of a physical, logical, or manual system. <br><br> A data flow diagram illustrates the movement and transformation of data between external entities and processes. The output from one external or process is the input to another. The data flow diagram also illustrates the temporary or permanent repositories (referred to as data stores or terminators) where data is stored within a system or an organization. |
| Details | An **external** (entity, source, sink) is a person, organization, automated system, or any device capable of producing data or receiving data. An external is an object which is outside of the system under analysis. Externals are the sources and/or destinations (sinks) of the data. <br><br> A **data store** is a collection of data where data may be read repeatedly and where it can be stored for future use. <br><br> A **process** can be a manual or automated activity performed for a business reason. <br><br> A **data flow** is the movement of data between an external, a process, and a data store. |
| Strengths | <ul><li>May be used as a discovery technique for processes and data or as a Technique for the verification of functional decompositions or data models.</li><li>Are excellent ways to define the scope of a system and all of the systems, interfaces, and user interfaces that attach to it. Allows for estimation of the effort needed to study the work.</li><li>Most users find these data flow diagrams relatively easy to understand.</li><li>Helps to identify duplicated data elements or misapplied data elements.</li><li>Illustrates connections to other systems.</li><li>Helps define the boundaries of a system.</li><li>Can be used as part of system documentation.</li><li>Helps to explain the logic behind the data flow within a system.</li></ul> |
| Limitations | <ul><li>Using data flow diagrams for large-scale systems can become complex and difficult for stakeholders to understand.</li><li>Different methods of notation with different symbols could create challenges pertaining to documentation.</li><li>Does not illustrate a sequence of activities.</li><li>Data transformations (processes) say little about the process or stakeholder.</li></ul> |
| Knowledge Areas | RLCM, RADD |

**Figure 10.13.1: Data Flow Diagram (Level 1) using Yourdon Notation**

Chapter 10 Techniques

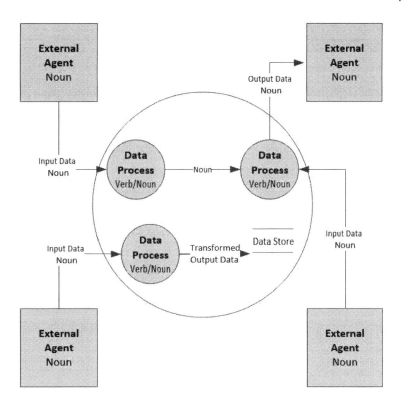

Figure 10.13.2: Data Flow Diagram using Yourdon Notation

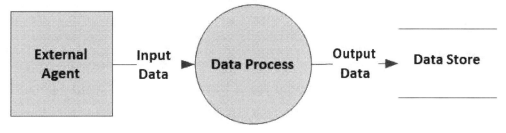

## 10.14 Data Mining

| | |
|---|---|
| Purpose | To improve decision making by finding useful patterns and insights from data. |
| Description | Data mining is an analytic process that examines large amounts of data from different perspectives and summarizes the data in such a way that useful patterns and relationships are discovered. The results of data mining techniques are generally mathematical models or equations that describe underlying patterns and relationships. |
| Details | The goal and scope of data mining is established either in terms of decision requirements for an important identified business decision, or in terms of a functional area where relevant data will be mined for domain-specific pattern discovery. Data mining tools work on an analytical dataset. This is generally formed by merging records from multiple tables or sources into a single, wide dataset. Once the data is available, it is analyzed. A wide variety of statistical measures are typically applied and visualization tools used to see how data values are distributed, what data is missing, and how various calculated characteristics behave.<br><br>There are a wide variety of data mining techniques, like classification and regression trees (CART), C5 and other decision tree analysis techniques, linear and logistic regression, neural networks, support sector machines, and predictive (additive) scorecards.<br><br>Once a model has been built, it must be deployed to be useful. Data mining models can be deployed in a variety of ways, either to support a human decision maker or to support automated decision-making systems. |
| Strengths | • Reveal hidden patterns and create useful insight during analysis—helping determine what data might be useful to capture or how many people might be impacted by specific suggestions.<br>• Can be integrated into a system design to increase the accuracy of the data.<br>• Can be used to eliminate or reduce human bias by using the data to determine the facts. |
| Limitations | • Applying some techniques without an understanding of how they work can result in erroneous correlations and misapplied insight.<br>• Access to big data and to sophisticated data mining tool sets and software may lead to accidental misuse.<br>• Many techniques and tools require specialist knowledge to work with.<br>• Some techniques use advanced math in the background and some stakeholders may not have direct insights into the results. A perceived lack of transparency can cause resistance from some stakeholders.<br>• Data mining results may be hard to deploy if the decision making they are intended to influence is poorly understood. |
| Knowledge Areas | EC, SA, SE |

## 10.15 Data Modeling

| | |
|---|---|
| Purpose | A pictorial diagram that describes the entities, classes or data objects relevant to a domain, the attributes that are used to describe them, and the relationships among them to provide a common set of semantics for analysis and implementation. |
| Description | A data model usually takes the form of a diagram that is supported by textual descriptions. It visually represents the elements that are important to the business (for example, people, places, things, and business transactions), the attributes associated with those elements, and the significant relationships among them. Data models are frequently used in elicitation and requirements analysis and design, as well as to support implementation and continuous improvement. |
| Details | There are several variations of data models:<br><br>• **Conceptual data model**: is independent of any solution or technology and can be used to represent how the business perceives its information.<br><br>• **Logical data model**: is an abstraction of the conceptual data model that incorporates rules of normalization to formally manage the integrity of the data and relationships.<br><br>• **Physical data model**: is used by implementation subject matter experts to describe how a database is physically organized.<br><br>The conceptual, logical, and physical data models are developed for different purposes and may be significantly different even when depicting the same domain. |
| Strengths | • Can be used to define and communicate a consistent vocabulary used by domain subject matter experts and implementation subject matter experts.<br>• Review of a logical data model helps to ensure that the logical design of persistent data correctly represents the business need.<br>• Provides a consistent approach to analyzing and documenting data and its relationships.<br>• Offers the flexibility of different levels of detail, which provides just enough information for the respective audience.<br>• Formal modeling of the information held by the business may expose new requirements as inconsistencies are identified. |
| Limitations | • Following data modeling standards too rigorously may lead to models that are unfamiliar to people without a background in IT.<br>• May extend across multiple functional areas of the organization, and so beyond the business knowledge base of individual stakeholders. |
| Knowledge Areas | EC, RCLM, RADD |

## 10.16 Decision Analysis

| | |
|---|---|
| Purpose | To assess a problem and possible decisions in order to determine the value of alternate outcomes under conditions of uncertainty. |
| Description | Decision analysis examines and models the possible consequences of different decisions about a given problem. A decision is the act of choosing a single course of action from several uncertain outcomes with different values. The outcome value may take different forms depending on the domain, but commonly include financial value, scoring, or a relative ranking dependent on the approach and evaluation criteria used by the business analyst. |
| Details | General components of decision analysis include:<br><br>• **Decision to be Made or Problem Statement**: a description of what the decision question or problem is about.<br>• **Decision Maker**: person or people responsible for making the final decision.<br>• **Alternative**: a possible proposition or course of action.<br>• **Decision Criteria**: evaluation criteria used to evaluate the alternatives.<br><br>Trade-offs become relevant whenever a decision problem involves multiple, possibly conflicting, objectives. Because more than one objective is relevant, it is not sufficient to simply find the maximum value for one variable (such as the financial benefit for the organization). When making trade-offs, effective methods include:<br><br>• **Elimination of dominated alternatives**: a dominated alternative is any option that is clearly inferior to some other option. If an option is equal to or worse than some other option when rated against the objectives, the other option can be said to dominate it. In some cases, an option may also be dominated if it only offers very small advantages but has significant disadvantages.<br>• **Ranking objectives on a similar scale**: one method of converting rankings to a similar scale is proportional scoring. Using this method, the best outcome is assigned a rating of 100, the worst a rating of 0, and all other outcomes are given a rating based on where they fall between those two scores. If the outcomes are then assigned weights based on their relative importance, a score can be assigned to each outcome and the best alternative assigned using a decision tree. |

## 10.16 Decision Analysis

| | |
|---|---|
| Strengths | - Provides business analysts with a prescriptive approach for determining alternate options, especially in complex or uncertain situations.
- Helps stakeholders who are under pressure to assess options based on criteria, thus reducing decisions based on descriptive information and emotions.
- Requires stakeholders to honestly assess the importance they place on different alternate outcomes in order to help avoid false assumptions.
- Enables business analysts to construct appropriate metrics or introduce relative rankings for outcome evaluation in order to directly compare both the financial and non-financial outcome evaluation criteria. |
| Limitations | - The information to conduct proper decision analysis may not be available in time to make the decision.
- Many decisions must be made immediately, without the luxury of employing a formal or even informal decision analysis process.
- The decision maker must provide input to the process and understand the assumptions and model limitations. Otherwise, they may perceive the results provided by the business analyst as more certain than they are.
- Analysis paralysis can occur when too much dependence is placed on the decision analysis and in determining probabilistic values. |
| Knowledge Areas | RCLM, SA, RADD, SE |

## 10.17 Decision Modeling

| | |
|---|---|
| Purpose | Depicts how repeatable business decisions are made. |
| Description | Decision models show how data and knowledge are combined to make a specific decision. Decision models can be used for both straightforward and complex decisions.<br><br>Decision tables and decision trees define how a specific decision is made. A graphical decision model can be constructed at various levels. A high-level model may only show the business decisions as they appear in business processes, while a more detailed model might show as-is or to-be decision making in enough detail to act as a structure for all the relevant business rules. |
| Details | There are several different approaches to decision modeling. Decision tables represent all the rules required to make an atomic decision. Decision trees are common in some industries, but are generally used much less often than decision tables.<br><br>Business decisions use a specific set of input values to determine a particular outcome by using a defined set of business rules to select one from the available outcomes. A decision table is a compact, tabular representation of a set of these rules. Each row (or column) is a rule and each column (or row) represents one of the conditions of that rule. When all the conditions in a particular rule evaluate to true for a set of input data, the outcome or action specified for that rule is selected.<br><br>Decision trees are also used to represent a set of business rules. Each path on a decision tree leaf node is a single rule. Each level in the tree represents a specific data element; the downstream branches represent the different conditions that must be true to continue down that branch. Decision trees can be very effective for representing certain kinds of rule sets, especially those relating to customer segmentation.<br><br>A decision requirements diagram is a visual representation of the information, knowledge, and decision making involved in a more complex business decision. Decision requirement diagrams contain the following elements: decisions, input data, business knowledge models, and knowledge sources. |
| Strengths | • Decision models are easy to share with stakeholders, facilitate a shared understanding, and support impact analysis.<br>• Multiple perspectives can be shared and combined, especially when a diagram is used.<br>• Simplifies complex decision making by removing business rules management from the process.<br>• Assists with managing large numbers of rules in decision tables by grouping rules by decision. This also helps with reuse.<br>• These models work for rules-based automation, data mining, and predictive analytics, as well as for manual decisions or business intelligence projects. |

Chapter 10 Techniques

## 10.17 Decision Modeling

| | |
|---|---|
| Limitations | - Adds a second diagram style when modeling business processes that contain decisions. This may add unnecessary complexity if the decision is simple and tightly coupled with the process.<br>- May limit rules to those required by known decisions and so limit the capture of rules not related to a known decision.<br>- Defining decision models may allow an organization to think it has a standard way of making decisions when it does not. May lock an organization into a current-state decision-making approach.<br>- Cuts across organizational boundaries, which can make it difficult to acquire any necessary sign-off.<br>- May not address behavioral business rules in a direct fashion.<br>- Business terminology must be clearly defined and shared definitions developed to avoid data quality issues affecting automated decisions. |
| Knowledge Areas | SA, RADD |

Figure 10.17.1: Decision Table Example

| Eligibility Rules | | |
|---|---|---|
| Loan Amount | Age | Eligibility |
| <=1000 | >18 | Eligible |
| | <=18 | Ineligible |
| 1000–2000 | >21 | Eligible |
| | <=21 | Ineligible |
| >2000 | >=25 | Eligible |
| | <25 | Ineligible |

### Figure 10.17.2: Decision Tree Example

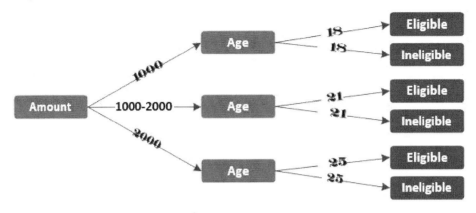

### Figure 10.17.3: Decision Requirements Diagram Example

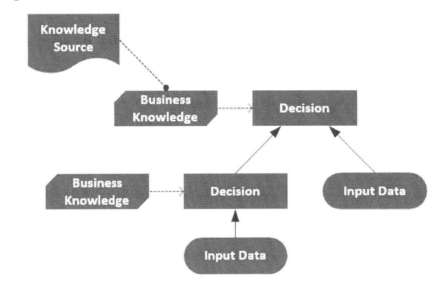

Chapter 10 Techniques

## 10.18 Document Analysis

| | |
|---|---|
| Purpose | To elicit business analysis information, including contextual understanding and requirements, by examining available materials that describe either the business environment or existing organizational assets. |
| Description | Document analysis may be used to gather background information in order to understand the context of a business need, or it may include researching existing solutions to validate how those solutions are currently implemented. |
| Details | The purpose, scope, and topics to be researched through document analysis are determined based on the business analysis information being explored. By researching a wide variety of source materials, the business analyst can ensure the need is fully understood in terms of the environment in which it exists. Document analysis about an existing solution may include reviewing business rules, technical documentation, training documentation, problem reports, previous requirements documents, and procedure manuals in order to validate both how the current solution works and why it was implemented in its current form. Document analysis can also help address information gaps that may occur when the subject matter experts (SMEs) for the existing solution are no longer present or will not be available for the duration of the elicitation process. |
| Strengths | • Existing source material may be used as a basis for analysis.<br>• The business analyst does not need to create content.<br>• Existing sources, although possibly outdated, can be used as a point of reference to determine what is current and what has changed.<br>• Results can be used to validate against the results of other requirements elicitation techniques.<br>• Findings can be presented in formats that permit ease of review and reuse. |
| Limitations | • Existing documentation may be out of date or invalid (incorrect, missing information, unreadable, unreviewed or unapproved).<br>• Authors may not be available for questions.<br>• Primarily helpful only for evaluating the current state, via review of as-is documentation.<br>• If there is a wide range of sources, the effort may be very time-consuming and lead to information overload and confusion. |
| Knowledge Areas | BAPM, EC, RLCM, SA, RADD, SE |

| 10.19 Estimation | |
|---|---|
| Purpose | To forecast the cost and effort involved in pursuing a course of action. |
| Description | Estimation is used to support decision making by predicting costs, benefits, and value of alternative options. Estimations typically are expressed as a single number, but can be expressed as a range (the minimum and maximum estimated values possible). |
| Details | Common estimation methods include:<br><br>• **Top-down**: examining the components at a high level in a hierarchical breakdown.<br><br>• **Bottom-up**: using the lowest-level elements of a hierarchical breakdown to examine the work in detail and estimate the individual cost or effort, and then summing across all elements to provide an overall estimate.<br><br>• **Parametric Estimation**: use of a calibrated parametric model of the element attributes being estimated. It is important that the organization uses its own history to calibrate any parametric model, since the attribute values reflect the skills and abilities of both its staff and the processes used to do work.<br><br>• **Rough Order of Magnitude (ROM)**: a high-level estimate, generally based on limited information, which may have a very wide confidence interval.<br><br>• **Rolling Wave**: repeated estimates throughout an initiative or project, providing detailed estimates for near-term activities (such as an iteration of the work) extrapolated for the remainder of the initiative or project.<br><br>• **Delphi**: uses a combination of expert judgment and history. There are several variations on this process, but they all include individual estimates, sharing the estimates with experts, and having several rounds of estimation until consensus is reached. An average of the three estimates is used.<br><br>• **PERT**: each component of the estimate is given three values: (1) Optimistic value, representing the best-case scenario, (2) Pessimistic value, representing the worst-case scenario, (3) Most Likely value. Then a PERT value for each estimated component is computed as a weighted average: (Optimistic + Pessimistic + (4 times Most Likely))/6.<br><br>The accuracy of an estimate is a measure of uncertainty that evaluates how close an estimate is to the actual value measured later. It can be calculated as a ratio of the width of the confidence interval to its mean value and then expressed as a percentage. ROM estimates are often no more than +50% to -50% accurate. |

## 10.19 Estimation

| | |
|---|---|
| Strengths | - Estimates provide a rationale for an assigned budget, time frame, or size of a set of elements.<br>- Without an estimate, teams making a change may be provided an unrealistic budget or schedule for their work.<br>- Having a small team of knowledgeable individuals provide an estimate by following a defined technique generally results in a closer predictor of the actual value than if an estimate was made by one individual.<br>- Updating an estimate throughout a work cycle, in which the estimated elements are refined over time, incorporates knowledge and helps ensure success. |
| Limitations | - Estimates are only as accurate as the level of knowledge about the elements being estimated. Without organization or local knowledge, estimates can vary widely from the actual values determined later.<br>- Using just one estimation method may lead stakeholders to have unrealistic expectations. |
| Knowledge Areas | BAPM, EC, RLCM, SA, RADD |

## 10.20 Financial Analysis

| | |
|---|---|
| Purpose | To understand the financial aspects of an investment, a solution, or a solution approach. |
| Description | Financial analysis is the assessment of the expected financial viability, stability, and benefit realization of an investment option. It includes a consideration of the total cost of the change as well as the total costs and benefits of using and supporting the solution.<br><br>Financial analysis is used to make a solution recommendation for a specific change initiative by comparing one solution or solution approach to others, based on analysis of the initial cost and the time frame in which those costs are incurred, expected financial benefits and the time frame in which they will be incurred, ongoing costs of using the solution and supporting the solution, risks associated with the change initiative, and ongoing risks to business value of using that solution. |
| Details | The **cost of a change** includes the expected cost of building or acquiring the solution components and the expected costs of transitioning the enterprise from the current state to the future state. This could include the costs associated with changing equipment and software, facilities, staff and other resources, buying out existing contracts, subsidies, penalties, converting data, training, communicating the change, and managing the roll out.<br><br>The **total cost of ownership (TCO)** is the cost to acquire a solution, the cost of using the solution, and the cost of supporting the solution for the foreseeable future.<br><br>**Value** is typically realized over time. The planned value could be expressed on an annual basis, or could be expressed as a cumulative value over a specific time period.<br><br>**Cost-benefit analysis** is a prediction of the expected total benefits minus the expected total costs, resulting in an expected net benefit (the planned business value). Assumptions about the factors that make up the costs and benefits should be clearly stated. The time period of a cost-benefit analysis should look far enough into the future that the solution is in full use, and the planned value is being realized.<br><br>The **return on investment (ROI)** of a planned change is expressed as a percentage measuring the net benefits divided by the cost of the change. One change initiative, solution, or solution approach may be compared to that of others to determine which one provides the greater overall return relative to the amount of the investment.<br><br>The **payback period** provides a projection on the time period required to generate enough benefits to recover the cost of the change. |

## 10.20 Financial Analysis

| | |
|---|---|
| Strengths | - Financial analysis allows executive decision makers to objectively compare very different investments from different perspectives.<br>- Assumptions and estimates built into the benefits and costs, and into the financial calculations, are clearly stated so that they may be challenged or approved.<br>- It reduces the uncertainty of a change or solution by requiring the identification and analysis of factors that will influence the investment.<br>- If the context, business need, or stakeholder needs change during a change initiative, it allows the business analyst to objectively re-evaluate the recommended solution. |
| Limitations | - Some costs and benefits are difficult to quantify financially.<br>- Because financial analysis is forward looking, there will always be some uncertainty about expected costs and benefits.<br>- Positive financial numbers may give a false sense of security—they may not provide all the information required to understand an initiative. |
| Knowledge Areas | BAPM, RLCM, SA, RADD, SE |

**Figure 10.20.1: Cost Benefit Analysis Example**

| Expected Benefits | Year 0 | Year 1 | Year 2 | Year3 |
|---|---|---|---|---|
| Revenue | | $ nnnn | $ nnnn | $ nnnn |
| Reduced operating cost | | nnnn | nnnn | nnnn |
| Time savings | | nnnn | nnnn | nnnn |
| Reduced cost of errors | | nnnn | nnnn | nnnn |
| Increased customer satisfaction | | nnnn | nnnn | nnnn |
| Decreased cost of compliance | | nnnn | nnnn | nnnn |
| Other | | nnnn | nnnn | nnnn |
| **Total Annual Benefits** | $ 0 | $ nnnn | $ nnnn | $ nnnn |
| Costs | | | | |
| Projected costs | $ nnnn | $ nnnn | $ nnnn | $ nnnn |
| Ongoing support | 0 | nnnn | nnnn | nnnn |
| New facilities | Nnnn | nnnn | nnnn | nnnn |
| Licensing | Nnnn | nnnn | nnnn | nnnn |
| Infrastructure changes | Nnnn | 0 | nnnn | 0 |
| Other | Nnnn | nnnn | nnnn | nnnn |
| **Total Costs** | $ nnnn | $ nnnn | $ nnnn | $ nnnn |
| | | | | |
| **Net Benefits** | - $ nnnn | $ nnnn | $ nnnn | $ nnnn |
| **Cumulative Net Benefits** | - $ nnnn | - $ nnnn | - $ nnnn | $ nnnn |

## 10.21 Focus Groups

| | |
|---|---|
| Purpose | To elicit ideas and opinions about a specific product, service, or opportunity in an interactive group environment. |
| Description | A focus group is a form of qualitative research. It is composed of pre-qualified participants whose objective is to discuss and comment on a topic within a context. The participants, guided by a moderator, share their impressions, preferences, needs, perspectives, and attitudes about a topic and discuss them in a group setting. This sometimes leads participants to re-evaluate their own perspectives in light of others' experiences. |
| Details | A **clear and specific objective** establishes a defined purpose for the focus group.<br><br>The **focus group plan** ensures that all stakeholders are aware of the purpose of the focus group and agree on the expected outcomes, and that the session meets the objectives.<br><br>A successful focus group session has **participants** who are willing to both offer their insights and perspectives on a specific topic and listen to the opinions of the other participants. A focus group typically has 6 to 12 attendees.<br><br>A **discussion guide** provides the moderator with a prepared script of specific questions and topics for discussion that meet the objective of the session.<br><br>The **moderator** is both skilled at keeping the session on track and knowledgeable about the initiative. Moderators are able to engage all participants and are adaptable and flexible. The moderator is an unbiased representative of the feedback process. The **recorder** takes notes to ensure the participant's opinions are accurately recorded.<br><br>The moderator **conducts the focus group** by guiding the group's discussion, follows a prepared script of specific issues, and ensures that the objectives are met.<br><br>The **results of the focus group** are transcribed as soon as possible after the session has ended. |
| Strengths | • The ability to elicit data from a group of people in a single session saves both time and costs as compared to conducting individual interviews with the same number of people.<br>• Effective for learning people's attitudes, experiences, and desires.<br>• Active discussion and the ability to ask others questions creates an environment in which participants can consider their personal view in relation to other perspectives.<br>• An online focus group is useful when travel budgets are limited and participants are distributed geographically.<br>• Online focus group sessions can be recorded easily for playback. |

## 10.21 Focus Groups

| | |
|---|---|
| Limitations | - In a group setting, participants may be concerned about issues of trust or may be unwilling to discuss sensitive or personal topics.
- Data collected about what people say may not be consistent with how people actually behave.
- If the group is too homogeneous their responses may not represent the complete set of requirements.
- A skilled moderator is needed to manage group interactions and discussions.
- It may be difficult to schedule the group for the same date and time.
- Online focus groups limit interaction between participants.
- It is difficult for the moderator of an online focus group to determine attitudes without being able to read body language.
- One vocal participant could sway the results of the focus group. |
| Knowledge Areas | EC, SA, RADD, SE |

## 10.22 Functional Decomposition

| | |
|---|---|
| Purpose | To manage complexity and reduce uncertainty by breaking down processes, systems, functional areas, or deliverables into their simpler constituent parts and allowing each part to be analyzed independently. |
| Description | Functional decomposition breaks down larger components into sub-components allows scaling, tracking, and measuring work effort for each of them. It also facilitates evaluation of the success of each sub-component as it relates to other larger or smaller components.<br><br>The depth of decomposition may vary depending on the nature of components and objectives. Functional decomposition assumes that sub-components can and do completely describe their parent components. Any sub-component can have only one parent component when developing the functional hierarchy. |
| Details | Objectives of functional decomposition both drive the process of decomposition and define what to decompose, how to decompose, and how deeply to decompose.<br><br>Functional decomposition applies to a wide variety of versatile subjects, such as business outcomes, work to be done, business process, function, business unit, solution component, activity, products and services, and decisions. |
| Strengths | • Makes complex endeavors possible by breaking down complex problems into feasible parts.<br>• Provides a structured approach to building a shared understanding of complex matters among a diverse group of stakeholders.<br>• Simplifies measurement and estimation of the amount of work involved in pursuing a course of action, defining scope of work, and defining process metrics and indicators. |
| Limitations | • Missing or incorrect information at the time decomposition is performed may later cause a need to revise the results of decomposition partially or entirely.<br>• Many systems cannot be fully represented by simple hierarchical relationships between components because the interactions between components cause emergent characteristics and behaviors.<br>• Every complex subject allows multiple alternative decompositions. Exploring all alternatives can be a challenging and time-consuming task, while sticking with a single alternative may disregard important opportunities and result in a sub- optimal solution.<br>• Performing functional decomposition may involve deep knowledge of the subject and extensive collaboration with diverse stakeholders. |
| Knowledge Areas | BAPM, RLCM, SA, RADD |

# 10.23 Glossary

| | |
|---|---|
| Purpose | Defines key terms relevant to a business domain. |
| Description | Glossaries are used to provide a common understanding of terms that are used by stakeholders. A term may have different meanings for any two people. A list of terms and established definitions provides a common language that can be used to communicate and exchange ideas. A glossary is organized and continuously accessible to all stakeholders. |
| Details | A term is included in the glossary when:<br>• the term is unique to a domain,<br>• there are multiple definitions for the term,<br>• the definition implied is outside of the term's common use, or<br>• there is a reasonable chance of misunderstanding. |
| Strengths | • A glossary promotes common understanding of the business domain and better communication among all stakeholders.<br>• Capturing the definitions as part of an enterprise's documentation provides a single reference and encourages consistency.<br>• Simplifies the writing and maintenance of other business analysis information including but not limited to requirements, business rules, and change strategy. |
| Limitations | • A glossary requires an owner to perform timely maintenance, otherwise it becomes outdated and may be ignored.<br>• It may be challenging for different stakeholders to agree on a single definition for a term. |
| Knowledge Areas | RADD |

## 10.24 Interface Analysis

| | |
|---|---|
| Purpose | To identify where, what, why, when, how, and for whom information is exchanged between solution components or across solution boundaries. |
| Description | An interface is a connection between two components or solutions. Most solutions require one or more interfaces to exchange information with other solution components, organizational units, or business processes. Interface types include:<br>• user interfaces, including human users directly interacting with the solution within the organization,<br>• people external to the solution such as stakeholders or regulators,<br>• business processes,<br>• data interfaces between systems,<br>• application programming interfaces (APIs), and<br>• any hardware devices. |
| Details | The business analyst can leverage other techniques, such as document analysis, observation, scope modeling, and interviews, in order to understand which interfaces need to be identified.<br>Business analysts identify what interfaces are needed in the future state for each stakeholder or system that interacts with the system.<br>Requirements for an interface are primarily focused on describing the inputs to and outputs from that interface, any validation rules that govern those inputs and outputs, and events that might trigger interactions. Interface definition includes:<br>• the name of the interface,<br>• the coverage or span of the interface,<br>• the exchange method between the two entities,<br>• the message format, and<br>• the exchange frequency. |
| Strengths | • By engaging in interface analysis early on, increased functional coverage is provided.<br>• Clear specification of the interfaces provides a structured means of allocating requirements, business rules, and constraints to the solution.<br>• Due to its broad application, it avoids over analysis of fine detail. |
| Limitations | • Does not provide insight into other aspects of the solution since the analysis does not assess the internal components. |
| Knowledge Areas | EC, RLCM, RADD |

## 10.25 Interviews

| | |
|---|---|
| Purpose | To elicit business analysis information from a person or group of people by asking relevant questions, and documenting the responses. |
| Description | The interview is a common technique for eliciting requirements. It involves direct communication with individuals or groups of people who are part of an initiative. The interview can also be used for establishing relationships and building trust between business analysts and stakeholders in order to increase stakeholder involvement or build support for a proposed solution. One-on-one interviews are the most common. In a group interview, the interviewer is careful to elicit responses from each participant. Interviews can be structured or unstructured. |
| Details | To prepare for interviews, the business analysts defines the goal of the interviews, produces a list of potential participants (stakeholders of the initiative), list of questions (open-ended and closed-ended) you wish to ask the interviewees, and sets up interview logistics. Then the business analyst conducts the interview, paying attention to the interview flow, and properly closing the interview. Interviews often require follow-up to ask questions not asked during the original interview. |
| Strengths | • Encourages participation by and establishes rapport with stakeholders.<br>• Simple, direct technique that can be used in a variety of situations.<br>• Allows the interviewer and participant to have full discussions and explanations of the questions and answers.<br>• Enables observations of non-verbal behavior.<br>• The interviewer can ask follow-up and probing questions to confirm their own understanding.<br>• Maintains focus through the use of clear objectives for the interview that are agreed upon by all participants and can be met in the time allotted.<br>• Allows interviewees to express opinions in private that they may be reluctant to express in public, especially when interview results are kept confidential. |
| Limitations | • Significant time is required to plan for and conduct interviews.<br>• Requires considerable commitment and involvement of the participants.<br>• Training is required to conduct effective interviews.<br>• Based on the level of clarity provided during the interview, the resulting documentation may be subject to the interviewer's interpretation.<br>• There is a risk of unintentionally leading the interviewee. |
| Knowledge Areas | BAPM, EC, RLCM, SA, RADD, SE |

## 10.26 Item Tracking

| | |
|---|---|
| Purpose | To capture and assign responsibility for issues and stakeholder concerns that pose an impact to the solution. |
| Description | Item tracking is an organized approach to address stakeholder concerns. Stakeholders may identify such item types as actions, assumptions, constraints, dependencies, defects, enhancements, and issues.<br><br>When a stakeholder concern is first raised, it is assessed to determine if it is viable. If viable, the concern is classified as a specific item type so that it can be better tracked and controlled by a process that works towards the item's closure. During its life cycle, an item is assigned to one or more stakeholders who are responsible for its resolution.<br><br>Item tracking tracks the item from the initial recording of the concern and its degree of impact to its agreed-upon closure. The item tracking record may be shared with stakeholders to ensure transparency and visibility into the status and progress of items in the record. |
| Details | Each recorded item may contain all or any of the following attributes for item tracking. Each item's resolution is undertaken as prescribed by stakeholder needs and according to any organizational process standards. |
| Strengths | • Ensures concerns around stakeholder requirements are captured, tracked, and resolved to the stakeholder's satisfaction.<br>• Allows stakeholders to rank the importance of outstanding items. |
| Limitations | • If not careful, the copious recording of data about items may outweigh any benefits realized.<br>• It may use time that could be better spent on other efforts and stakeholders could become mired in details and statistics. |
| Knowledge Areas | BAPM, RLCM, SA, RADD, SE |

# Chapter 10 Techniques

## 10.27 Lessons Learned

| | |
|---|---|
| Purpose | To compile and document successes, opportunities for improvement, failures, and recommendations for improving the performance of future projects or project phases. |
| Description | A lessons learned session (also known as a retrospective) helps identify either changes to business analysis processes and deliverables or successes that can be incorporated into future work. These techniques can also be beneficial at the close of any milestone within the effort.<br><br>Lessons learned sessions can include any format or venue that is acceptable to the key stakeholders and can be either formal facilitated meetings with set agendas and meeting roles or informal working sessions. If there are noteworthy successes, a celebration may be included in a lessons learned session. |
| Details | Lessons Learned Sessions can include a review of business analysis activities or deliverables, the final solution, service, or product, automation or technology that was introduced or eliminated, impact to organizational processes, performance expectations and results, positive or negative variances, root causes impacting performance results, and recommendations for behavioral approaches. |
| Strengths | • Useful in identifying opportunities or areas of improvement.<br>• Assists in building team morale after a difficult period.<br>• Reinforces positive experiences and successes.<br>• Reduces risks for future actions.<br>• Provides tangible value or metrics as a result of the effort.<br>• Recognizes strengths or shortcomings with the project structure, methodology, or tools that were used. |
| Limitations | • Honest discussion may not occur if participants try to assign blame during these sessions.<br>• Participants may be reluctant to document and discuss problems.<br>• Proactive facilitation may be required to ensure that the discussions remain focused on solutions and improvement opportunities. |
| Knowledge Areas | BAPM, EC, SA, RADD, SE |

## 10.28 Metrics and Key Performance Indicators (KPIs)

| | |
|---|---|
| Purpose | To measure the performance of solutions, solution components, and other matters of interest to stakeholders. |
| Description | A metric is a quantifiable level of an indicator that an organization uses to measure progress. An indicator identifies a specific numerical measurement that represents the degree of progress toward achieving a goal, objective, output, activity, or further input. A key performance indicator (KPI) is one that measures progress towards a strategic goal or objective. Reporting is the process of informing stakeholders of metrics or indicators in specified formats and at specified intervals. |
| Details | An indicator displays the result of analyzing one or more specific measures for addressing a concern about a need, value, output, activity, or input in a table or graphical form. Each concern requires at least one indicator to measure it properly.<br><br>Stakeholder interests are also important. Certain indicators may help stakeholders perform or improve more than others. Over time, weaknesses in some indicators can be identified and improved.<br><br>When establishing an indicator, business analysts will consider its source, method of collection, collector, and the cost, frequency, and difficulty of collection. Secondary sources of data may be the most economical, but to meet the other characteristics of a good indicator, primary research such as surveys, interviews, or direct observations may be necessary. The method of data collection is the key driver of a monitoring, evaluation, and reporting system's cost. |
| Strengths | • Establishing a monitoring and evaluation system allows stakeholders to understand the extent to which a solution meets an objective, as well as how effective the inputs and activities of developing the solution (outputs) were.<br>• Indicators, metrics, and reporting also facilitate organizational alignment, linking goals to objectives, supporting solutions, underlying tasks, and resources. |
| Limitations | • Gathering excessive amounts of data beyond what is needed will result in unnecessary expense in collecting, analyzing, and reporting. It will also distract project members from other responsibilities. On Agile projects, this will be particularly relevant.<br>• A bureaucratic metrics program fails from collecting too much data and not generating useful reports that will allow timely action. Those charged with collecting metric data must be given feedback to understand how their actions are affecting the quality of the project results.<br>• When metrics are used to assess performance, the individuals being measured are likely to act to increase their performance on those metrics, even if this causes sub-optimal performance on other activities. |
| Knowledge Areas | BAPM, SA, RADD, SE |

## 10.29 Mind Mapping

| | |
|---|---|
| Purpose | To articulate and capture thoughts, ideas, and information. |
| Description | Mind mapping is a form of note taking that captures thoughts, ideas, and information in a non-linear diagram. Mind maps use images, words, color, and connected relationships to apply structure and logic to thoughts, ideas, and information. A mind map has a central main idea supported by secondary ideas (or topics), followed by as many layers of ideas (or sub-topics) as necessary to fully capture and articulate the concept. Connections are made between ideas by branches that typically have a single keyword associated with them that explain the connection.<br><br>Mind maps can be developed individually or as a collaboration exercise. They can be created on paper or with the use of specialized software.<br><br>There is no standardized format for a mind map. The intent of a mind map is to capture information in a fashion closely resembling how our minds process information. |
| Details | The **main topic** of a mind map is the thought or concept that is being articulated. The main topic is positioned in the center of the images so that multiple topics and associations can branch off.<br><br>**Topics** are thoughts or concepts that expound upon or further articulate the main topic. Their association with the main topic is expressed through a branch (connected line) that has a keyword associated with it. There can be as many or as few topics as required to fully explore the thought or concept of the main topic.<br><br>**Sub-topics** are thoughts or concepts that expound upon or further articulate the topic and directly relate to the main topic. Their association with the topic is expressed through a branch (connected line) that has a keyword associated with it. There can be as many or as few sub-topics as required to fully explore the thought or concept of the main topic.<br><br>**Branches** are the associations between the main topic, topics, and sub-topics.<br><br>**Keywords** are single words used to articulate the nature of the association of topics or sub-topics connected by a branch.<br><br>**Color** may be used to categorize, prioritize, and analyze topics, sub-topics, and their associations. There is no defined color standard for mind maps.<br><br>**Images** can be used in mind maps to express larger volumes of information that are unable to be expressed in short topic headings. Images are useful in stimulating creativity and innovation by generating additional thoughts, ideas, and associations. |

## 10.29 Mind Mapping

| Strengths | - Can be used as an effective collaboration and communication tool.<br>- Summarizes complex thoughts, ideas, and information in a way that shows the overall structure.<br>- Associations and sub-topics facilitate understanding and decision making.<br>- Enable creative problem solving by articulating associations and generating new associations.<br>- Can be helpful in preparing and delivering presentations. |
|---|---|
| Limitations | - Can be misused as a brainstorming tool, and the related documenting of ideas and creating associations may inhibit idea generation.<br>- A shared understanding of a mind map can be difficult to communicate. |
| Knowledge Areas | BAPM, EC, SA, RADD |

**Figure 10.29.1: The Taxonomy of a Mind Map**

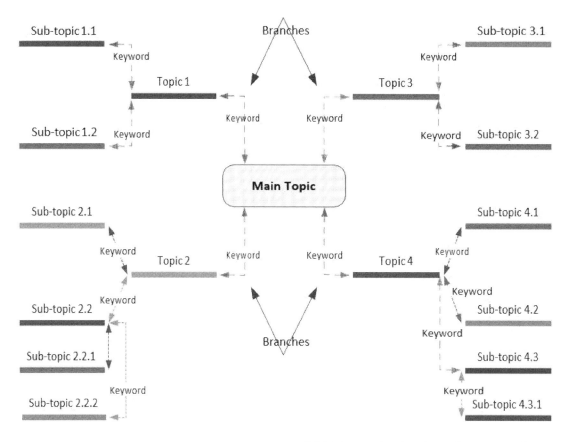

© 2015 International Institute of Business Analysis

# Chapter 10 Techniques

## 10.30 Non-Functional Requirements Analysis

| | |
|---|---|
| Purpose | To examine the requirements for a solution that define how well the solution must perform. |
| Description | Non-functional requirements (also known as quality attributes or quality of service requirements) specify criteria that can be used to judge the operation of a system rather than specific behaviors (which are referred to as the functional requirements). They augment the functional requirements of a solution, identify constraints on those requirements, or describe quality attributes a solution must exhibit when based on those functional requirements.<br><br>Non-functional requirements are generally expressed in textual formats as declarative statements or in matrices. Declarative non-functional requirements statements will typically have a constraining factor to them. |
| Details | Common categories of non-functional requirements include:<br><br>• **Availability**: degree to which the solution is operable and accessible when required for use.<br>• **Compatibility**: degree to which the solution operates effectively with other components in its environment, such as one process with another.<br>• **Functionality**: degree to which the solution functions meet user needs, including aspects of suitability, accuracy, and interoperability.<br>• **Maintainability**: ease with which a solution or component can be modified to correct faults, improve performance, or adapt to a changed environment.<br>• **Performance Efficiency**: degree to which a solution or component performs its designated functions with minimum consumption of resources. Can be defined based on the context or period, such as high-peak, mid- peak or off-peak usage.<br>• **Portability**: ease with which a solution or component can be transferred from one environment to another.<br>• **Reliability**: ability of a solution or component to perform its required functions under stated conditions for a specified period of time.<br>• **Scalability**: degree with which a solution is able to grow or evolve to handle increased amounts of work.<br>• **Security**: aspects of a solution that protect solution content or solution components from accidental or malicious access, use, modification, destruction, or disclosure.<br>• **Usability**: ease with which a user can learn to use the solution.<br>• **Certification**: constraints on the solution that are necessary to meet certain standards or industry conventions.<br>• **Compliance**: regulatory, financial, or legal constraints which can vary based on the context or jurisdiction.<br>• **Localization**: requirements dealing with local languages, laws, currencies, cultures, spellings, and other characteristics, which requires attention to the context.<br>• **Service Level Agreements**: agreed upon constraints of the organization using the solution.<br>• **Extensibility**: the ability of a solution to incorporate new functionality. |

## 10.30 Non-Functional Requirements Analysis

| | |
|---|---|
| Strengths | - Clearly states the constraints that apply to a set of functional requirements.
- Provides measurable expressions of how well the functional requirements must perform, leaving it to the functional requirements to express what the solution must do or how it must behave. This will also have a strong influence on whether the solution is accepted by the users. |
| Limitations | - The clarity and usefulness of a non-functional requirement depends on what the stakeholders know about the needs for the solution and how well they can express those needs.
- Expectations of multiple users may be quite different, and getting agreement on quality attributes may be difficult because of the users' subjective perception of quality. For example, what might be 'too fast' to one user might be 'too slow' to another.
- A set of non-functional requirements may have inherent conflicts and require negotiation. For example, some security requirements may require compromises on performance requirements.
- Overly strict requirements or constraints can add more time and cost to the solution, which may have negative impacts and weaken adoption by users.
- Many non-functional requirements are qualitative and therefore may be difficult to be measured on a scale, and may garner a degree of subjectivity by the users as to how they believe the particular requirements ultimately meet their needs. |
| Knowledge Areas | RADD, SE |

# Chapter 10 Techniques

## 10.31 Observation

| | |
|---|---|
| Purpose | To elicit information by viewing and understanding activities and their context. |
| Description | It is used as a basis for identifying needs and opportunities, understanding a business process, setting performance standards, evaluating solution performance, or supporting training and development. |
| | Observation of activities, also known as job shadowing, involves examining a work activity firsthand as it is performed. There are two approaches for observation: active and passive. |
| Details | A clear and specific objective establishes a defined purpose of the observation session. Preparing for an observation session involves planning the observation approach based on the objectives and deciding who should be viewed performing which activities at what times. |
| | Before the observation session explain why the observation is being conducted, reassure the participant that their personal performance is not being judged and that the results of this observation, among others, will be evaluated as a whole, inform the participant that they can stop the observation at any time, and recommend the sharing of any reasoning or concerns while performing the activity or soon afterwards. |
| | During the observation session attentively watch the person perform the activity and note typical and atypical tasks or steps, the manner in which any tools are used, and information content, record what is seen, the time taken to perform the work, its quality, any process anomalies, and the observer's own concerns or questions, and ask probing questions either while the work is being performed or soon after the observation session. |
| | After the observation session, review the notes and data recorded from the observation and follow up with the participant to obtain answers to any remaining questions or to fill any gaps. Sharing these notes and data with participants may be helpful in obtaining answers to any questions or easing any concerns the participant may have. |
| Strengths | • Observers can gain realistic and practical insight about the activities and their tasks within an overall process.<br>• Instances of informally performed tasks as well as any workarounds can be identified.<br>• Productivity can be viewed firsthand and realistically compared against any established performance standards or metrics.<br>• Recommendations for improvement are supported by objective and quantitative evidence. |

## 10.31 Observation

| | |
|---|---|
| Limitations | - May be disruptive to the performance of the participant and the overall organization.
- Can be threatening and intrusive to the person being observed.
- While being observed, a participant may alter their work practices.
- Significant time is required to plan for and conduct observations.
- Not suitable for evaluating knowledge-based activities since these are not directly observable. |
| Knowledge Areas | BAPM, EC, SA, SE |

## 10.32 Organizational Modeling

| | |
|---|---|
| Purpose | to describe the roles, responsibilities, and reporting structures that exist within an organization and to align those structures with the organization's goals. |
| Description | An organizational model defines how an organization or organizational unit is structured. An organizational model is a visual representation of the organizational unit which defines the boundaries of the group (who is in the group), the formal relationships between members (who reports to whom), the functional role for each person, and the interfaces (interaction and dependencies) between the unit and other units or stakeholders. |
| Details | There are three pre-eminent organizational models:<br><br>**Functionally-oriented**: group staff together based on areas of expertise and generally encourage a standardization of work or processes within the organization. Functional organizations are beneficial because they seem to facilitate cost management and reduce duplication of work, but are prone to develop communication and cross-functional coordination problems ("silos").<br><br>**Market-oriented**: may be intended to serve particular customer groups, geographical areas, projects, or processes rather than grouping employees by common skills or expertise. Market-oriented structures permit the organization to meet the needs of its customers, but are prone to developing inconsistencies in how work is performed.<br><br>**The Matrix Model**: has separate managers for each functional area and for each product, service, or customer group. Employees report to a line manager, who is responsible for the performance of a type of work and for identifying opportunities for efficiency in the work, and to a market (or product, service, or project) manager, who is responsible for managing the product or service across multiple functional areas. A challenge of the matrix model is that each employee has two managers (who are focused on different goals) and accountability is difficult to maintain. |
| Strengths | • Organizational models are common in most organizations.<br>• Including an organizational model in business analysis information allows team members to provide support. Future projects may benefit from knowing who was involved in this project and what their role entailed. |
| Limitations | • Organizational models are sometimes out of date.<br>• Informal lines of authority, influence, and communication not reflected in the org chart are more difficult to identify and may conflict with the organizational chart. |
| Knowledge Areas | BAPM, EC, SA, RADD, SE |

## 10.33 Prioritization

| | |
|---|---|
| Purpose | To facilitate stakeholder decisions and to understand the relative importance of business analysis information. |
| Description | Prioritization is a process used to determine the relative importance of business analysis information. The importance may be based on value, risk, difficulty of implementation, or other criteria. These priorities are used to determine which business analysis information should be targeted for further analysis, which requirements should be implemented first, or how much time or detail should be allocated to the requirements. |
| Details | Grouping consists of classifying business analysis information according to predefined categories such as high, medium, or low priority. Many requirements management tools support listing the priority category as an attribute of a requirement.<br><br>Ranking consists of ordering business analysis information from most to least important. Some adaptive approaches involve the explicit sequencing of requirements in an ordered list (a product backlog).<br><br>Time boxing or budgeting prioritizes business analysis information based on the allocation of a fixed resource.<br><br>The negotiation approach involves establishing a consensus among stakeholders as to which requirements will be prioritized. |
| Strengths | • Facilitates consensus building and trade-offs and ensures that solution value is realized and initiative timelines are met. |
| Limitations | • Some stakeholders may attempt to avoid difficult choices and fail to recognize the necessity for making trade-offs.<br>• The solution team may intentionally or unintentionally try to influence the result of the prioritization process by overestimating the difficulty or complexity of implementing certain requirements.<br>• May be subjective due to metrics and key performance indicators not being available when prioritizing items. |
| Knowledge Areas | RLCM, SE |

# Chapter 10 Techniques

## 10.34 Process Analysis

| | |
|---|---|
| Purpose | Assesses a process for its efficiency and effectiveness, as well as its ability to identify opportunities for change. |
| Description | Process analysis is used for various purposes including:<br>• recommending a more efficient or effective process,<br>• determining the gaps between the current and future state of a process,<br>• understanding factors to be included in a contract negotiation,<br>• understanding how data and technology are used in a process, and<br>• analyzing the impact of a pending change to a process.<br>A number of frameworks and methodologies exist that focus on process analysis and improvement methods, such as Six Sigma and Lean. Methods for process improvement include value stream mapping, statistical analysis and control, process simulation, benchmarking, and process frameworks. |
| Details | Identifying gaps and areas to improve helps to identify what areas are in scope for analysis. Identifying the root cause of the gaps and improvement areas ensures that the solution addresses the right gap and area. Generating options and alternative solutions to solve for the gap or area of improvement helps the team evaluate and see different points of view for improving the process. |
| Strengths | • Ensures solutions address the right issues, minimizing waste.<br>• Many different techniques and methodologies can be used and provide teams with great flexibility in approach. |
| Limitations | • Can be time-consuming.<br>• There are many techniques and methodologies in process analysis. It can be challenging to decipher which to use and how rigorously to follow them, given the scope and purpose.<br>• May prove ineffective at process improvement in knowledge or decision-intensive processes. |
| Knowledge Areas | BAPM, EC, SA, SE |

## 10.35 Process Modeling

| | |
|---|---|
| Purpose | Is a standardized graphical model used to show how work is carried out and is a foundation for process analysis. |
| Description | Process models describe the sequential flow of work or activities. A business process model describes the sequential flow of work across defined tasks and activities through an enterprise or part of an enterprise. A system process model defines the sequential flow of control among programs or units within a computer system. A program process flow shows the sequential execution of program statements within a software program. A process model can also be used in documenting operational procedures.<br><br>Process models can be used to:<br><br>• describe the context of the solution or part of the solution,<br>• describe what actually happens, or is desired to happen, during a process,<br>• provide an understandable description of a sequence of activities to an external observer,<br>• provide a visual to accompany a text description, and<br>• provide a basis for process analysis.<br><br>A process model can be used to define the current state of a process (also known as an as-is model) or a potential future state (also known as a to-be model). A model of the current state can provide understanding and agreement as to what happens now. A model of the future state can provide alignment with what is desired to happen in the future. |
| Details | Many different notations are used in process modeling. The most commonly used notations include Flowcharts and Value Stream Mapping (VSM), Data Flow diagrams and Unified Modeling Language™ (UML®) diagrams, Business Process Model and Notation (BPMN), Integrated DEFinition (IDEF) notation and Input, Guide, Output, Enabler (IGOE) diagrams, and SIPOC and Value Stream Analysis.<br><br>Process models typically contain some or all of the following key elements:<br><br>• **Activity**: an individual step or piece of work that forms part of the business process.<br>• **Event**: a zero-time occurrence which initiates, interrupts, or terminates an activity or task within a process or the process itself.<br>• **Directional Flow**: a path that indicates the logical sequence of the workflow. In general, diagrams are drawn to show the passage of time in a consistent fashion.<br>• **Decision Point**: a point in the process where the flow of work splits into two or more flows (paths), which may be mutually exclusive alternatives or parallels. A decision can also be used to locate rules where separate flows merge together.<br>• **Link**: a connection to other process maps.<br>• **Role**: a type of person or group involved in the process. |

## 10.35 Process Modeling

| | |
|---|---|
| Strengths | • Appeals to the basic human understanding of sequential activities.<br>• Most stakeholders are comfortable with the concepts and basic elements of a process model.<br>• The use of levels can accommodate the different perspectives of various stakeholder groups.<br>• Effective at showing how to handle a large number of scenarios and parallel branches.<br>• Can help identify any stakeholder groups that may have otherwise been overlooked.<br>• Facilitates the identification of potential improvements by highlighting "pain points" in the process structure (i.e. process visualization). Likely to have value in its own right. They provide documentation for compliance purposes and can be used by business stakeholders for training and coordination of activities.<br>• Can be used as a baseline for continuous improvement.<br>• Ensures labelling consistency across artifacts.<br>• Provides transparency and clarity to process owners and participants on activity responsibilities, sequence and hand-overs. |
| Limitations | • To many people in IT, a formal process model tends to reflect an older and more document-heavy approach to software development. Therefore, project time is not allocated to developing a process model, especially of the current state or problem domain.<br>• Can become extremely complex and unwieldy if not structured carefully. This is especially true if business rules and decisions are not managed separately from the process.<br>• Complex processes can involve many activities and roles; this can make them almost impossible for a single individual to understand and 'sign off'.<br>• Problems in a process cannot always be identified by looking at a high-level model. A more detailed model with reference to metadata (such as path frequency, cost, and time factors) is usually required. It is often necessary to engage with stakeholders directly to find the operational problems they have encountered while working with a process.<br>• In a highly dynamic environment where things change quickly, process models can become obsolete.<br>• May prove difficult to maintain if the process model only serves as documentation, as stakeholders may alter the process to meet their needs without updating the model. |
| Knowledge Areas | BAPM, EC, RLCM, SA, RADD, SE |

## 10.36 Prototyping

| | |
|---|---|
| Purpose | To elicit and validate stakeholder needs through an iterative process that creates a model or design of requirements. It is also used to optimize user experience, to evaluate design options, and as a basis for development of the final business solution. |
| Description | Prototyping is a proven method for product design. It works by providing an early model of the final result, known as a prototype. Prototyping is used to identify both missing or improperly specified requirements and unsubstantiated assumptions by demonstrating what the product looks like and how it acts in the early stages of design.<br><br>Prototypes can be non-working models, working representations, or digital depictions of a solution or a proposed product. They can be used to mock up websites, serve as a partially working construct of the product, or describe processes through a series of diagrams (such as workflow). Business rules and data prototypes can be used to discover desired process flow and business rules. Data prototyping can be used for data cleansing and transformation. |
| Details | There are two common approaches to prototyping: throw-away and evolutionary (or functional).<br><br>Each of the following can be considered a form of prototyping:<br><br>• **Proof of Principle or Proof of Concept**: is a model created to validate the design of a system without modeling the appearance, materials used in the creation of work, or processes/workflows ultimately used by the stakeholders.<br><br>• **Form Study Prototype**: is used to explore the basic size, look, and feel of a product that will be manufactured, without creating actual functionality. It is used to assess ergonomic and visual factors using a sculptural representation of the product made from inexpensive materials. This type of prototype may also be used to model a workflow or navigation at a high level in order to identify gaps or inconsistencies in the possible solution of the properties (for example, appearance, configuration).<br><br>• **Usability Prototype**: is a product model created to test how the end user interacts with the system without including any of the properties (for example, appearance, configuration).<br><br>• **Visual Prototype**: is a product model created to test the visual aspects of the solution without modeling the complete functionality.<br><br>• **Functional Prototype**: is a model created to test software functionality, qualities of the system for the user (for example, appearance), and workflow. It is also referred to as a working model and is used both to simulate business processes and business rules and to evaluate software function calls.<br><br>The following is a list of commonly used methods for prototyping:<br><br>• **Storyboarding**: is used to visually and textually detail the sequence of activities by summing up different user interactions with the solution or enterprise. |

## 10.36 Prototyping

| | |
|---|---|
| | • **Paper Prototyping**: uses paper and pencil to draft an interface or process.<br>• **Workflow Modeling**: depicts a sequence of operations that are performed and usually focuses solely on the human aspect.<br>• **Simulation**: is used to demonstrate solutions or components of a solution. It may test various processes, scenarios, business rules, data, and inputs. |
| Strengths | • Provides a visual representation for the future state.<br>• Allows for stakeholders to provide input and feedback early in the design process.<br>• When using throw-away or paper prototyping methods, users may feel more comfortable being critical of the mock-up because it is not polished and release-ready.<br>• A narrow yet deep vertical prototype can be used for technical feasibility studies, proof of concept efforts, or to uncover technology and process gaps. |
| Limitations | • If the system or process is highly complex, the prototyping process may become bogged down with discussion of 'how' rather than 'what', which can make the process take considerable time, effort, and facilitation skill.<br>• Underlying technology may need to be understood or assumed in order to initiate prototyping.<br>• If the prototype is deeply elaborate and detailed, stakeholders may develop unrealistic expectations for the final solution. These can range from assumed completion dates to higher expectations of performance, reliability, and usability.<br>• Stakeholders may focus on the design specifications of the solution rather than the requirements that any solution must address. This can, in turn, constrain the solution design. Developers may believe that they must provide a user interface that precisely matches the prototype, even if more elegant technology and interface approaches exist. |
| Knowledge Areas | EC, SA, RADD, SE |

## 10.37 Reviews

| | |
|---|---|
| Purpose | To evaluate the content of a work product. |
| Description | Different types of reviews are conducted for business analysis work products, and uses these dimensions: objectives, techniques, and participants. Each review is focused on a work product, not the skills or actions of the participants. For a completed work product, the objective of the review is usually to remove defects or inform the reviewers about the content. For work in process, the review may be conducted to resolve an issue or question. |
| Details | Objectives are clearly communicated to all participants prior to the review. Reviews can be formal or informal. The techniques used during a review are selected to support the objectives of the review. Participant roles involved in any particular review depend on the objectives of the review, the selected technique, and any organizational standards that may be in place. |
| Strengths | <ul><li>Can help identify defects early in the work product life cycle, eliminating the need for expensive removal of defects discovered later in the life cycle.</li><li>All parties involved in a review become engaged with the final outcome; they have a vested interest in a quality result.</li><li>Desk checks and pass around reviews can be performed by a reviewer at a convenient time, rather than interrupting work in progress to attend a meeting.</li></ul> |
| Limitations | <ul><li>Rigorous team reviews take time and effort. Thus, only the most critical work products might be reviewed using inspection or formal walkthrough techniques.</li><li>Informal reviews by one or two reviewers are practical in terms of the effort required, but they provide less assurance of removing all significant defects than using a larger team and more formal process.</li><li>For desk checks and pass around reviews it may be difficult for the author to validate that an independent review was done by each participant.</li><li>If review comments are shared and discussed via e-mail there may be many messages to process, which makes it difficult for the author to resolve disagreements or differences in suggested changes.</li></ul> |
| Knowledge Areas | BAPM, EC, RLCM, RADD |

## 10.38 Risk Analysis and Management

| | |
|---|---|
| Purpose | To identify areas of uncertainty that could negatively affect value, analyzes and evaluates those uncertainties, and develops and manages ways of dealing with the risks. |
| Description | Failure to identify and manage risks may negatively affect the value of the solution. Risk analysis and management involves identifying, analyzing, and evaluating risks. Where sufficient controls are not already in place, business analysts develop plans for avoiding, reducing, or modifying the risks, and when necessary, implementing these plans.<br><br>Risk management is an ongoing activity. Continuous consultation and communication with stakeholders help to both identify new risks and to monitor identified risks. |
| Details | Risks are discovered and identified through a combination of expert judgment, stakeholder input, experimentation, past experiences, and historical analysis of similar initiatives and situations. The goal is to identify a comprehensive set of relevant risks and to minimize the unknowns. Risk identification is an ongoing activity. Each risk can be described in a risk register that supports the analysis of those risks and plans for addressing them.<br><br>Analysis of a risk involves understanding the risk, and estimating the level of a risk. Sometimes controls may already be in place to deal with some risks, and these should be taken into account when analyzing the risk.<br><br>The risk analysis results are compared with the potential value of the change or of the solution to determine if the level of risk is acceptable or not.<br><br>Some risks may be acceptable, but for other risks it may be necessary to take measures to reduce the risk. |
| Strengths | • Can be applied to strategic risks which affect long-term value of the enterprise, tactical risks which affect the value of a change, and operational risks which affect the value of a solution once the change is made.<br>• An organization typically faces similar challenges on many of its initiatives. The successful risk responses on one initiative can be useful lessons learned for other initiatives.<br>• The risk level of a change or of a solution could vary over time. Ongoing risk management helps to recognize that variation, and to re-evaluate the risks and the suitability of the planned responses. |
| Limitations | • The number of possible risks to most initiatives can easily become unmanageably large. It may only be possible to manage a subset of potential risks.<br>• There is the possibility that significant risks are not identified. |
| Knowledge Areas | BAPM, EC, RLCM, SA. RADD, SE |

## 10.39 Roles and Permissions Matrix

| | |
|---|---|
| Purpose | To ensure coverage of activities by denoting responsibility, to identify roles, to discover missing roles, and to communicate results of a planned change. |
| Description | Role and permission allocation involves identifying roles, associating these with solution activities, and then denoting authorities who can perform these activities. |
| Details | To identify roles for either internal or external stakeholders, review any organizational models, job descriptions, procedure manuals, and system user guides, and meet with stakeholders to uncover additional roles. |
| | Use functional decomposition to break down each function into sub-parts, process modeling to better understand the workflow and division of work among users, and use cases to represent tasks. |
| | Authorities are actions that identified roles are permitted to perform. |
| Strengths | • Provides procedural checks and balances, as well as data security, by restricting individuals from performing certain actions. |
| | • Promotes improved review of transaction history, in that audit logs can capture details about any assigned authorities at the time. |
| | • Provides documented roles and responsibilities for activities. |
| Limitations | • Need to recognize the required level of detail for a specific initiative or activity; too much detail can be time-consuming and not provide value, too little detail can exclude necessary roles or responsibilities. |
| Knowledge Areas | RADD, SE |

Figure 10.39.1: Roles and Permissions Matrix

| Roles and Permissions Matrix / Activity | Role Group 1 | Administrator | Manager | Role Group 2 | Sales | Customer |
|---|---|---|---|---|---|---|
| Create new account | | X | X | | | X |
| Modify account | | X | X | | | X |
| Create order | | X | X | | X | X |
| View reports | | X | X | | X | |
| Create reports | | X | X | | X | |

© 2015 International Institute of Business Analysis

## 10.40 Root Cause Analysis

| | |
|---|---|
| Purpose | To identify and evaluate the underlying causes of a problem. |
| Description | Root cause analysis is a systematic examination of a problem or situation that focuses on the problem's origin as the proper point of correction rather than dealing only with its effects. It applies an iterative analysis approach in order to take into account that there might be more than one root cause contributing to the effects. Root cause analysis looks at the main types of causes such as people (human error, lack of training), physical (equipment failure, poor facility), or organizational (faulty process design, poor structure). |
| Details | A fishbone diagram (also known as an Ishikawa or cause-and-effect diagram) is used to identify and organize the possible causes of a problem. This tool helps to focus on the cause of the problem versus the solution and organizes ideas for further analysis. The diagram serves as a map that depicts possible cause-and- effect relationships. |
| | The five whys is a question asking process to explore the nature and cause of a problem. The five whys approach repeatedly asks questions in an attempt to get to the root cause of the problem. This is one of the simplest facilitation tools to use when problems have a human interaction component. |
| Strengths | • Helps to maintain an objective perspective when performing cause-and-effect analysis. |
| | • Enables stakeholders to specify an effective solution at the appropriate points for corrective action. |
| Limitations | • Works best when the business analyst has formal training to ensure the root causes, not just symptoms of the problem, are identified. |
| | • May be difficult with complex problems; the potential exists to lead to a false trail and/or dead–end conclusion. |
| Knowledge Areas | BAPM, SA, RADD, SE |

## 10.41 Scope Modeling

| | |
|---|---|
| Purpose | To define the nature of one or more limits or boundaries and place elements inside or outside those boundaries. |
| Description | Scope models are commonly used to describe the boundaries of control, change, a solution, or a need. These models may show elements that include:<br>• **In-scope**: the model identifies a boundary as seen from inside, as well as the elements contained by that boundary (for example, functional decomposition).<br>• **Out-of-scope**: the model identifies a boundary as seen from outside, as well as the elements that are not contained by that boundary (for example, context diagram).<br>• **Both**: the model identifies a boundary as seen from both sides, as well as elements on both sides of the boundary (for example, venn diagram or use case model). |
| Details | Scope models are typically used to clarify the span of control, relevance of elements, and where effort will be applied. Typically, business analysts are concerned with elements that will be altered as part of a change, as well as external elements that are relevant to the change. The purpose of analysis defines the appropriate level of abstraction at which scope elements are described. A proper level of detail provides a meaningful reduction of uncertainty while preventing 'analysis paralysis' at a scope definition stage. Exploring relationships between potential scope elements helps to ensure completeness and integrity of the scope model by identifying their dependencies or by discovering other elements involved in or impacted by the change. At a time of scope modeling, the validity of the model heavily relies on assumptions such as the definition of needs, causality of outcomes, impact of changes, applicability, and feasibility of the solution. The resulting scope model should include explicit statements of critical assumptions and their implications. |
| Strengths | A scope model facilitates agreement as a basis for:<br>• defining contractual obligations,<br>• estimating the project effort,<br>• justifying in-scope/out-of-scope decisions in requirements analysis, and<br>• assessing the completeness and impact of solutions. |
| Limitations | • An initial, high-level model can lack a sufficient level of granularity, particularly for boundary elements, that is needed to ensure clear scope identification.<br>• Once a scope is defined, changing it may be difficult due to political reasons and contractual obligations. Meanwhile, many factors can affect the scope validity before the targets are achieved. Such factors as wrong initial assumptions, situation change, evolution of stakeholder needs, or technology innovations may cause a need for revising the scope partially or entirely.<br>• Traditional scope models cannot address common complex boundaries, such as a horizon (a boundary that is completely dependent on the position of the stakeholder). |
| Knowledge Areas | BAPM, RLCM, SA, RADD |

## 10.42 Sequence Diagrams

| | |
|---|---|
| Purpose | To model the logic of usage scenarios by showing the information passed between objects in the system through the execution of the scenario. |
| Description | A sequence diagram shows how processes or objects interact during a scenario. The classes required to execute the scenario and the messages they pass to one another (triggered by steps in the use case) are displayed on the diagram. The sequence diagram shows how objects used in the scenario interact, but not how they are related to one another. Sequence diagrams are also often used to show how user interface components or software components interact. |
| Details | A **lifeline** represents the lifespan of an object during the scenario being modeled in a sequence diagram.<br><br>An **activation box** represents the period during which an operation is executed.<br><br>A **message** is an interaction between two objects. Message types are:<br><br>• **Synchronous Call**: transfers control to the receiving object. The sender cannot act until a return message is received.<br>• **Asynchronous Call**: (also known as a signal) allows the object to continue with its own processing after sending the signal. The object may send many signals simultaneously, but may only accept one signal at a time. |
| Strengths | • Shows the interaction between the objects of a system in the chronological order that the interactions occur.<br>• Shows the interaction between the objects in a visual manner that allows the logic to be validated by stakeholders with relative ease.<br>• Use cases can be refined into one or more sequence diagrams in order to provide added detail and a more in-depth understanding of a business process. |
| Limitations | • Time and effort can be wasted creating a complete set of sequence diagrams for each use case of a system, which may not be necessary.<br>• Have historically been used for modeling system flows and may be considered too technical in other circumstances. |
| Knowledge Areas | RADD |

## 10.43 Stakeholder List, Map, or Personas

| | |
|---|---|
| Purpose | To analyze stakeholders and their characteristics. |
| Description | This analysis is important in ensuring that the business analyst identifies all possible sources of requirements and that the stakeholder is fully understood so decisions made regarding stakeholder engagement, collaboration, and communication are the best choices for the stakeholder and for the success of the initiative. |
| | This analysis is important in ensuring that the business analyst identifies all possible sources of requirements and that the stakeholder is fully understood so decisions made regarding stakeholder engagement, collaboration, and communication are the best choices for the stakeholder and for the success of the initiative. |
| | Common types of stakeholder characteristics that are worth identifying and analyzing include: |
| | • level of authority within the domain of change and within the organization, |
| | • attitudes toward or interest in the change being undertaken, |
| | • attitudes toward the business analysis work and role, and |
| | • level of decision-making authority. |
| Details | A **stakeholder list** can be developed using a number of techniques. Brainstorming and interviews are two common techniques that can be used. The goal is to ensure a thorough list is produced because this list is central to both stakeholder analysis activities and the planning work the business analyst performs for elicitation, collaboration, and communication. |
| | **Stakeholder maps** are diagrams that depict the relationship of stakeholders to the solution and to one another. There are many forms of stakeholder maps, but two common ones include: |
| | • **Stakeholder Matrix**: maps the level of stakeholder influence against the level of stakeholder interest. |
| | • **Onion Diagram**: indicates how involved the stakeholders are with the solution, which stakeholders will directly interact with the solution or participate in a business process, which are part of the larger organization, and which are outside the organization. |
| | Another popular stakeholder matrix is the **RACI matrix**. RACI stands for the four types of responsibility that a stakeholder may hold on the initiative: Responsible, Accountable, Consulted, and Informed. When completing a RACI matrix, it is important to ensure that all stakeholders or stakeholder groups have been identified. Further analysis is then conducted to assign the RACI designation in order to specify the level of responsibility expected from each stakeholder and/or group. |
| | A **persona** is defined as a fictional character or archetype that exemplifies the way a typical user interacts with a product. Personas are helpful when there is a desire to understand the needs held by a group or class of users. |

Chapter 10 Techniques

## 10.43 Stakeholder List, Map, or Personas

| | |
|---|---|
| Strengths | • Identifies the specific people who must be engaged in requirements elicitation activities.<br>• Helps the business analyst plan collaboration, communication, and facilitation activities to engage all stakeholder groups.<br>• Useful to understand changes in impacted groups over time. |
| Limitations | • Business analysts who are continuously working with the same teams may not utilize the stakeholder analysis and management technique because they perceive change as minimal within their respective groups.<br>• Assessing information about a specific stakeholder representative, such as influence and interest, can be complicated and may feel politically risky. |
| Knowledge Areas | BAPM, EC, RADD |

Figure 10.43.1: Stakeholder Matrix

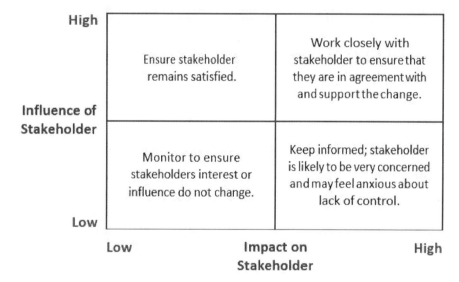

Figure 10:43.2: Stakeholder Onion Diagram

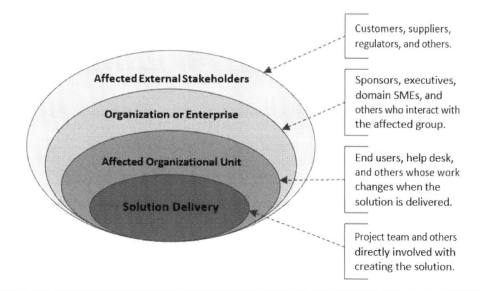

ECBA™ Certification Study Guide 307

## 10.44 State Modeling

| | |
|---|---|
| Purpose | To describe and analyze the different possible states of an entity within a system, how that entity changes from one state to another, and what can happen to the entity when it is in each state. |
| Description | An entity is an object or concept within a system. The life cycle of every entity has a beginning and an end. In a state model a state is a formal representation of a status. It is used when it is necessary to have a precise and consistent understanding of an entity that has complex behavior and complex rules about that behavior.<br><br>A state model describes:<br><br>• a set of possible states for an entity,<br>• the sequence of states that the entity can be in,<br>• how an entity changes from one state to another,<br>• the events and conditions that cause the entity to change states, and<br>• the actions that can or must be performed by the entity in each state as it moves through its life cycle. |
| Details | An entity has a finite number of states during its life cycle, although it can be in more than one state at a time. Each state is described with a name and the activities that could be performed while in that state.<br><br>How the entity changes or transitions from one state to another could be determined by the steps of a process, by business rules, or by information content. The sequence of states of an entity are not always linear; an entity could skip over several states or revert to a previous state, perhaps more than once.<br><br>A state diagram shows the life cycle of one entity, beginning when the entity first comes into existence and moving through all of the different states that the entity may have until it is discarded and no longer of use.<br><br>A state table is a two-dimensional matrix showing states and the transitions between them. It can be used during elicitation and analysis either as an alternative, a precursor, or a complement to a state diagram. It is a simple way to get started on a state model in order to elicit the state names and event names from the domain subject matter experts. |
| Strengths | • Identifies business rules and information attributes that apply to the entity being modeled.<br>• Identifies and describes the activities that apply to the entity at different states of the entity.<br>• Is a more effective documentation and communication tool than plain text, especially if the entity being described has more than a few states, transitions, and conditions governing those transitions. |

## 10.44 State Modeling

| | |
|---|---|
| Limitations | - Is usually only used to understand and communicate about information entities that are perceived to be complex; simple entities may be understood without the time and effort required to build a state model.
- Building a state model appears simple at the start, but achieving a consensus among domain SMEs about the details required by the model can be difficult and time-consuming.
- A high degree of precision about states and transitions is required to build a state diagram; some domain SMEs and business analysis practitioners are uncomfortable trying to describe such a level of detail. |
| Knowledge Areas | RADD |

Figure 10:44:1: State Transition Diagram

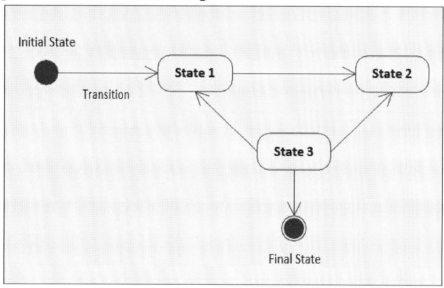

## 10.45 Survey or Questionnaire

| | |
|---|---|
| Purpose | To elicit business analysis information (e.g., customers, products, work practices, and attitudes) from a group of people in a structured way and in a relatively short period of time. |
| Description | A survey or questionnaire presents a set of questions to stakeholders and subject matter experts (SMEs), whose responses are then collected and analyzed in order to formulate knowledge about the subject matter of interest. The questions can be submitted in written form or can be administered in person, over the telephone, or using technology that can record responses.<br><br>There are two types of questions used in a survey or questionnaire:<br><br>• **Close-ended**: the respondent is asked to select from a list of predefined responses, such as a Yes/No response, a multiple-choice selection, a rank/order decision, or a statement requiring a level of agreement. This is useful when the anticipated range of user responses is fairly well defined and understood. The responses to close-ended questions are easier to analyze than those gained from open-ended questions because they can be tied to numerical coefficients.<br><br>• **Open-ended**: the respondent is asked to answer questions in a free form without having to select an answer from a list of predefined responses. Open-ended questions are useful when the issues are known and the range of user responses is not. Open-ended questions may result in more detail and a wider range of responses than closed-ended questions. The responses to open-ended questions are more difficult and time-consuming to categorize, quantify, and summarize as they are unstructured and often include subjective language with incomplete or superfluous content.<br><br>Questions should be asked in a way that does not influence the response data. They should be expressed in neutral language and should not be structured or sequenced to condition the respondent to provide perceived desirable answers. |
| Details | An effective survey or questionnaire requires detailed planning in order to ensure that the needed information is obtained in an efficient manner. When preparing for a survey or questionnaire, business analysts do the following:<br><br>• **Define the objective**: a clear and specific objective establishes a defined purpose of the survey or questionnaire.<br><br>• **Define the target survey group**: identifying the group to be surveyed in terms of population size and any perceived variations (for example, culture, language, or location) helps identify factors that can impact survey design.<br><br>• **Choose the appropriate survey or questionnaire type**: the objective of the survey or questionnaire determines the appropriate questions.<br><br>• **Select the sample group**: consider both the survey or questionnaire type and the number of people in the identified user group in order to determine if it is necessary and feasible to survey the entire group.<br><br>• **Select the distribution and collection methods**: determine the appropriate communication mode for each sample group. |

## 10.45 Survey or Questionnaire

|  |  |
|---|---|
|  | • **Set the target level and timeline for response**: determine what response rate is acceptable and when it should be closed or considered complete. If the actual response rate is lower than the acceptable threshold, the use of the survey results may be limited.<br>• **Determine if the survey or questionnaire should be supported with individual interviews**: as a survey or questionnaire does not provide the depth of data that can be obtained from individual interviews, consider either pre- or post-survey or questionnaire interviews.<br>• **Write the survey questions**: ensure that all the questions support the stated objectives.<br>• **Test the survey or questionnaire**: a usability test on the survey identifies errors and opportunities for improvement.<br><br>When distributing the survey or questionnaire it is important to communicate the survey's objectives, how its results will be used, as well as any arrangements for confidentiality or anonymity that have been made.<br><br>When documenting the results of the survey or questionnaire collate the responses, summarize the results, evaluate the details and identify any emerging themes, formulate categories for encoding the data, and break down the data into measurable increments. |
| Strengths | • Quick and relatively inexpensive to administer.<br>• Easier to collect information from a larger audience than other techniques such as interviews.<br>• Does not typically require significant time from the respondents.<br>• Effective and efficient when stakeholders are geographically dispersed.<br>• When using closed-ended questions, surveys can be effective for obtaining quantitative data for use in statistical analysis.<br>• When using open-ended questions, survey results may yield insights and opinions not easily obtained through other elicitation techniques. |
| Limitations | • To achieve unbiased results, specialized skills in statistical sampling methods are needed when surveying a subset of potential respondents.<br>• The response rates may be too low for statistical significance.<br>• Use of open-ended questions requires more analysis.<br>• Ambiguous questions may be left unanswered or answered incorrectly.<br>• May require follow-up questions or more survey iterations depending on the answers provided. |
| Knowledge Areas | BAPM, EC, SA, RADD, SE |

## 10.46 SWOT Analysis

| | |
|---|---|
| Purpose | To evaluate an organization's strengths, weaknesses, opportunities, and threats to both internal and external conditions. |
| Description | SWOT analysis is used to identify the overall state of an organization both internally and externally. SWOT analysis serves as an evaluation of an organization against identified success factors. By performing SWOT in a disciplined way, stakeholders can have a clearer understanding of the impact of an existing set of conditions on a future set of conditions.<br><br>A SWOT analysis can be used to evaluate an organization's current environment, share information learned with stakeholders, identify the best possible options to meet an organization's needs, identify potential barriers to success and create action plans to overcome barriers, adjust and redefine plans throughout a project as new needs arise, identify areas of strength that will assist an organization in implementing new strategies, develop criteria for evaluating project success based on a given set of requirements, identify areas of weakness that could undermine project goals, and develop strategies to address outstanding threats. |
| Details | SWOT is an acronym for Strengths, Weaknesses, Opportunities, and Threats:<br><br>• **Strengths (S)**: anything that the assessed group does well. May include experienced personnel, effective processes, IT systems, customer relationships, or any other internal factor that leads to success.<br>• **Weaknesses (W)**: actions or functions that the assessed group does poorly or not at all.<br>• **Opportunities (O)**: external factors of which the assessed group may be able to take advantage. May include new markets, new technology, changes in the competitive marketplace, or other forces.<br>• **Threats (T)**: external factors that can negatively affect the assessed group. They may include factors such as the entrance into the market of a new competitor, economic downturns, or other forces.<br><br>Beginning a SWOT analysis with opportunities and threats sets the context to identify strengths and weaknesses. |
| Strengths | • Is a valuable tool to aid in understanding the organization, product, process, or stakeholders.<br>• Enables business analysts to direct the stakeholders' focus to the factors that are important to the business. |
| Limitations | • The results of a SWOT analysis provide a high-level view; more detailed analysis is often needed.<br>• Unless a clear context is defined for the SWOT analysis the result may be unfocused and contain factors which are not relevant to the current situation. |
| Knowledge Areas | SA, RADD, SE |

**Figure: 10.46.1: SWOT Analysis Matrix**

|  | **Opportunities**<br>• Opportunity<br>• Opportunity<br>• Opportunity | **Threats**<br>• Threat<br>• Threat<br>• Threat |
|---|---|---|
| **Strengths**<br>• Strength<br>• Strength<br>• Strength | **SO Strategies**<br><br>How can the group's strength be used to exploit potential opportunities? SO strategies are fairly straightforward to implement. | **ST Strategies**<br><br>How can the group use its strengths to ward off potential threats? Can the threats be turned into opportunities? |
| **Weaknesses**<br>• Weakness<br>• Weakness<br>• Weakness | **WO Strategies**<br><br>Can the group use an opportunity to eliminate or mitigate a weakness? Does the opportunity warrant the development of new capabilities? | **WT Strategies**<br><br>Can the group restructure itself to avoid the threat? Should the group consider getting out of this market? WT strategies involve worst-case scenarios. |

© 2015 International Institute of Business Analysis

## 10.47 Use Cases and Scenarios

| | |
|---|---|
| Purpose | Describes how a person or system interacts with the solution being modeled to achieve a goal. |
| Description | Use cases describe the interactions between the primary actor, the solution, and any secondary actors needed to achieve the primary actor's goal. Use cases are usually triggered by the primary actor, but in some methods may also be triggered by another system or by an external event or timer. |
| | A use case describes the possible outcomes of an attempt to accomplish a particular goal that the solution will support. It details different paths that can be followed by defining primary and alternative flows. The primary or basic flow represents the most direct way to accomplish the goal of the use case. Use cases are written from the point of view of the actor and avoid describing the internal workings of the solution. |
| | Use case diagrams are a graphical representation of the relationships between actors and one or more use cases supported by the solution. |
| | A scenario describes just one way that an actor can accomplish a particular goal. Scenarios are written as a series of steps performed by actors or by the solution that enable an actor to achieve a goal. A use case describes several scenarios. |
| Details | A **use case diagram** visually depicts the scope of the solution, by showing the actors who interact with the solution, which use cases they interact with, and any relationships between the use cases. |
| | **Relationships** between actors and use cases are called associations. Two types of relationships between use cases are extend and include. |
| | The use case has a unique **name**. The name generally includes a verb that describes the action taken by the actor and a noun that describes either what is being done or the target of the action. |
| | The **goal** is a brief description of a successful outcome of the use case from the perspective of the primary actor. |
| | An **actor** is any person or system external to the solution that interacts with that solution. Each actor is given a unique name that represents the role they play in interactions with the solution. A use case is started by an actor, referred to as the primary actor for that use case. Other actors who participate in the use case in a supporting role are called secondary actors. |
| | A **precondition** is any fact that must be true before the use case can begin. |
| | A **trigger** is an event that initiates the flow of events for a use case. |
| | The **flow of events** is the set of steps performed by the actor and the solution during the execution of the use case. |
| | A **post-condition** is any fact that must be true when the use case is complete. The post-conditions must be true for all possible flows through the use case, including both the primary and alternative flows. |

## 10.47 Use Cases and Scenarios

| | |
|---|---|
| Strengths | - Use case diagrams can clarify scope and provide a high-level understanding of requirements.<br>- Use case descriptions are easily understood by stakeholders due to their narrative flow.<br>- The inclusion of a desired goal or outcome ensures that the business value of the use case is articulated.<br>- Use case descriptions articulate the functional behavior of a system. |
| Limitations | - The flexibility of the use case description format may lead to information being embedded that would be better captured using other techniques such as user interface interactions, non-functional requirements, and business rules.<br>- Decisions and the business rules that define them should not be recorded directly in use cases, but managed separately and linked from the appropriate step.<br>- The flexible format of use cases may result in capturing inappropriate or unnecessary detail in the attempt to show every step or interaction.<br>- Use cases intentionally do not relate to the design of the solution and as a result, significant effort may be required in development to map use case steps to software architecture. |
| Knowledge Areas | RLCM, RADD, SE |

**Figure 10.47.1: Use Case Diagram**

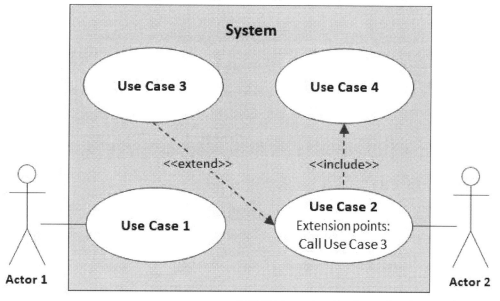

© 2015 International Institute of Business Analysis

## 10.48 User Stories

| | |
|---|---|
| Purpose | To represent a small, concise statement of functionality or quality needed to deliver value to a specific stakeholder. |
| Description | User stories capture the needs of a specific stakeholder and enable teams to define features of value to a stakeholder using short, simple documentation. They can serve as a basis for identifying needs and allow for the prioritizing, estimating, and planning of solutions. With a focus on stakeholder value, user stories invite exploration of the requirements by promoting additional conversations with stakeholders and grouping functional requirements for delivery. User stories can be used to capture stakeholder needs and prioritize development of solutions, as a basis of estimating and planning solution delivery, as a basis for generating user acceptance tests, as a metric for measuring the delivery of value, as a unit for tracing related requirements, as a basis for additional analysis, and as a unit of project management and reporting. |
| Details | The title of the story describes an activity the stakeholder wants to carry out with the system.<br><br>There is no mandatory structure for user story statements of value. The most popular format includes three components: Who, What, Why.<br><br>User stories help teams to explore and understand the feature described in the story and the value it will deliver to the stakeholder. The story itself doesn't capture everything there is to know about the stakeholder need and the information in the story is supplemented by further modeling as the story is delivered.<br><br>A user story may be supported through the development of detailed acceptance criteria. Acceptance criteria define the boundaries of a user story and help the team to understand what the solution needs to provide in order to deliver value for the stakeholders. Acceptance criteria may be supplemented with other analysis models as needed. |
| Strengths | • Easily understandable by stakeholders.<br>• Can be developed through a variety of elicitation techniques.<br>• Focuses on value to stakeholders.<br>• A shared understanding of the business domain is enhanced through collaboration on defining and exploring user stories.<br>• Tied to small, implementable, and testable slices of functionality, which facilitates rapid delivery and frequent customer feedback. |

## 10.48 User Stories

| | |
|---|---|
| Limitations | Tied to small, implementable, and testable slices of functionality, which facilitates rapid delivery and frequent customer feedback. |
| | • This conversational approach can challenge the team since they do not have all the answers and detailed specifications upfront. |
| | • Requires context and visibility; the team can lose sight of the big picture if stories are not traced back through validation or supplemented with higher- level analysis and visual artifacts. |
| | • May not provide enough documentation to meet the need for governance, a baseline for future work, or stakeholder expectations. Additional documentation may be required. |
| Knowledge Areas | RLCM, RADD |

## 10.49 Vendor Assessment

| | |
|---|---|
| Purpose | To assess the ability of a vendor to meet commitments regarding the delivery and the consistent provision of a product or service. |
| Description | When solutions are in part provided by external vendors there may be a need to ensure that the vendor is financially secure, capable of maintaining specific staffing levels, compliant with standards, and able to commit appropriate skilled staff to support the solution. |
| | A vendor assessment is conducted to ensure that the vendor is reliable and that the product and service meet the organization's expectations and requirements. The assessment may be formal through the submission of a Request for Information (RFI), Request for Quote (RFQ), Request for Tender (RFT), or Request for Proposal (RFP). It may also be very informal through word of mouth and recommendations. The standards of the organization, the complexity of the initiative, and the criticality of the solution may influence the level of formality in which vendors are assessed. |
| Details | A common reason for using third-party vendors is that they can provide knowledge and expertise not available within the organization. It may be desirable to target vendors with expertise in particular methodologies or technologies with the goal of having that expertise transferred to people within the enterprise. |
| | The licensing or pricing model is taken into account in cases where a solution or solution component is purchased from or outsourced to a third-party vendor. |
| | It is important to be able to compare each vendor with the competitors and decide with which market players the organization wants to get involved. |
| | Terms and conditions refer to the continuity and integrity of the provided products and services. The organization investigates whether the vendor's licensing terms, intellectual property rights and technology infrastructure are likely to turn into challenges if the organization later chooses to transition to another supplier. |
| | Vendors' experience with other customers may provide valuable information on how likely it is that they will be able to meet their contractual and non-contractual obligations. Vendors can also be evaluated for conformance and compliance with external relevant standards for quality, security, and professionalism. |
| Strengths | - Increases the chances of the organization to develop a productive and fair relationship with a suitable and reliable vendor, and to improve long-term satisfaction with the decision. |
| Limitations | - May be consuming in regards to time and resources.
- Does not prevent risk of failure as the partnership evolves.
- Subjectivity may bias the evaluation outcome. |
| Knowledge Areas | SA, RADD, SE |

# 10.50 Workshops

| | |
|---|---|
| Purpose | To bring stakeholders together in order to collaborate on achieving a predefined goal. |
| Description | A workshop is a focused event attended by key stakeholders and subject matter experts (SMEs) for a concentrated period of time. A workshop may be held for different purposes including planning, analysis, design, scoping, requirements elicitation, modeling, or any combination of these. A workshop may be used to generate ideas for new features or products, to reach consensus on a topic, or to review requirements or designs.<br><br>Workshops generally include a representative group of stakeholders, a defined goal, interactive and collaborative work, a defined work product, and a facilitator.<br><br>Workshops can promote trust, mutual understanding, and strong communication among the stakeholders and produce deliverables that structure and guide future work efforts. |
| Details | When preparing for a workshop, define the purpose and desired outcomes, identify key stakeholders to participate, identify the facilitator and scribe, create the agenda, determine how the outputs will be captured, schedule the session and invite the participants, arrange room logistics and equipment, send the agenda and other materials in advance to prepare the attendees and increase productivity at the meeting, and if appropriate, conduct pre-workshop interviews with participants.<br><br>To ensure that all participants have a common understanding, facilitators generally begin the workshop with a statement of its purpose and desired outcomes. Some workshops may also start with an easy or fun task to break the ice and get the participants comfortable working together. Throughout the workshop, the facilitator maintains focus by frequently validating the session's activities with the workshop's purpose and outcomes.<br><br>After the workshop, the facilitator follows up on any open action items that were recorded at the workshop, completes the documentation, and distributes it to the workshop attendees and any stakeholders who need to be kept informed of the work done. |
| Strengths | • Can be a means to achieve agreement in a relatively short period of time.<br>• Provides a means for stakeholders to collaborate, make decisions, and gain a mutual understanding.<br>• Costs are often lower than the cost of performing multiple interviews.<br>• Feedback on the issues or decisions can be provided immediately by the participants. |
| Limitations | • Stakeholder availability may make it difficult to schedule the workshop.<br>• The success of the workshop is highly dependent on the expertise of the facilitator and knowledge of the participants. |

## 10.50 Workshops

|  | • Workshops that involve too many participants can slow down the workshop process. Conversely, collecting input from too few participants can lead to the overlooking of needs or issues that are important to some stakeholders, or to the arrival at decisions that don't represent the needs of the majority of the stakeholders. |
|---|---|
| Knowledge Areas | BAPM, EC, RLCM, SA, RADD, SE |

## Techniques Pop-up Quiz

1. The business analyst needs to produce numerous ideas from stakeholders to generate ideas on handling the current issue at hand. Which technique should the business analyst use?

    a. Interviews

    b. Focus groups

    c. Brainstorming

    d. Interface analysis

2. Which of the following best describes the requirements review process?

    a. A formal presentation ending with sign-off by all stakeholders after which no further requirements will be elicited.

    b. A working session where invited stakeholders review and discuss a set of requirements.

    c. An agile process for continually identifying and refining requirements.

    d. A group of impacted stakeholders identify 'must have' functionality.

3. What are the roles of participants of a workshop?

    a. Participants, facilitator, scribe, timekeeper, and sponsor.

    b. Stakeholders, business analyst, note taker, and timekeeper.

    c. Participants, business analyst, and sponsor.

    d. Stakeholders, manager, business analyst, and note taker.

4. The business analyst is creating a prototype to explore the basic look and feel of the software product without creating actual functionality. Which type of prototype is the business analyst building?

    a. Visual prototype

    b. Functional prototype

    c. Form study prototype

    d. Usability prototype

5. In order to make a buy vs. build decision the sponsor wishes you, the business analyst, to give an estimate of the cost of building the product in-house. There are three teams of developers that could build the product; so you decide to ask each team to create an estimate of the cost if they were assigned to build the product. As a business analyst, you are not going to use the three estimates that come back as a decision of which team to award the job of building the product, but to develop a single estimate for the sponsor. Which estimation method are you using?

    a. PERT estimation

    b. Rough order of magnitude (ROM) estimation

    c. Delphi estimation

    d. Rolling wave estimation

6. The business analyst is creating a model of the sequential flow of work or activities through the organization; which type of model is the business analyst creating?

    a. Activity diagram

    b. Interface model

    c. Organizational model

    d. Process model

## Answers to Pop-up Quiz

| Question | Answer | Description |
|---|---|---|
| 1 | C | BABOK section 10.5.1. The aim of brainstorming is to produce numerous new ideas, and to derive from them themes for further analysis. |
| 2 | B | BABOK section 10.37.2. Reviewers may be peers, especially for work in process, or stakeholders, who validate that the work product is complete and correct. |
| 3 | A | BABOK section 10.50.3.2. |
| 4 | C | BABOK section 10.36.3.2. Form Study Prototype: is used to explore the basic size, look, and feel of a product that will be manufactured, without creating actual functionality. |
| 5 | A | BABOK section 10.19.3.1. You have created three points of estimation: Optimistic, Pessimistic, and Most likely. You can use the PERT formula to create one estimate for the sponsor. |
| 6 | D | BABOK section 10.35.2. A business process model describes the sequential flow of work across defined tasks and activities through an enterprise or part of an enterprise. |